55-8033

6-23-60

as france goes

HARPER & BROTHERS NEW YORK

as france goes

by
DAVID SCHOENBRUN

To Dorothy

who designed the jacket, edited the
copy and gave courage to the author of this
book, with a skill and devotion for
which he is eternally grateful.

contents

vii

ACKNOWLEDGMENTS

Every page of this book merits an acknowledgment of some kind to my colleagues of the press and radio, to government officials and to the fascinating people of France among whom I live. To a special few, however, I owe a particular debt that I can never repay but which I hereby gratefully acknowledge:

Louis Beaugey, Jean Béliard, David K. E. Bruce, Buu Hoi, Blair Clark, C. V. Clifton, Patricia Davenport, Jean Delcroix, Brigitte Gros, Guillaume Guindey, Etienne Hirsch, Alex Karmel, Claude de Kemoularia, Eve and Harry Labouisse, George Marton, Jean Monnet, David Seymour, Jeanne-Paul Sicard, W. D. Tomlinson, William Tyler, Roger Vaurs, Theodore H. White.

Not all of these good people would agree with all of the opinions herein expressed. In some cases they would disagree strongly and many a wonderful hour have I spent in argument with them. It is, therefore, not the fault of these intelligent and well-informed men and women if this book contains errors and if its author is obtuse and opinionated. However, anything accurate or enlightening in this text may well be attributed to those whose inspiration I have acknowledged.

In the preparation of the final manuscript I am most heavily indebted to the principal editors of this book: my wife and John Appleton, of Harper & Brothers, who made many valuable suggestions and corrections; to my colleague Alexander Kendrick of CBS, who read and criticized most constructively all three drafts of the manuscript; finally to Mrs. Joseph Wertheimer, Mrs. Benjamin Wohlgemuth and Miss Patricia Davenport, who typed the manuscripts and who each made very useful suggestions for improving the copy, the most frequent of which was: "strike this out."

Among the many friends who helped there is one without whom I can truly say this book would never have been written: S. M. Bessie, of Harper & Brothers, editor, publisher, guide and moral support, who never lost faith even when I did, and whose own knowledge of France and the French is unsurpassed.

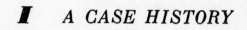

I   *A CASE HISTORY*

1 A Case of World Concern

The *John S. Cropper* rolled easily on the gentle swell of the Mediterranean, just off the coast of the French Riviera. Overhead a cloudless,
sapphire sky was streaked with pink as dawn advanced from Italy.
From the land came the scent of jasmine and honey and the rustle
of a thousand wings as the larks rose to greet the sun. A soldier from
Tennessee, leaning over the rail next to me, said: "Man, is this ever
a place for an invasion."

For thousands of years, soldiers from foreign lands have looked
across the frontiers of France and said, perhaps more elegantly, but no
more truly: "Man, is this ever a place for an invasion." The U.S.
Seventh Army, combat-packed and ready to jump off from our Liberty
Ships on that lovely dawn of August 15, 1944, was following the path
that Greeks and Romans, Norsemen, Huns and Arabs had beaten to
the doors of France through history.

Off to starboard we could see the villas of Fréjus, rose clusters in
the lush, green hills. General Caesar called it "Forum Julii" when
he pitched his winter camp there two thousand years before General
Eisenhower. Beyond view, to port, lay Marseilles, the western flank of
our projected landing line. Greek settlers, from Phocaea, named it
Massilia when they opened a trading post there, six hundred years
before Christ.

Whatever the name, whatever the motive, for two millennia France
has been a magnet that attracted hundreds of millions of men to her
flowered shores and fertile valleys.

Those who came and left never forgot their sojourn in France.
Many an invader stayed on, enchanted by the beauty of the land
and the culture of its people. Thousands of Roman soldiers never
returned to Rome. Unlike their General Caesar, they said: "I came,

3

I saw, I was conquered." Or, as General Pershing's men used to sing:
"How yuh gonna keep 'em down on the farm after they've seen
Paree?"

⚬↝⚬

France, say the classic geography texts, is shaped like a hexagon. A
more colorful but no less accurate image would describe France as
an emerald, sparkling on the finger of the Eurasian Peninsula. France
is as green as Ireland, without Ireland's rain and mist. France has a
climate as varied as that of continental United States, without
America's extremes of heat and cold. The south of France is the
best of California, the north of France, the best of New England.

You can find Maine fishing villages in Brittany, Wisconsin dairy-
land in Normandy, Texas oil fields in Aquitania. You can ski in the
Alps before breakfast, swim in the Mediterranean after lunch and
attend a gala première in a Paris theater all in one day, for France
is a small country. From north to south, or east to west, all France
can be traversed in a two-hour flight.

From one corner of the hexagon to another, France is linked by
valleys and rivers.

The Rhone connects the Jura plains and Alpine regions with
Marseilles. The Garonne carries the wines and brandies of Aquitania
from the Atlantic port of Bordeaux to the tables of the world. The
longest, loveliest river of France, the Loire, meanders through six
hundred miles of farmland and woods, from central France to the
west Atlantic coast. Above its banks rise the crenelated walls and
turrets of historic, medieval châteaux, illumined by hidden arclights,
so that they rise out of the trees like illustrations in a fairy tale. All
of France is a stage, every Frenchman a scenic designer.

The heart of France is in the great, central depression, the Ile de
France. The heart of this heart is Paris and its arteries are the Marne
and the Seine, carrying the life stream of the nation to and from its
capital.

The most fertile fields of fertile France encircle Paris; to the south
the gardens of the Loire valley; to the east and southeast the green-
gold vineyards of Champagne and Burgundy; to the southwest the
thick, black loam of the Beauce wheatfields, as rich a soil as can be
found even in the great plains of America; to the west, the rolling

pasturelands of Normandy, flecked with bright, red poppies, luminous mustard and the soft, white and pink blossoms of the apple orchards.

ᔕᔪ

If France enjoys all the natural blessings that make life sweet, it also suffers all the curses that plague nature: the worm in the luscious apple, the blight always threatening to destroy the crops, the sharks in the azure waters. France is a rich country but it is inhabited by a great many poor people. It is a Catholic country but it fears and mistrusts the political influence of the Church of Rome. France is a democracy whose biggest political party is Communist; it is a republic whose people adore royalty. The French have their heads in the clouds and their feet stuck in the mud. France behaves like the legendary floogie-bird, which flies backward because it is afraid to see where it is going but is fascinated by where it has been.

The brilliance yet the waste of its genius makes France the most bewildering, provocative and irritating of all countries. No other nation has so won the affection and suffered the contempt of the rest of the world as that complex of contradictions known as France, the country which incites the envy of its enemies and the despair of its friends.

The Spaniards, trying to scratch some sustenance out of their sandy, rock soil, look across the Pyrenees at France and sigh with envy, "France is not a country, it is a garden."

The Germans, despite their power, their rising graphs of production, look dreamily across the Rhine and say, "Happy as God in France."

The British look down their noses at the "savages in Calais," but give a Briton twenty pounds and a passport and he will walk, ride, fly or, if necessary, swim to Calais and from there to the British "colonies" at Nice, Monte Carlo and Menton. To paraphrase George Bernard Shaw, the British would agree that "France is a wonderful country. It's a shame to waste it on the French."

Americans, too, flock to France every spring and summer. Department of Commerce statistics reveal that France is the favorite mecca of the American tourist, who visits France in greater numbers than any other country. Like the British, Americans look down upon the French as an inferior race, lazy, immoral and inefficient. France, for most Americans, is a land of bad women and bad plumbing. Yet, for some mysterious reason, they keep coming back for more each year. Apparently Americans dislike the French but love France.

The Americans and the French are constantly carping at each other but no two peoples have a longer record of mutual friendship. America has never made war on France and France is the only major power in the world that has never made war—hot or cold—upon America. Americans have had to fight against the British, the Spaniards, the Italians, the Germans, the Japanese and the Chinese. No hot war has engendered more hatreds than the cold war with Russia. France, alone, has been the ally of the United States, from the day our country declared its independence.

There is no more poignant document in the history of America than the letter sent by General George Washington to his military envoy in Paris, on April 9, 1781:

We are at this hour suspended in the balance. . . . Our troops are fast approaching nakedness. Our hospitals are without medicines and our sick without nutrition. In a word, we are at the end of our tether, and now or never our deliverance must come.

It did come—from France, in our darkest hour.

In the many years that I have been a reporter and commentator on French affairs for an American audience I have been called on constantly to answer questions that betray an emotional barrier to understanding; emotions only too justified by the frictions and frustrations of dealing with the unpredictable and often maddening French. In recent years the questions indicate a basic mistrust as well as misunderstanding of France.

"Will the French fight?" "Is France a reliable ally?" "How can we trust a nation where one out of four people vote Communist?" "Why are the French atheists?" "Why can't they keep a government in office?" "Why don't they give independence to the Algerians?" "Why did they quit fighting in Indochina?" "Why should we keep on giving them money when they won't even pay their own taxes?" Even such trivia as: "Why do they have two-hour lunches and why don't their elevators work?"

These questions do not surprise me. I could add a half-dozen of my own. Some fifteen years of living among the French have taught this reporter how irritating they can be. I spend a good part of my working day stuck in elevators or being chased down the boulevards of Paris by cars that use the sidewalks as highways. I have seen French officials whom I wined and dined for weeks walk past me without recognition. I have flown in fighter-bomber missions with French squadrons and crouched in terror on the floor, not because of German flak, but because of the constant danger of collision in the undisciplined, unco-ordinated French flying formation. As much as any American I know that the criticisms of contemporary France are based on accurate observations, the angry questions justified. Yet I have also learned that the questions are often incomplete and superficial, for nothing is quite as it seems in France, where every valid generalization has its opposite, which is equally valid. Almost every question one can ask about France and the French can be answered with a "Well, yes and no," or "Well, they do and they don't."

Why don't the French pay their taxes? Well, they do and they don't. The French national tax burden is as heavy as that of the United States, but it is inequitably shared and indirectly assessed. Tax evasion is practiced by peasants and shopkeepers, who are hard to control, but most Frenchmen pay very heavy taxes.

Why do they eat two-hour lunches? For one thing because they do not take morning coffee breaks and afternoon teatime recesses like the Americans and the British. For another, they work later. The offices of New York empty out as though someone had shouted fire exactly at five o'clock. In Paris men and women stay at their posts until six, seven and even eight o'clock for top executives. Also, Frenchmen do not eat two-hour lunches except when they are entertaining visiting Americans. They normally use the extra hour at lunch for rest or shopping or other personal chores.

Are the French anti-American? In words, yes; in deeds, no. They criticize us, as we do them, but are always on our side when it really counts. Moreover, most Americans do not know that the French are more anti-French than anti-anyone else. No people are so self-critical as the French. They are certainly just as rude to each other as to foreigners. In recent years the rudeness reached such proportions that Paris authorities organized a *"Croisade de l'Amabilité"* and gave prizes to anyone they found being amiable or just normally polite.

The imaginative Paris police equipped a special car, which they baptized Geneviève, to cruise around looking for motorists who drove considerately and pedestrians who observed the safety zones for crossing the broad boulevards of Paris. When an inspector saw one he would chase the model citizen, while Geneviève would honk with delight. The inspector would leap out as soon as he had caught up with his quarry and present the amiable and virtuous Parisian with a gold coin—a louis d'or.

Public behavior in Paris has not improved notably despite the amiability crusade. However public manners, while indicative of a people's mood, is not the most reliable barometer of reliability or courage. The people who pat you on the back most effusively are sometimes just waiting for a chance to stick a knife into your ribs just when you trust them most. The French do not fawn upon you but they do not foul you either. They say what they want to say right to your face.

The fact is that the nerves of the French have been stretched taut for years by wars in Europe, Asia and Africa. France is the only country in the world that has been at war nonstop ever since 1939. It is all the more amazing therefore that anyone should ask the question: "Will the French fight?" What else have they been doing in this century, indeed for the past thousand years? The French have demonstrated their fighting courage many, too many times in history. Verdun is a badge of courage that any nation could wear with pride. There, for eleven bloody months, more than a half-million men were locked in a deathly embrace. Who gave ground? The tough, disciplined Germans or the soft, undisciplined French?

Verdun was less than fifty years ago, only a brief moment in history. Has a nation with such a record suddenly become a nation of cowards and weaklings? I think not. On the contrary the French are more foolhardy than cowardly. They fight too much, not too little. The real question to ask is a political one. It is not "Will the French fight?" but "What will the French fight for?"

They say they will *not* fight a crusade against Russia or against Communism. They say they *will* fight against Russian aggression and Communist subversion. They have already given proof of this determination. Although one out of four French citizens votes Communist the Communists were thrown out of the government and purged from the army and the police in the spring of 1947 and have been unable to win their way back since. The Communists failed in their avowed aim to keep France out of the Atlantic Pact and failed again when they swore to keep the Atlantic Alliance head-quarters out of France. Is it not more to the credit, than the discredit, of the democratic French that they were able to stand fast against the challenge of so many Communist voters and that they participated fully in the Atlantic Treaty Organization despite both internal threats and the external menace of the Red Army, poised for attack only two hundred miles from France's frontiers?

Perhaps, despite all this evidence, the French are too sapped by past wars to go to war again, too divided internally to defend democracy from Communist subversion. Perhaps. I would suggest, however, that it would be as unwise to write France off prematurely as it would be to put our security entirely in their hands. This is the most fundamental question to ask: just how important is France to the military alliance and above all to the civilization which that alliance was designed to protect and preserve?

∽

In the chain of alliances that bind the democratic nations France is one of the most important links. When America decided in the fall of 1950 that we had to send our troops and our top commanders back to Europe it was to France that we looked first. It was in Rocquencourt, just twelve miles outside Paris, that General Eisen-hower set up SHAPE, the peacetime successor to his wartime com-mand SHAEF, also headquartered in Paris.

General Eisenhower did not choose Paris for his headquarters, or France as the key area in the alliance, because he liked French cooking and wines. He chose France because geographically, politi-cally and strategically France is the linchpin of any Continental coalition.

The Supreme Commander was convinced of this when he set up SHAPE. In his very first briefing to his staff General Eisenhower instructed his planners to consider every possible strategy for defend-ing Europe, on any geographical line, without regard for national or political considerations. "It is our duty to consider every eventuality," said Eisenhower. But, he predicted, the planners would come to the inevitable conclusion that the only defense possible would have to be based on France, which was the hub of Europe and the turntable of Eurafrica.

Every top commander, then and since, has confirmed Eisenhower's original estimate: Montgomery, Ridgway and Gruenther all based their strategy on France, rejecting every suggestion to by-pass the French. Such suggestions were made regularly, during the period of France's hesitations on European Union and particularly when the French Assembly rejected the rearmament of Germany in EDC.

General Gruenther, in an interview with me at the time, stated: "France is essential to the Atlantic Alliance. We need and want German troops but not as a substitute for the French. No defense of Europe is possible without the participation of France."

France is the vital link not because of its size or strength but because of the strategic location of France's frontiers.

In the east, France is tied to Europe by the umbilical cord of the Rhine and the rocky spine of the Alps. No would-be conqueror of Europe can ever rest easy while France is free.

In the north, France looks across the narrowest span of the Channel to England. An atomic-rocket platform at Calais can make England uninhabitable.

On the west, France commands a thousand miles of Atlantic coast, with deep-water, all-weather ports. It is Europe's gateway to America.

The southern shores of France command a vital stretch of the Mediterranean. Naval and air bases, from Marseilles to Villefranche, are within short striking distances of Spain, Italy and North Africa.

Europe cannot be secure if hostile powers control the Mediterranean coast of Africa, and France is the only Western power that still has a foothold, albeit precarious, on the African coast, which is the flank of the Atlantic armies and an important platform for the United States Strategic Air Force.

In the fall of 1956 the dispute between the Western powers and Egypt over the Suez Canal gave greater prominence to the problems and values of French North Africa. France's success or failure at solving her North African conflicts are of the greatest interest to her allies. Crises, like that of Suez, are a constant strain on the alliance of the West. The French and British invasion of Egypt in November, 1956, almost set off World War III.

Once it was said by a European statesman: "When France has a cold the world sneezes." France is no longer the dominant power of Europe nor is Europe the dominant area of the world, but it is still true that the health of France and of Europe affects security and peace everywhere.

∾

In the creative fields of human endeavor France has long been the heartland of the West. Since the Italian Renaissance all roads have led to Paris. From every corner of Europe, and from many in Asia, have come students, writers, painters, architects and engineers to study in Paris. More than half a million foreign students have enrolled at the Sorbonne, more than at any other university in the world.

No other capital has been so often painted, photographed, written about and rhapsodized, not only for its physical beauties but for the climate of intellectual curiosity and creativeness that has made France unique. France has achieved a cultural community, a sort of mental melting pot, that America has achieved politically.

Peoples from all over the world, who emigrate to the United States, rapidly become American. One generation is enough to make the son of an Italian immigrant as American as the sons of Englishmen or Germans, and each of them different from the people of their fathers' birthplaces. This is the genius of America, and its essential political strength.

People from all over the world, who emigrate to France, do not become French. They remain what they were politically and ethnically but they are transformed culturally. This is the genius of France and its essential spiritual strength.

The great masters of modern art are all Parisian, but not all French. Picasso the Spaniard, Modigliani the Italian, Van Gogh the Dutchman, never lost the color of their individual national characteristics but all became French in their creative qualities.

Is there any song more homespun American than "Home, Sweet Home"? John Howard Payne wrote it in Paris. It was in Paris that James Farrell sired that most American boy, *Studs Lonigan*. James Fenimore Cooper wrote lovingly of *The Prairie* of America, while sitting at a sidewalk café in Paris. James Joyce and Gertrude Stein, Hemingway and Dos Passos, John Steinbeck and Irwin Shaw, every generation of writers and artists from Leonardo da Vinci to Picasso has seen some of its geniuses make the pilgrimage to Paris.

Perhaps the most controversial and most publicized literary movement of the mid-twentieth century, existentialism, was launched in liberated Paris by Jean-Paul Sartre and Albert Camus. Many critics now dismiss Sartre as unimportant and existentialism as a heated-over hash of Hegelian concepts. Yet even those who argue that Sartre is not an original nor even a clear thinker might agree that he forced people to think, provoking a debate about the meaning of life instead of the means to wipe out all life on earth. France has long been the foyer of experimental movements in all fields, and whether they are all useful or genuine or lasting is not necessarily the essential issue. In these movements France is seeking, examining, thinking and prodding others to think.

The cultural influence of France has not been confined to the West alone. Two of the greatest modern writers of Japan were profoundly influenced by their visits to Paris. Nagai's *Tales of France* has become one of the modern classics of Japan. Yakomitsu wrote some of his major works in Paris and Seritzawa entitled one book *I Want to Die in Paris*. Many more Japanese, however, prefer to live in Paris. Some two hundred Japanese artists and musicians are studying in Paris today.

The Chinese no longer come to Paris as they once did but they are not staying away by choice. Before the advent of the Communist regime many Chinese came regularly to Paris. Chinese scholars and democratic, revolutionary leaders, in the nineteenth and early twentieth centuries, were enthusiastic admirers of the French philosophers. They ranked two of them in their highest order, just below Confucius. They called them Masters Lu and Man, or, in French, Jean-Jacques Rousseau and Montesquieu.

ᐤᴗ

Paris is not inhabited exclusively by writers and artists, nor have the French given the world only poems, paintings and pastry.

Doctors listen to the heartbeats of the world through a French instrument called the stethoscope, designed by Dr. Laënnec in 1819. The blind of the world can read, thanks to a Frenchman named Louis Braille, himself a blind man. Each time you drink a glass of pasteurized milk you are toasting a great French biologist, whose work on asepsis revolutionized medicine. A measure of electrical current has immortalized the name of French physicist André-Marie Ampère.

French chemist Nicéphore Niepce invented photography in the early 1800's. Fifty years later the world was delighted with another French photographic invention, the daguerreotype—or, as our parents used to call it, "the old-fashioned tintype"—a creation of French artist Louis-Jacques Daguerre. Perhaps the greatest development of the photographic process was cinematography, pioneered by Louis Lumière. The latest innovation in the cinematic arts also came from France: CinemaScope.

Neon lights are another import from France, an invention of French physicist Georges Claude, at the turn of this century. The adding machine, the first airship, the balloon, the gyroscope, the screw propeller, smokeless powder, the phosphorus match, the machine gun, rayon, the sewing machine and the thermometer—all French inventions.

There is no field of human enterprise more characteristic of the modern world than atomic science, and in this field the French have been among the great pioneers for more than a half-century.

Henri Becquerel ushered in the Atomic Age, in 1896, when he discovered the radioactivity of uranium salts, in his Paris laboratory at the Museum of Natural History. Pierre and Marie Curie carried his work forward in a giant stride with the discovery of radium two years later. Marie Curie became the first person, and only woman, in history to win the Nobel Prize twice.

Her daughter, Irène Curie, brought a third Nobel Prize to the family trophy room in 1935 when she demonstrated that substances could be made artificially radioactive through nuclear bombardment. And in 1939, in the laboratory of the Collège de France, Franz Halban and Lew Kowarski, working under the direction of Irène Curie's husband, Frédéric Joliot, proved that a chain reaction takes place in the splitting of an atom, a discovery that led directly to the American decision to make an atom bomb.

ᘒ

It is in the field of politics that France demonstrated the vital role it occupies in world affairs. Europe had remained untouched by the revolutions of England and America. Yet every crown slipped and every throne trembled when the guillotine fell on the neck of Louis XVI of France. As for the people of Europe, they rejoiced at the news and celebrated the dawn of the millennium.

Men danced in the streets of Rome, Vienna and Prague as well as in the streets of Paris. The poet Wordsworth wrote: "Bliss was it in that dawn to be alive." In Britain Fox called the French Revolution "the greatest event that has ever happened in this world, and how much the best." In Copenhagen a Danish father called in his sons and, with tears in his eyes, told them that "poverty would vanish, the lowliest would begin the struggles of life on equal terms with the mightiest, with equal arms, on equal grounds."

The Revolution did not realize the aspirations of the Danish father, except in one respect: the people were given arms and were able to fight against the mightiest armies of Europe. It was Lazare Carnot, the Revolution's Minister of War, who first conceived the idea of national conscription, of a "citizens' army." He rallied the people of France to defend their Republic against the professional soldiers of the European coalition. One million two hundred thousand citizens answered his call and France became history's first "nation in arms."

The concept of individual rights, as well as the concept of the nation-state, grew out of the French Revolution. The Declaration of the Rights of Man was adopted in Paris in August, 1789, two months before the American Bill of Rights was presented to the Congress in New York, and some two years before the Bill of Rights was ratified by enough states to enter into force.

The drafters of our Constitution were influenced both by British liberalism and French radicalism. Locke's original phrase, "the right to person and property," was changed by Jefferson to the more idealistic French concept and became "life, liberty and the pursuit of happiness." The American Constitution asserts that all men are born equal. The French went even further in the Rights of Man, stating that "men are born *and remain* free and equal in rights."

There was, however, a significant difference between the French and American revolutions, one that is still of the greatest importance. It was first pointed out by England's Edmund Burke, the fervent advocate of the American Revolution and the equally fervent adversary of the French. Burke saw the essential difference between the two:

The American Revolution was republican, the French democratic. The American revolutionary philosophers were as concerned about putting a rein on the unbridled will of the people as they were about safeguarding the people's rights. The French, however, were experimenting with *pure democracy*, which Burke insisted would destroy the traditions, loyalties and faiths that were the foundations of a stable community.

This dilemma of democracy is as burning an issue today as it was in 1789. America's "Loyalty Boards" are a modern version of the French Revolution's "Committee of Public Safety." No one has yet found the final, perfect solution to the problem of providing maximum security to the State and maximum freedom for its people.

In France, above all, the search is an agonizing one, for France is a restless spirit, ever asking for the universal truth, yet ever doubting that there is one. It is a quality that free men can both deplore and admire, for, although doubt is destructive if unresolved, doubt is also an essential element of democracy. Doubt is not permitted in a slave state.

&

Despite its doubts France is the only major power on the Continent of Europe that has remained loyal to its democratic traditions in this century of totalitarianism. In the past fifty years Russia has gone Communist, Italy Fascist, Germany Nazi, Spain Phalangist. France, alone, of the principal Continental powers, never succumbed to the madness that seized Europe, and stood with Britain and America in the democratic community.

France did succumb physically to the forces of evil. We can regret this but we cannot write off forty million Frenchmen because they were overrun by eighty million Germans. Those same Germans were powerful enough to fight off the combined might of England, Russia *and* the United States for almost a full year. Mighty as we are, we have never fought the Germans alone, and, as a veteran of the last war against the Germans, I can only say: "Thank God!"

It is now generally agreed by the overwhelming majority of Americans that we can no longer live safely in isolation. "Fortress America" would not long be a free America. Alone in a hostile world we would have to mobilize our resources and manpower so totally as to destroy our American way of life. We could live on, certainly, but it is a question as to whether life would be worth living in lead-lined cellars, inside the vacuum tube of a radar screen.

Yet, as we have seen, this is a danger we might face if France should fall or go totalitarian.

This is not only unpleasant to admit, it is frightening. No American can view with anything but alarm the idea that any part of our security is in the shaky hands of the French.

The French, more than anyone, know that their hands are unsteady. "France is the sick man of Europe," elder statesman Paul Reynaud told his fellow deputies in Parliament in the summer of 1953. In the winter of 1956 France is sicker than ever, torn by civil war in Algeria and civil strife inside metropolitan France. The fevers that have racked France this century have not abated; they are rising.

There can be no doubt that France is sick. The question is: How sick? What is the nature of the sickness? What are its causes, and what are the chances for a cure?

It is the purpose of this study to examine those questions, to try to find out what is wrong with France, and why, and where France is going. The examination is motivated by the basic assumption that as France goes, so go the plans and hopes of many other nations, for the case of France is a case of world concern. The story of France is, however, much more than a case to be examined, more than a matter of security. It would be no less important, no less fascinating if it were no concern of anyone but the French. We can all learn much that is meaningful to ourselves and to our own society from the triumphs and the tragedies of the people who, as much as any, made the world in which we live.

ᔕᕈ

This inquiry into the crises of France will be conducted on the principles of a case history. A case history, unlike a history, is not a narrative, nor does it seek to document all the important events or developments in a selected period of time. It attempts, rather, to describe and explain the actions of a group in terms of the influences that motivate its behavior. In a case history events of the past are important only as they affect the present. From this perspective, relatively obscure figures sometimes become more important than the giants of history. General Boulanger, for example, is a more potent influence on contemporary France than Joan of Arc. The specter of that aspirant dictator haunted the drafters of the Fourth Republic's Constitution and became a very live ghost when General de Gaulle seemed on the verge of attempting a Boulangist coup. In this respect Napoleon III has been a more important influence on contemporary France than his more illustrious uncle, Bonaparte.

The present of any country can only be fully understood in terms of its past. Friendships and enmities, group habits of action and thought are passed down from generation to generation. No European could hope to understand such American phenomena as the "solid South," the isolationist Middle West, the internationalist East, or a dozen other aspects of American life, without some knowledge of the Civil War, the social competition among succeeding waves of European immigrants and a host of factors deeply rooted in the folklore of America and the subconscious of Americans. Similarly modern France is the end product of some two thousand years of turbulent history that have left their mark on the land and in the minds and hearts of the people.

This case history of France, therefore, will endeavor to take into account historical forces wherever they are pertinent to the contemporary scene. The diagnostic approach is not, however, meant literally to be a medical or psychiatric examination. No nation can be prodded, weighed or psychoanalyzed as an individual can. Yet many of the questions pertaining to the state of health of an individual are pertinent to the health of a nation. Coal, iron and oil are essential ingredients of a national economy just as vitamins and proteins are essential to an individual's strength. There are national phobias and illusions just as there are individual psychoses. It is the aim of a case history to seek out those physical and psychological elements that contribute to a nation's growth or decline.

When an individual goes to a doctor for a "checkup," the first question he is asked is not: What seems to be the trouble? A doctor wants to know your past medical history before he probes into your present maladies: What childhood diseases have you had? Any major operations, chronic complaints or record of illness in the family? These are the vital statistics that a doctor needs for a full knowledge of his patient. Since a nation is a group of individuals the same information is useful for an appreciation of its state of health and a prognosis of its evolution.

How old is France? What are the chronic crises of French life? What maladies have afflicted the young Fourth Republic? Of what disease did its parent die and are there any hereditary traces? What are the scars of past wars, the passions and prejudices of history that influence present policies? These, I am convinced, are the basic questions that must be kept constantly in mind when examining any aspect of contemporary French society. This study, therefore, is neither a history nor a journalistic report. It is rather a picture of France and the French in the present, considered as an integral outgrowth of the past, with the hope that it will illumine the trends rather than predict the events of the future.

2 *Family History of the Case*

France is the land of the living past where nothing is ever forgotten and little is ever learned.

On a cold, misty Sunday in December, 1953, a solemn group of men marched to early Mass in the Royal Chapel of the Palace of Versailles. A crowd of spectators, lined up along the cobblestoned road outside the Palace, saw with surprise, at the head of the procession, the trim figure of Foreign Minister Georges Bidault, Catholic party leader, and that day a candidate for the presidency of the Republic.

Bidault, a former history teacher in the Lycée of Louis-le-Grand, could not have forgotten that it was there in Versailles, and in the Royal Chapel itself, that much of the passion and conflict that sparked the French Revolution had been kindled. He could not have forgotten that in 1905 the Third Republic of France had formally decreed the separation of Church and State and specifically banned the celebration of Mass in the Royal Chapel.

Why then did Georges Bidault walk deliberately to that Chapel, opening up the old wound of religious conflict? Why had he apparently learned so little, he who was so learned a man? What force drove him to the Chapel of Versailles, in the heat of an election for the highest office of the Republic, with the certain knowledge that his defiant act would intensify the already bitter contest for the presidency?

The answer goes directly to the root of understanding France and French political behavior which so mystifies foreign observers, who never cease wondering how a people who make a cult of rationalism can behave so irrationally. The clue to the mystery is the role that

19

history plays in the lives of the French. History was one of the inner forces propelling Bidault forward to Mass in Versailles.

To Americans, all history is ancient. America is the country of tomorrow. France, however, is the land of yesterday, and to the French all history is contemporary. The past, for the French, is one with the present, in a continuous stream of life whose conflicts are rarely fully resolved, whose passions rise and fall like tides. The defeated never reconcile themselves to defeat; the victors can never be generous, for they are never secure in their victory. Thus old sores never heal completely and historic conflicts remain contemporary through the generations, so that we see the religious conflicts of the Versailles of 1789 re-enact themselves in the Versailles of 1953.

France is thus one country where history does repeat itself, where it is part of each man's family album.

You cannot escape from history in France. It is all around you, in the newspapers and on the billboards and boulevards of Paris. The briefest promenade through Paris is a journey through yesterday. Its street names read like the table of contents of a history text: the Street of the Fourth of September, the Twenty-fifth of August, the Twenty-ninth of July; the Square of the Republic, of the Resistance, of Sebastopol and of Stalingrad; and a metro station called Alesia, so that no Frenchman might forget the battle in which Caesar defeated Vercingetorix and subjugated all Gaul.

The French do not limit history to their own national events and heroes. Their great men share the streets of Paris with men from other lands. Up on the Trocadéro heights France's greatest soldier, Marshal Foch, looks eternally at one of America's most beloved heroes, Ben Franklin, who sits serenely in an armchair on the corner of the street that bears his name, and where, legend insists, he once flew his kite and talked about electricity with French chemist Lavoisier. To the left of Foch is the tree-lined Avenue du Président Wilson, where, midway down the hill, General George Washington rides a stone horse. Paris is the world's greatest public museum.

The homes of the French are museums, too. I have lived in Paris apartments whose bric-a-brac and family memorabilia rivaled the collection of the Musée Carnavalet. I shall never forget the day that the owner of such an apartment came to pay me a "courtesy call," which I sensed was an investigation to determine whether I was taking care of her treasures. As the charming old lady sank into a tapestry-covered armchair in the salon, she caressed its carved arms lovingly and sighed: "Ah, this is a proper chair, Monsieur. It is Laleu. They do not make them like this now. It is one of the few good things I have left, you know. I lost everything in the Revolution."

I found it difficult not to smile at her extraordinary use of the personal pronoun. *She* had lost everything in a revolution that took place a century before her birth, and still felt the loss keenly and personally.

This personal identification of Frenchmen with their past is an essential element of French psychology. There is hardly a family in France that has not suffered loss, from the relatively insignificant loss of an armchair to the grievous loss of every male member of the family, in the endless series of invasions, wars and revolutions that have racked France for centuries.

ତ⍵

The roots of the French family tree are buried deep in the alluvial clay of prehistory. The first of our species, Homo sapiens, lived in France some twenty-five thousand years ago and developed there one of the earliest human cultures in the periods known as the Aurignacian and Magdalenian.

The Magdalenian inhabitant of the land that was to become France was a talented sculptor and artist. He fashioned figurines of reindeer horn and was the first draftsman to use shading to suggest depth and angled lines to denote distance. Magdalenian man created a fishhook and a needle from bone splinters and thread from reindeer sinew. He organized a large-scale flint "industry." He traveled and traded over large areas; necklaces of Mediterranean shells, of Magdalenian design, have been found north of the River Loire. Britain's distinguished archaeologist Gordon Childe believes that "the Magdalenian culture of France is the most brilliant achievement of that long episode known to archaelogy."[1]

Magdalenian culture finally died, however, leaving only a few bones, flints, cave paintings and a lesson for future French scholars to ponder on: the price of failure to adapt to a changing environment is the decay of a civilization. For, when the glaciers receded and the reindeer and

[1] Gordon Childe, *Man Makes Himself.*

bison moved north, the overspecialized hunter's culture of the last
Ice Age could not survive. Most of the Magdalenians moved north on
the reindeer trail where the Ice Age environment, for which they were
fitted, still existed. The modern Eskimo is believed to be their descendant.

Some stayed in France, mainly in the central and southern plains,
particularly the Dordogne region, which had been the most populous
center of their society. They were joined there by a new wave of mi-
grants from the damp woodlands beyond the Danube. The stocky,
broad-headed Danubian invaders conquered the tall artists of the
Dordogne, but were themselves soon attacked by another horde of
invaders from the Baltic.

For five thousand years, wave after wave of invasions rolled regularly over France, each invading horde settling down, merging with
its predecessors, constantly renewing the blood stream of France.
Celts, Iberians, Phoenicians, Greeks and Goths migrated to France,
mixing with the descendants of the Magdalenians, to produce short
Frenchmen and tall Frenchmen, longheads and broadheads, blonds
and brunettes, making of France a huge melting pot of peoples, so
that it is absurd today to talk of a Frenchman in any terms other than
political or cultural.

There is no French race, no French stock, not even a French type.
There is a common cultural, historical heritage that is uniquely
French, but, in terms of a family tree, France is a hybrid, whose seeds
came from Asia, Africa and Europe. The flowering of French culture
is the result of millennia of cross-pollenization. Perhaps that is one
reason why there is virtually no racism in France. The French know
they are, in the words of their own great historian Seignobos, "a race
of half-breeds." Seignobos thought this was a mark of French superiority, because, he wrote, "mongrels are often more intelligent than
purebred dogs."

ᔕᕗ

For Frenchmen, the real history of their country begins with the
greatest invasion of all that long period: the arrival of the Celts. All
that happened earlier is prehistory to them, for the Celts are the
people that the primer books refer to as "our ancestors, the Gauls."

The name of their ancestors they owe, however, to Roman writers, who called the Celtic warriors "Galli," and that was the name that survived in France after the Roman conquest.

The Celts came to France from the well-worn invasion routes of Eastern Europe. Their greatest immigration to France, for it was more of a mass immigration than an invasion, started about 600 B.C. and continued in successive waves for more than three centuries. They moved across France, gradually pushing the Iberians back to the southwest corner, near the Pyrenees, driving the Ligurians up into the foothills of the Alps, and pinning the Greeks to their port of Massilia. Everywhere else in France the Celts held sway, masters of the wide fertile plains, the rolling basins and thick forests of the country.

There is an old but still heated dispute among scholars on the real role these Celtic warriors played in the development of modern France. It is generally agreed that Gaul grew in population to some ten millions of people in the three centuries of Celtic rule, but it is also argued that there were at least three million people living in France before the Celts came, so that the phrase, "our ancestors, the Gauls," seems to be a historical exaggeration.

What is important, however, for the purposes of our analysis, which seeks to find those periods of history that leave a permanent mark upon the land and the people, is that the Gauls are accepted by most of the French people as their true ancestors and that their alleged virtues and skills are extolled in children's history books, thus entering the consciousness of Frenchmen at the most impressionable age. Whether the Gauls did, or did not, invent the cask, the two-wheeled cart and the mattress is of importance only to a few specialists. What is important to an understanding of modern France is that the French people actually do believe that the Gauls invented the cask, the cart and mattress, and that they consider these to be early proofs of French ingenuity.

What is true for the mattress is equally true for soap, the cloak and trousers, all of which are claimed as Gallic inventions by French historians who specialize in popularizing history. So much has been written of the art of the Gauls, their pottery, goldworking, their brilliant dyes, jewels and filigreed silver, their rainbow-tinted glasses and enamels, that it has become a national conviction that France is, always has been, and always will be the land of art and sensitivity, above all others, and that, somehow, French civilization is intrinsically superior to all others.

The civilization of France is, of course, a heritage of which any man can be proud. It has given the French comfort and courage in moments of adversity. Yet this historical heritage has also been abused to the point of being used as an opium, a dream-escape into a glorious past, instead of an inspiration and challenge to be maintained and even surpassed.

Nostalgia for the past is a sign of old age, and, in that sense, as in others, France is an old nation. France has both the strength and the weakness of old age. The wisdom and moderation that come with maturity are characteristic of the individual Frenchman, but so are the cynicism of old age that undermines faith and the rigidity of old age that brakes progress. The French feel themselves to be old, constantly refer to France as the "oldest national community." They count their age as at least two thousand years, tracing their origins back to Caesar's conquest of Gaul.

∽

Before Caesar came to conquer and to unite, the Gauls lived in a chaotic, tribal society. The Gallic peoples had no government. Authority was at the base, in the family unit. Even the chiefs of tribes were elected by the families and had little authority over them. The Gauls, however, had a highly developed sense of justice and individual liberty. In Roman and Greek civilizations, contemporary with Gaul, all members of the family might be held accountable for the crimes of any individual in it, whereas in Gaul only the guilty one was punished for his crimes, a basic principle of justice too frequently violated in our so-called modern world.

Responsibility of the citizen and his right to personal freedom were also basic principles of Gallic society. It was, however, an anarchic society that went to the opposite extreme of carrying the love of liberty to the dangerous threshold of irresponsibility. This distortion of liberty to libertarianism is one of the basic weaknesses of French society today, and attributed by many Frenchmen to the heritage of the Gauls. The Gauls would have no king. They barely tolerated a leader, a state of mind not unlike that of present-day Frenchmen who barely tolerate a premier, and never for very long.

The first great reportage on Gallic society was written by Julius Caesar. Anyone who has lived in Western Europe in the past decade would not regard as ancient history the observation noted in Caesar's *Commentaries:* "All Gaul is divided into three parts. One part is inhabited by the Belgians, another by the Aquitanians, and the third part by those who, in their own language, call themselves the Celts, and whom we call the Gauls." Caesar concluded: "The bravest of these people are the Belgians because they are furthest removed from the civilization and refinements of the Southland. Traders rarely go to their lands and, when they do, they never buy from them those things likely to soften their hearts, because they are continually at war with the Germans, who are their nearest neighbors, across the River Rhine."

Caesar eventually discovered, as others were to discover in great battles throughout history, from Troyes to Poitiers to Verdun, that the Gauls were not so soft as they seemed. He had entered Gaul as a friend, to help the Celts repel a German invasion, but, that mission accomplished, Caesar had turned on his allies and ordered them to surrender their territory to him. They did not yield, however. The Celts were just as ready to resist Caesar as they had been to resist the Germans.

Vercingetorix, leader of the Arverni tribe, offered to lead the other tribes in a resistance movement. All but one, the Aedui, rallied to his call. The Aedui collaborated with the Romans—there were collaborators in those days, too, just as there were resistants.

The campaign was unequal from the start. General Caesar had a trained professional army, well organized, with central communications and services of supply. Vercingetorix commanded an irregular band of partisans. Yet the war lasted for seven years. Vercingetorix led the Gauls in a campaign of guerrilla warfare, the first recorded instance of a "scorched earth" policy to deny the invader bases of operation. He was finally captured, tortured and assassinated by the Romans, who gave him a martyr's death and a guaranteed immortality in French history.

There is thus a hallowed tradition of resistance in France. All through French history women and men have arisen to resist the invaders, from Ste Geneviève, the patron saint of Paris, who saved the city from Attila, through Joan of Arc, Clemenceau and Charles de Gaulle. The Vercingetorix symbol is one of the strongest motivating forces of modern French society. His act of resistance to Caesar was the first significant act of French history, a lesson the French have taken to their hearts as well as their minds.

∽

If the Gauls resisted Roman military domination, they did not resist for long the lures of Roman civilization. Roman historian Tacitus noted: "To habituate the natives to well-being and peacefulness Agricola helped them to construct temples, markets, houses, baths, congratulating and rewarding those who co-operated in these projects, making his rigor felt by those who resisted. . . . Little by little the Bretons were seduced even by our faults, by our taste for strolling under porticoes, by our baths, by the delicacies and refinements of our banquets." The only real conflict between the Gauls and the Roman administrators came when the Romans imposed a land tax on the Gallic farmers. This they bitterly resisted from the first. The peasant of France, perhaps the most stubbornly consistent of men, is still resisting the tax collectors of the State today as his Gallic ancestor did two thousand years ago.

Aside from the paying of taxes, the Gauls enthusiastically Romanized themselves and were granted positions in the colonial hierarchy until it was not clear whether Rome was occupying Gaul or merely being tolerated by the Gauls. In fact, the western half of the Roman Empire became, in time, the Gallo-Roman Empire, a unique development that occurred nowhere else in the dominion of Rome.

The influence of that collaboration and Romanization of Gallic society on contemporary France is considerable. The French preoccupation with statute law, in contrast with the Anglo-Saxon tradition of common law, derives from Rome. The French are obsessed with words, with written texts, to fix the citizens' relations to the State. That is one of the basic reasons why there is so notable a lack of community spirit in France. The Frenchman is not concerned about the possible effect of his actions on his neighbors. He feels free to do anything not explicitly forbidden by law.

Laws, however, are not holy. What man makes man can break. The Frenchman, therefore, feels no moral compunction to obey the law. He obeys out of fear of punishment rather than a positive desire to conform. Traffic regulations in Paris, for example, state that when two cars approach a crossroads at the same time, priority belongs to the one on the right. If there is no policeman around to enforce that law, both cars proceed on the basic principle of French society: *"Chacun pour soi"*—"Every man for himself." As a consequence, the streets of Paris are littered with the wreckage of violated priorities at crossroads.

In France the tradition of Roman law combined with the normally anarchic nature of the Gauls to block the development of a community spirit. There are other forces, of course, that contribute to the divisions of France, but many of them grew out of the Gallo-Roman soil.

The Roman conquest of Gaul, therefore, left permanent marks upon the country and its inhabitants. The highways of France still follow the Roman pattern just as the French *"père de famille"* is a Roman paterfamilias. Rome gave France its language, its laws, and even its religion, for when Rome finally embraced Christianity, the people of its Gallic provinces followed suit. Perhaps the greatest gift of Rome to the Gauls was three centuries of peace, the Pax Romana, the longest period of freedom from invasion the land has ever known, before or since.

∽

The end of the Pax Romana was followed by three centuries of invasion from across the Rhine. The "German question," for the French, is some fifteen hundred years old. Some non-French historians ridicule the notion of a "German problem" existing a millennium before the existence of anything resembling a German nation. This may be academically accurate but this thesis fails to take into account the reality of national myths. As we noted in the case of Gallic inventiveness, the myth is often more powerful than the truth. The French believe in an ancient enmity with the Germans and this belief is a trauma that blocks contemporary attempts to establish friendly, normal relations between the two peoples.

The "Germans," striking at Rome's frontiers for years, lusting for the riches they could see through the holes they punched, were fierce, nomadic warriors. Tacitus described them as believing it was "a sign of cowardice to win by the sweat of their brows what they might just as well obtain by spilling blood." The German tribes were constantly at war, with each other or with their neighbors. They frequently infiltrated Gaul by offering their services as mercenaries to fight off some other Germanic tribe.

Over the years large numbers of Germans came to settle in Gaul, on the banks of the Escaut and the Rhine and in the Alpine villages. One tribe particularly, the Franks, came to settle in great numbers in Gaul, both as soldiers and as agricultural laborers. The greatest influx of Germanic peoples came in the fourth century, when Attila the Hun rode down from the Asiatic steppes to terrify even the warlike Germans, who fled into neighboring Gaul.

In modern phraseology, to meet the "threat from the East" the Romans formed a "European Army" to stop Attila's aggression. Roman General Aëtius commanded mixed legions of Gauls, Alans, Norsemen, Franks and Burgundians. Attila, too, recruited German troops for his Mongol Army. Thus Aëtius had the Visigoths on his side and Attila had the Ostrogoths in his camp—a fifth-century preview of the West Germans in the Atlantic Alliance camp and the East Germans in the Russian bloc. The armies met near Orléans in a surprise attack by Aëtius that drove Attila back to Troyes, where, after a fierce battle, the Huns broke ranks and retreated beyond the Rhine. The united Roman coalition, composed mainly of German shock troops, had saved Rome from the Eastern hordes.

After having helped defeat Attila, the Visigoths stayed on in Gaul, some of them settling in the northern half, some moving south. The Vandals went on to conquer regions of Spain and Africa, the Angles and the Saxons crossed the Channel to the Celtic island of Britain, while the Burgundians settled down in the Vosges Mountains and the plains of the Jura. For French historians and politicians today this is a historic parallel, whose significance is obvious. In modern terms it means to the French that a European coalition, built around German troops, to meet the threat from Russia, would, if successful, result in the Germans swallowing up France and the small Benelux states. The historic parallel may be a fantasy but the fears are very real and frequently revived. Frenchmen have not yet forgotten that during the last German occupation the major Nazi propaganda line was Hitler's "New Europe," presented as a reincarnation of Charlemagne's Empire.

On June 20, 1940, just two days after de Gaulle called on Frenchmen to resist the Germans, the *Berliner Borsenzeitung* published an editorial proposing that "we must go back to Charlemagne to find the model for a new Europe." The Nazi editorialist wrote: "In the time of Charlemagne the West was unified in a great Empire directed by the Germans. The victory of 1940 consecrates the supremacy of the eastern Franks over the western Franks and gives them the right to organize and lead the old continent."

The collaborationist press of France picked up this Nazi propaganda theme and all through the occupation Frenchmen were urged to "end the quarrel of the Franks and reunite the family."

General de Gaulle, too, used the memory of the Franks to argue for French control of the Saar. Speaking at Bayeux on June 18, 1947, he claimed that the Saar must "take its place alongside us, the sons of the Franks."

The French and Germans both claim the first great Frankish general, Chlodwig, as their own. French historians translated Chlodwig's name into Latin, as Clovis. It survives in French as Louis, in German as Ludwig. The tribe of people Clovis defeated in battle were the Alammani and that name lives on in French as *"allemands"* —the Germans.

Clovis became a convert to Christianity and was baptized at Reims. He fought from then on in the name of the Pope, crushed all rivals and made the Franks supreme throughout all Gaul. His domain was called the kingdom of the Franks. Modern France was the product of this union of Roman Gaul and Frankish Gaul. France, south of the River Loire, down to the Mediterranean, is strongly "Latin" in temperament and culture; France, north of the Loire, particularly the territory between the Rhine and the Somme, is distinctly "Frankish," that is Germanic, in temperament and culture.

A synthesis of the two evolved through the ages as France grew to be a unique national community, but the dualism of its heredity was never completely eradicated and its conflicting characteristics are still manifest in French life today.

The Roman-Frankish union reached its highest point of glory under the regime of Charles Martel and his sons. He was a palace official whose very name symbolized the dualism of the era: Charles (from the German word for "valiant") and Martel (from the French word for "hammer"). It was Charles the Hammer who raised and led the Frankish Army that met and defeated the Arab invaders, near Poitiers, in one of the great battles of history. Charles, like Clovis, had been baptized a Christian, so that his victory over Islam was a religious victory, and was to contribute to a close union of King and Church in France.

Charles himself was not a king and did not claim the throne, even after his defeat of the Saracens. His son Pepin, however, was elected by the Franks as their king. Pepin advanced the union of the temporal and spiritual powers by requesting consecration of his sovereignty by the Pope, who crowned him at Saint-Denis. The final union of the Crown and the Cross was achieved by Pepin's son, Charles, who was to earn the title "Magnus," the Great King. Carolus Magnus lives in French history as Charlemagne and in German history as Karl der Grosse. Both nations also claim him as one of their early national heroes.

Like his father and grandfather, Charlemagne was a great warrior. His armies struck deep into Europe, east to the Oder River, then south through the Austrian marshes to the Dalmatian coast. He conquered Italy, and on Christmas night, on the eve of the ninth century, Charlemagne knelt in prayer at St. Peter's and the Pope set a golden crown upon his head, and called him Emperor.

Charlemagne, despite the legends of his greatness, suffered from the fatal weakness of other "barbarians" who had conquered Rome: he had no organizing ability for any enterprise but war. His so-called "Empire" was only a series of subject territories and peoples, and his troops were stretched too far, too thinly to preserve their power. At Charlemagne's death a fight for succession took place among the heirs throughout the Empire, and in that conflict a decision of enormous importance was taken, that influenced the course of European history for one thousand years. Many of the agonies of modern Europe trace back to the fight for power among three grandsons of Charlemagne.

Charlemagne's three grandsons were called Louis the German, Charles the Bald and Lothar. Each aspired to his throne but none was strong enough alone to impose his will on the others. They had to compromise their differences.

Louis the German, a prince of the eastern lands, made a pact with his brother Charles, who ruled west of the Rhine. Their pact was written and signed at Strasbourg on the Rhine, in the year 841, and has come down in history as the Oath of Strasbourg. It is the first document to be inscribed in the language of the people, Romansh, instead of Latin; as such it is considered to be the birth certificate of the French language. In it the two brothers pledged to support each other against the third brother, Lothar.

Within two years Lothar was forced to abandon his claims. He met with his brothers to agree on a division of the Empire among the three of them. They met in Verdun and negotiated one of the most fateful treaties in world history. To Louis the German was ceded all the territories of the eastern Frankish realm: modern Germany. Charles the Bald was confirmed as king of the western lands: modern France. And the first European "buffer state" was granted to the unfortunate Lothar, a long, thin slice of land from the North Sea down to the Swiss-Italian Alps. It was called by his name, Lotharinge, or in modern French "Lorraine." Lothar did not hold it long. Buffer states have always been short-lived.

The "peace pact" of the Treaty of Verdun in the year 843 led directly to war, as so many peace pacts do. The descendants of Louis the German and Charles the Bald never stopped fighting about Lorraine and Alsace, and killing each other in family quarrels. The statesmen who are trying today to create a new community of Europe are, in effect, seeking to annul the ancient Treaty of Verdun and restore the unity that prevailed before the grandsons of Charlemagne carved up his domain.

∞

The history of France, as a territory identified by that name and unified by a central power, began long after Charlemagne. The name "France" was not used in the political sense until the end of the tenth century.

At that time Louis V, last of the Carolingian dynasty, died without

an heir. The Archbishop of Reims called an assembly of the lords at
Senlis, south of Paris, and urged them to elect a new king. He told
them: "Take for chief the Duke of the Franks, glorious by his actions,
his family and his valiant men-at-arms."

There were two major claimants for the kingdom: the uncle of
Louis V and the great-grandson of Robert the Strong. Louis's uncle
called upon the Germans to help him conquer the realm of the western Franks. His forces marched as far as Paris, where they had to pull
up before the army of the opposite claimant: Hughes, Duke of
France, Count of Paris and Orléans. The assembled lords, faced with
the choice of throwing their support to a German-backed prince or a
French duke, chose Hughes.

Elected king, Hughes chose the dynastic name Capet, because, as
Abbot of the old Gallic sanctuary of Saint Martin, he possessed the
holy relic of the "bishop's cape," thus reaffirming the union of scepter
and miter. So began the great Capetian dynasty, which extended the
domain of France from the basin of Paris through all of Gaul.

His sons were strong and fertile men and for the first three centuries of the dynasty the crown passed regularly from father to son,
with an average reign of thirty years. This gave the Capetian kings
time and power to build a firm foundation and extend their domain.
The Capets were absolute monarchs, determined to centralize power
in their own hands, and consequently reduce the power of the rival
dukes. In all, the dynasty lasted 341 years. In that period the Capetians
gave the French people their first sense of a common destiny.

The centralizing work of the Capetians was continued and height-
ened by their later successors, the Bourbon kings of France, whose
dynasty began in 1589. The Bourbon imposition of one-man rule
forever after left a mark of fear on the French consciousness. It is one
of the reasons for weak government in France today. The Constitution makes the executive a servant of the legislative, subject to instant
dismissal, to a great extent because of Frenchmen's traditional hatred
and fear of central authority.

The first, and perhaps most ruthless, absolute ruler in French history
was not a king although he used a king as his puppet. The specter of
Cardinal Richelieu still haunts the French today.

Richelieu set out to destroy every real or potential rival of the central authority inside France. He fought the Protestants and reduced their last armed cities to rubble. He went to war against the last of the feudal lords who still dared challenge the king's power, destroyed their castles and all strong points in which they might put up resistance to the king's authority. King Louis XIII was one of the weakest of the Bourbons, but thanks to Richelieu his reign was one of the most spectacular.

A prince of the Church, Richelieu was, at the same time, a soldier and an empire-builder. In terms of French influence in the world of his day, he served his nation well. He chartered colonial companies that established French trading posts in Africa, Asia and the Americas. He made France the dominant power in Europe. French history has thus given Richelieu an exalted position among the heroes of the country.

However, Richelieu, the dictator, with his elaborate network of spies and police agents, also left a heritage of mistrust and fear of tyranny, as have so many other admired but feared heroes of France. The fact that he was a cardinal has also served to provoke the fears of anticlericalists in France. Today it is apparent that the majority of the French people believe they have a vested interest in a weak, unstable executive power, and a clear separation of Church and State, as a result of the lessons of French history.

Yet one of the most admired figures in all French history was one of the most absolute and tyrannical of rulers, Louis XIV, the "Sun King." Under his reign France reached the peak of world political and cultural eminence. His court was the most brilliant in Europe and men came from every country to marvel at the beauty and grandeur of Versailles, and then return home to copy it.

All over Europe little imitation Versailles were built, at Potsdam, Schönbrunn and St. Petersburg. Boileau, Racine, La Fontaine, Molière, Lully, Mansart and Le Nôtre wrote the poems, plays and music, built the mansions, gardens and parks that set the standards for the entire Western world. French became the language of all the courts and the language of diplomacy, in the closing years of the Bourbon monarchy. No single place in modern history has ever seen the grandeur that was Versailles.

Frenchmen today, even the most fervent Republicans, revere the memory of Versailles. They suffer from a kind of historical schizophrenia, worshiping both the royal splendor of Versailles and the grandeur of the Revolution against that same royalty.

One of the great public events in France, early in 1954, was the première of the motion picture, *Si Versailles m'était conté*, which purported to tell the history of modern France through a re-enactment of events that took place in Versailles Palace, from the time of Louis XIV to Clemenceau. It was fascinating for a foreign observer to go to the cinema to watch the reaction of the public. I must have seen the picture—a three-hour-long extravaganza—at least six times, and each time the applause came at the same moments, no matter what movie house I was in, from the "palaces" of the Champs Elysées to the most proletarian neighborhood cinemas.

The loudest applause and cheers always came near the end when the camera moved into the Hall of Mirrors to find Clemenceau, the "Tiger" of France, last of the victorious leaders of French democracy. Next strongest applause, invariably, was for Napoleon. For Louis XIV there was no applause at all, but there was, instead, an intense interest and a great curiosity that, somehow, was more impressive than the cheers. People would lean forward on their seats, comment on the costumes, the wigs, the beautiful ladies of the court, laugh delightedly at Louis's witticisms and particularly buzz about the grand manner with which he informed Madame de Maintenon that he would honor her by allowing her to become his mistress.

In the lobby, after the show, men and women would stand looking around at the stills of the picture they had just seen, talking about the glory that was France under Louis XIV. Arguments would start about historical errors in the script. For almost a month the literary review *Figaro Littéraire* ran several pages of letters and interviews by distinguished historians and statesmen, discussing the merits and faults of Sacha Guitry's version of French history in that cinematic superproduction. The picture earned the largest box-office receipts ever brought in by any French film.

The nostalgia for the days of French supremacy is very great in these gray, frustrating days of French decline.

The decline had already begun to set in during the reign of Louis

XIV. His was a last brilliant burst of glory of the monarchs of France. With him ended a chapter of French history that began with Hughes Capet, almost eight hundred years before. In that long period the country of France was conceived. In the Revolution against the Bourbon dynasty the nation of France was born.

3 *The Case of the Three*
Republics

A nation is an almost undefinable thing.

Nationalism is determined by neither race nor language. The Danes, Norwegians and Swedes, the Irish and the Scots, are members of the same subspecies of man but of different nations. Spaniards and Mexicans speak the same language but are separated physically and politically. The Swiss, however, are united physically and politically but speak three different languages.

Most people think of a nation as a community of citizens living within fixed geographical frontiers, under one flag, to which all pledge allegiance, and which each is sworn to defend, even with his life, if need be. This is the generally accepted concept of a nation in the twentieth century.

It is an accurate definition as far as it goes. Yet a nation is much more than a frontier, a flag or a political community. My daughter, born and raised in Paris, speaking French as her mother tongue from birth, always considered herself to be an American, long before she came to America and learned to speak English, to the point of refusing to utter another word of French.

The simple logic of a child led her to understand instinctively what complicated adult minds forget: that a nation is above all a family of peoples sharing a common cultural heritage, united by a common destiny. Since my daughter's mother and father, and our entire family, are American this meant to her that she was an American. This is the real meaning of the word "motherland" to denote a nation, that is, a family rather than just a community of citizens.

This was the concept of the fathers of the American nation, expressed in the words "We, the people of the United States." Americans were members of a family before and after the American

Revolution and this tradition of family relations persisted through the years. Frenchmen who visit America are always astonished at the unity achieved overnight after bitter fights in political conventions and campaigns, such as the Eisenhower-Taft rift that split the Republican party in the summer of 1952 and the Stevenson-Truman-Harriman battle in the summer of 1956, that briefly split the Democratic party. Frenchmen find it difficult to understand that these were family quarrels which affected neither the basic unity of the party nor that of the nation once elections were over.

Frenchmen are not members of a family, not since the Revolution that split them apart. Before 1789 the peoples living on the territory of France were united by central authority, by the bonds of the kingdom and of the Church. However, when the temporal authority became despotic and when the spiritual authority allied itself with the monarchy, the French rebelled against both with equal fury. More importantly, the rebels failed to distinguish between the symbols of authority and authority itself, confusing the king with one-man government, the Church with religion. Thus they revolted against all personal and spiritual authority, which left nothing but anarchy.[1]

Americans, too, revolted against a tyrannical king, but the Americans then chose a man of the people to be president, with the executive authority if not the personal power of a king. They continued to put their faith in God as the ultimate Supreme Being.

The French, on the contrary, killed their king and rejected the supremacy of God. In the place of the king they put an institution, the sovereign National Assembly, a committee of many men, rather than one man, to make certain that no man could ever again become their master. This is still the basic principle of government in France. In place of God, as Supreme Being, the revolutionists elevated the Nation to supremacy, and substituted for the Christian faith a new religion, democracy, which they were sure would bring about Utopia and banish fear and misery.

---

[1] British historian David Thomson, in his study *Democracy in France*, commented that "the overturn of royal sovereignty meant the destruction of the only power which had held together the diverse, dispersed powers of Church, nobility and 'parliaments.'" American historian, Crane Brinton, in his *Decade of Revolution*, observed that "the French Revolution did destroy, as completely as it can be destroyed, the nexus of loyalities, which had once made the old regime an authority."

In France, however, the Revolution did not banish poverty, did not bring heaven to earth.

Government by committee proved no less tyrannical and considerably less efficient than one-man government. The will of the people had a strong, articulate voice but a paralyzed body. This body, the National Assembly, was divided against itself. Instead of representing all the people—an absurd theory predicated on the premise that all people have exactly the same interests and opinions—it degenerated into special-interest groups, with deputies from different regions and of different social classes warring among themselves. This is an inherent characteristic of parliamentary democracy but its defects are overcome, or at least attenuated, in those democracies that instituted counterbalances, in independent executive and judicial powers. In France, however, the leaders of the Revolution refused to limit the "sovereignty of the people" in any way. The legislative power was supreme, the executive its servant.

Each of the succeeding three Republics of France preserved this basic principle of the First Republic. Every attempt to limit the legislative power was defeated by the "people's representatives," jealous of their own prerogatives and fearful of some new tyranny, ever lurking in the background, ready to destroy French democracy.

These historic fears were kept constantly alive by the series of revolutions and counterrevolutions that exploded in France every generation since 1789.

The experiment in constitutional monarchy, after the fall of the Bastille, ended when Louis XVI was beheaded in 1793. The subsequent First Republic of France was drowned in the blood of the Terror within a year. The Terror degenerated into the Directory, which became an easy victim of Napoleon's *coup d'état* in 1799. The French torch of liberty, which had once enflamed the hopes of all Europe, became in Napoleon's hands a torch of war that put all Europe to flame. Napoleon himself lasted only one generation and by 1814 the Bourbon dynasty was restored to the throne of France by the victorious allies. In the space of only twenty-five years Frenchmen had lived under the Bourbons, the Republic, the Convention, the Commune, the Directory, the Empire and finally ended up exactly where they had begun, under the rule of the Bourbons.

The Bourbon Restoration had little popular support, owing its existence to foreign powers. There was a moment of panic when, in 1815, Bonaparte escaped from Elba and marched triumphantly back to Paris, while Louis XVIII ran for his life. That fantastic "Hundred Days" episode ended at Waterloo, in one of the most extraordinary battles of history. The Bourbons came nervously back but they did not last much longer. In 1830 Charles X, last of the Bourbons, was driven into exile by a second French Revolution.

Only a few months before, however, Charles had taken a fateful decision, which was to affect the future of France: he sent an expeditionary corps to Algiers. In July, 1830, French soldiers conquered and annexed Algeria while the people in Paris were busy overthrowing the last of the Bourbons. The Bourbons have long since gone but the French Republic is today fighting a desperate war in Algeria to preserve the Bourbon legacy.

The Revolution of 1830 was a return to 1789 and the principle of constitutional monarchy, with a prince of the Orléans family, Louis-Philippe, becoming king. The experiment lasted eighteen years. Its principal achievement was the consolidation of the conquest of Algeria and little else. A new nobility of the bourgeoisie came to power in the reign of Louis-Philippe, whom the people called "King of the Bourgeois." The bourgeoisie was as self-assured and selfish as the nobility of the old pre-1789 regime. When some of the working-class deputies demanded an extension of the franchise, the King's First Minister, Guizot, replied: "If you want a vote, get rich."[2]

In February, 1848, the poor people of Paris revolted again, ending the experiment in constitutional monarchy. King Louis-Philippe, last of the French kings, fled to England, and closed the royal history of France on a comic note by traveling under the most common of all commoners' names, Mr. Smith.

The Revolution of 1848 was a return to the principles of 1793, of the First Republic, the abortive "Republic of Virtue." The people of Paris, who had led the revolts of 1789, 1793 and 1830, had each time been cheated of their victory. In 1848 they were determined to create a state that was truly of, by and for the people. The Second Republic was proclaimed to be the first "democratic and social Republic" of Europe.

The right to a job became one of the new and most important of

[2] Albert Guérard, *France: A Short History*, New York, W. W. Norton, 1946.

the "Rights of Man." National workshops—in modern American terms, P.W.A. projects—were created to give jobs to the unemployed. The chief of government, who promoted the reform program, was the poet Lamartine, and the head of the Republic's "brain trust" was the Socialist economist Louis Blanc. The Second Republic, even more than the First, was a precursor of the present Fourth Republic of France, although modern politicians constantly declaim their devotion to the principles of 1789. 1789 in France is a magic date, as 1776 is in America, but it has become a memory to revere rather than a set of principles to follow.

The workshop project was a failure, ruined by poor administration and discredited by boondoggling. The poor got poorer, the rich, richer. Before the Second Republic was six months old the barricades were up again in the streets of Paris and another revolution seemed imminent. The rest of the country, however, closed ranks against the Paris proletariat, in an alliance of the merchant middle class and the farmers against the "Reds." Lamartine's Government resigned. General Cavaignac, fresh from a campaign of repression in Algeria, led the troops against the workers and crushed the insurrection. The "democratic and social Republic" was no longer democratic nor social.

The approval of the Constitution in November was an anticlimax, for its principles now echoed hollowly over the bloodstained cobblestones of the capital. The new Constitution provided the framework of an American-style presidential government, France's first experiment in direct election of an executive, but it had none of the checks-and-balances of the American Constitution. The result, as French democrats had long feared, was a return to one-man dictatorship.

The election was won by Prince Louis-Napoleon, nephew of Bonaparte, with a tremendous popular majority. Louis-Napoleon soon made himself into a Caesar, emulating his illustrious uncle. First he disenfranchised some three million workers, then he dissolved the legislature and scheduled new elections. The merchants and peasants, safely controlling the majority, re-elected their strong-man idol, and cheered "the new Emperor."

On December 2, 1852, Louis-Napoleon formally became Napoleon III, the "elected Emperor" of the French. The Second Republic was dead. Long live the Second Empire!

The Second Empire was not, however, long-lived. Louis-Napoleon thought he was a new Bonaparte but he was not. He drained France's strength in a series of wars, in the Crimea, in Austria and in the mad adventure in Mexico, where Louis's protégé Maximilian was briefly enthroned by a French expeditionary corps and then dethroned by Mexican bullets. A few years later, in 1870, another protégé of Louis-Napoleon, Count Bismarck of Prussia, ended the comedy of his Empire by invading and defeating France.

The fall of Napoleon III completed a fifty-year cycle of two monarchies, two republics and one empire. Once again France was back in 1789, in search of a regime in which men could live at peace and in freedom.

There was a bitter battle between those who wanted to restore the monarchy, the "good old days," and those who still had not lost faith in the Republic, arguing, with some justice, that the previous republics had not lasted long enough to prove their worth. The Republicans won the argument by accident and by default.

The royalists had won a large majority in the Assembly but were split between those who wanted to restore the Bourbons, in the person of the grandson of Charles X, and those who favored the grandson of Louis-Philippe, of the Orléans dynasty. While the Bourbons fought the Orléanists, the Republicans were able to draft a liberal Constitution and regain popular support. In the 1876 general elections the Republicans won a clear majority.

Royalist President Marshal MacMahon thereupon dissolved the Assembly and called new elections, in true dictatorial style. However, the French were weary of soldiers and dictators. They voted Republican, albeit by a smaller majority, and the Marshal's coup failed. The French had had another lesson in the weakness of the Republic and the danger of presidential government. Never again would they allow a president or a premier, or any one man, to have real executive power. In this series of events lie the deep-rooted psychoses that account for the present spectacle of French political crises, with cabinets rising and falling every few months.

I have often been asked in my career as a commentator of French affairs: why can't the French keep a government in office? The answer might be put this way: because Richelieu and Louis XIV were vain and arbitrary despots; because Robespierre was a fanatic and

Bonaparte a megalomaniac; because Louis-Napoleon was an apprentice Caesar; because Cavaignac, MacMahon and Boulanger epitomized the military dictator; because, in short, every monarch, politician or soldier who ever held executive power in France used it to disenfranchise the people and impose his personal will upon the nation.

Thus the people of France have become convinced that they have a vested interest in weak and unstable government. The cabinet crisis in France is a kind of bloodless revolution. The "no confidence" vote in Parliament, that brings down a premier, is the dry guillotine of the twentieth century.

ᕫᕤᕬ

The technique of the bloodless revolution and the dry guillotine was developed into a fine art under the Third Republic. More than a thousand cabinet ministers were victims of the "political terror" that executed governments on the average of one every four months.

The ministers, however, developed a countertechnique of their own. Like a phoenix rising from its ashes, a minister would fall from office only to return immediately under a new premier, to serve in a different capacity. Minister of Justice in the Cabinet of Premier Y would become Minister of the Interior in the Cabinet of Premier Z, while ex-Premier Y would be reincarnated as Minister of Foreign Affairs.

A cabinet crisis was thus not really a crisis, it was a game of musical chairs or, if you like, an ingenious, political pressure valve, which permitted the deputies and the public to blow off steam without blowing up the country. Foreigners, particularly the British and Americans, never ceased to marvel at the capers of the French. The only conclusion they could reach was that Frenchmen were irresponsible lunatics and that no sane man could possibly comprehend the French political system.

In fact the system, with all its defects and disadvantages, was not insane. It corresponded to the particular circumstances of French national life. France was not Britain nor America, neither in geography, nor in history, nor in temperament. Britons lived in a tight, little island which could not produce enough food to feed itself. Britons had to live in harmony and organize their trade with the world in order to exist. America, through most of its formative years, was also an island fortress, protected from the stormy currents of world affairs by its two great ocean-moats.

France, through most of its long life, was, on the contrary, the storm center of a violent world. Located at the very tip of the Eurasian Peninsula, where it looks out on the Atlantic world and on Africa, France was subject to all the crosstides and riptides of history.

The fertile land of France was a treasurehouse of self-sufficiency before the industrial Age of Steel. The French could afford the luxury of anarchy. Habits long acquired are difficult to change and Frenchmen felt no compulsion to change their habits, just so long as the nation grew stronger and more prosperous every generation. And this was the miracle of France, for, despite the surface changes of its political regimes, France was one of the most stable and prosperous societies in the world, right up to the First World War.

Kings and Caesars rose and fell in France but the true rulers of French society were the bourgeois merchants and farmers. They were the real victors of 1789. The urban middle classes, who had achieved great economic power even before 1789, won political power in the Revolution and held on to it thereafter. The kings and dictators only reigned, the merchants ruled in France. For the rural middle class the Revolution was the culmination of their greatest aspirations, for the peasant acquired land in 1789, and land is life to the farmer.

The peasant was thereafter content to leave legislative control to his allies, the urban producer and merchant, whose vision of Paradise, like his own, was a Pearly Gate of tariffs, behind which thrifty and sober angels could make a high profit with a peacefully low production. "No sweat, no imports, no taxes" was the bourgeois vision of heaven on earth, the middle-class motto that replaced "Liberty, equality, fraternity."

The devil, in the person of the proletariat, began to threaten the earthly Paradise of the French bourgeois in the mid-nineteenth century, with the advent of the Industrial Revolution, the one form of revolution which the French middle classes feared. In 1848 and again in 1870 the merchants and peasants joined forces to crush insurrections by the workers of Paris.

The Paris workers were almost all Socialists in the nineteenth

century, and then, after the Russian Revolution, most of them
became Communists. The middle classes, seeing their privileges and
power threatened, made precisely the same mistake that the old
nobility had made when it was challenged by the bourgeoisie in 1789.
It refused to share its privileges, refused to change with the times.

In other countries, like Britain and America, the mercantile
capitalism of the past was beginning to evolve from the industrial
to the managerial era and to develop a new social and democratic
capitalism to meet the new challenge. In France, however, the
retrograde merchants and peasants fought the workers instead
of fighting Communism. The resultant social pressures strained the
fabric of the Republic to the breaking point.

At this critical moment in French history, World War I exploded.
It was a war from which France never completely recovered.

From 1914 to 1918 France lost 1,400,000 men killed, 4,000,000
wounded and 500,000 taken prisoner, a total of almost 6,000,000
men, almost 75 per cent of all the men mobilized. The destruction
of property and public works was equally tremendous. More than
five million homes and factories were destroyed or badly damaged.
The total cost to France of the First World War in terms only of
physical destruction and war costs exceeded $500,000,000,000.

Not only were her homes destroyed, her men killed and maimed,
but these losses engendered other losses. The death of a young man
means the loss of the children he would have sired. The best part
of an entire generation of French citizens was not born. It is no
mere coincidence that Frenchmen won twenty-eight Nobel Prizes for
science and literature from 1901 to 1939 but only four awards from
1939 to 1953. The boys who should have been in class in the
twenties, to emerge as leaders in the forties, were never conceived.

While France was still rebuilding the wreckage of the First World
War, the second one broke out in 1939.

Casualties in World War II cost France 500,000 soldiers and
300,000 civilians killed. Another 40,000 Frenchmen were killed in the
Resistance movement. Nearly 2,000,000 Frenchmen were enslaved
as forced laborers in Germany, where almost 200,000 of them died.
Of those who came back, three out of four were broken in body.
As for the children who grew up in France during the occupation,
they were wasted with disease and undernourishment.

The briefest list of German economic looting in France in two occupations, that of 1871 and of 1940, is monumental. In 1871 the French had to pay the Prussians a war indemnity of one billion dollars. One cannot even approximate the loss involved in the German annexation of Alsace-Lorraine. In the second occupation, from 1940 to 1944, the Germans requisitioned more than two billion dollars' worth of agricultural products and almost two billions more of industrial products. When France was starving and tuberculosis had shot up to 300 per cent of normal, the German Army took 150,000,000 *dozen* eggs and 300,000 tons of fruit out of France. French industry was wrecked by the Germans who stole almost all the machine tools of France. No nation in modern times has suffered the terrible losses of men and matériel lost by France in the three wars with Germany, from 1870 to 1940.[3]

Germany, too, suffered heavy losses, particularly in the Second World War, but Germany had twice as many men between the ages of twenty and sixty as France had, so that proportionate losses were less and replacement more rapid. Germany also had the good fortune to lose both wars, so that the "victor," France, had to maintain costly military establishment and reconstruction programs, while "defeated" Germany was being rebuilt by the Allies. After 1945 Germany was able to devote all her energies to productive efforts rather than the nonproductive rearmament program that drained the French economy.

It was a miracle, in politically volatile France, that the Republic could survive such killing blows. Yet it did, from 1871 to 1940. Its collapse in 1940 was brought about by the military defeat and not by an internal revolution. The autocratic, imitation-Nazi "État Français" of doddering Marshal Pétain and cynical, corrupt Pierre Laval never took root in French soil, nor in the hearts of most Frenchmen. At the liberation it disappeared like a bad dream, leaving only a haunting feeling of shame.

There never was the slightest doubt, throughout the years of occupation, that the Republic would be restored as soon as France was liberated. The only question was whether the Third Republic

[3] Figures on manpower losses supplied by the Ministry of Labor, on matériel losses by the Ministry of Economic Affairs.

should be revived, by simply erasing the Vichy statutes, or whether a new Fourth Republic should be created.

This question was put to the people of France by referendum on October 21, 1945. By an overwhelming majority of more than twenty-five to one the French voted in favor of a Fourth Republic, rather than the resurrection of the Third. Another regime was going to make its bow on the crowded stage of French history.

4 Birth of the Fourth Republic

On June 18, 1940, forty million Frenchmen mourned the fall of France. The government had fled to Bordeaux and had transferred executive authority from civilian leadership to aged Marshal Pétain, a prelude to surrender, the next morning, to the Germans.

Frenchmen, turning on their radios for the evening news, knew that only a miracle could save them from disaster, but few Frenchmen believed any longer in miracles.

Yet a miracle did occur, as they so often have for France in her darkest hours. A voice spoke to them, a deep, solemn but confident voice, coming from the last capital of Europe that still defied the Nazis, London.

"Has the last word been spoken? Must hope die now? Is our defeat decisive? No," the voice thundered, "nothing is lost for France!"

This was the "immortal message of June 18," the radio appeal to Frenchmen to take heart, to resist the Germans, delivered by General Charles de Gaulle. It was the message that lived on in history in the oft-cited phrase, "France has lost a battle, not the war."

De Gaulle never pronounced that phrase in exactly those words. What he said was, "This war has not ended with the battle of France. This war is a world war," but the shorter, more dramatic version that lived on was close enough to what de Gaulle actually had said to be valid.

De Gaulle did more that night than reassure his compatriots that the fight would continue. He called upon them to join the fight, to escape to England, where they would be welcomed in the common cause: "I, General de Gaulle at present in London, invite French officers and men, who are in British territory, or who might come there, with or without their arms, I invite engineers and skilled

workers of the armament industry, who are in British territory, or
who might come there, to put themselves in touch with me. Whatever
happens, the flame of French resistance must not and will not be
extinguished."

The news that Charles de Gaulle was in London, organizing a
resistance movement, spread rapidly through France that night. The
next day, the day of Pétain's surrender, every Frenchman who
could get near a radio set twisted the dials anxiously, searching for
"*La Voix de Londres,*" the famous BBC news channel, over which
de Gaulle had spoken. They were not disappointed. The Voice
spoke again: "Every Frenchman who still bears arms has the absolute
duty of continuing resistance. . . . Soldiers of France, wherever you
are, ARISE!"

This was the voice of history, the voice of Clemenceau, of Joan
of Arc, of Vercingetorix, of all the heroes of France who had led
the resistance against a foreign invader. What Frenchman could fail
to miss this symbolism? De Gaulle himself consciously evoked
history, when he chose as his flag the Cross of Lorraine, the Cross
of Saint Joan.

His cry of defiance and of hope echoed throughout the world
and Charles de Gaulle became overnight a hero to Britons and to
Americans, as well as to the French. Later, Winston Churchill,
his patience strained to the breaking point by de Gaulle's in-
tractability, was to sigh, "Of all the crosses I have to bear, that of
Lorraine is the heaviest," but in June of 1940 the Cross of Lorraine
burdened no man. It was held high by strong and willing hands and
cheered by millions who had not lost faith in France.

∽

Inevitably a new myth was written into the history books of
France, the myth of the Resistance, of men rising spontaneously
throughout the land to answer the call of de Gaulle. Many men did
arise but many, many more did not.

There is no better judge of what happened to de Gaulle's appeal
than one of his closest associates, one of the most patriotic of all
Frenchmen I have ever known: Philippe Barrès denounced the myth
in his biography of Charles de Gaulle, published at the liberation.

Barrès wrote:

Here we must face a cruel truth, but one which only augments the grandeur of de Gaulle: his appeals from London, echoing around the world through the sinister silence of the French disaster, seemed certain to stir many hearts, inspire many men to action, hundreds of thousands of men, in France and in the French Empire. Alas, no! Such was not the case at the outset. Volunteers did come, by the thousands, brave men who did honor to the General. But it was not a great wave. Such a wave was not possible. France, in July, 1940, was too stupefied, too crushed, too much a prisoner of the German invaders.

It is sad, for one who still remembers with a thrill the voice of June 18, to call the Resistance a myth. It is, however, necessary, I believe, to separate the myths from the realities. The reality of the Resistance, which later did grow into a powerful inspiring force, was glorious enough without exaggeration. It was, however, very different from the myth of an immediate uprising of all Frenchmen. This is a distinction to be drawn not only for the sake of historical accuracy, which by itself would be enough reason, but also to help understand what happened later, after the liberation and the birth of the Fourth Republic.

Above all it is necessary to note that the early resistance movement was no more general than it was immediate. The Communists, who were later to boast of their heroism and patriotism, did not join the Resistance in June, 1940, because they were still the political allies of the Nazis, still following the Soviet line, based upon the Ribbentrop-Molotov Pact. Only *after* the Nazi invasion of Russia, one full year later, did the Communist leaders suddenly remember that they were Frenchmen, and that a man named de Gaulle had called on Frenchmen to arise and fight the Germans.

Many French Communists were patriots and did join the Resistance in the early days, but their party had no right to take credit for their heroism, for the Communist party made no move to encourage its members to answer de Gaulle's appeal. When the party finally did join in, the Communist underground was brilliantly organized and highly effective, as all Communist undergrounds are. It thus was later able to campaign as the "Party of the Martyrs," boasting that seventy-five thousand Communists had died fighting in the maquis for the liberation of France.

This myth endured for years, still endures today. But it is a myth. The Communists have never published the names of their

seventy-five thousand martyrs, although they have often been challenged to do so. The total names ever published by them does not
reach the figure of five hundred. Yet they were able to exploit this
myth so effectively that at the liberation the Communist party was
by far the biggest, strongest, most popular party in France.

The myth had another, equally important, result. It enabled
hundreds of thousands of active collaborators and millions of passive
spectators to pretend to have been secret members or sympathizers
of the Resistance.

When I came to France, as a soldier in the liberating armies, I
found that every Frenchman claimed to be a "Résistant." Everyone
could boast of a patriot hidden in his barn, or a Jew saved from
the extermination camp, or some cunning act of sabotage of Vichy.
Only the most fanatic, active collaborators ever admitted their
collaboration.

Others, particularly those who worked for Pétain and the Vichy
regime, claimed to have been secret agents of the underground,
sending through intelligence information, gathered in their work,
which explained their service to Vichy. This was a convenient and
plausible myth. There were indeed many secret agents inside Vichy
and many more Frenchmen who played the "double game," col-
laborating with the Germans and aiding the Resistance at the same
time, so that they could not lose no matter which side won.

This truth was well known in France but it was rarely discussed
in the early days because wartime leaders feared it might besmirch
the glorious name of the Resistance and lower the prestige of France.
Perhaps they were right to allow the myth to develop, for in time
of war men need inspiration. However, they were wrong, I feel,
to let it stand unchallenged after the liberation, for it gave both
the Communists and the collaborators a cover under which they
could steal back into the fold of the Republic and be given another
chance to wreck French democracy, a chance they did not fail to
exploit.

∽

General de Gaulle never gave up hope despite the failure of his
countrymen to rise as one to resist the Germans. Enough Frenchmen
did arise to give validity to his "Free French" movement in London.

However, de Gaulle did not succeed in winning full Allied recognition of this movement. There was no French "government-in-exile" in London, as there were Czech, Belgian and Polish governments-in-exile. The legal government of France was in France, in Vichy, a hard fact that no myth could deny.

The parliamentarians of France, the duly authorized representatives of the people, had voted full powers to Pétain. The Third Republic was not murdered. It committed suicide. This was the principal, legal argument for the creation of a Fourth Republic, rather than the automatic resurrection of the Third.

The liberators of France, however, decided that this issue should be resolved by the people of the country. It was agreed that the question would be submitted to the electorate in a national referendum.

The vote was held on October 21, 1945. Two questions were put to the public:

1. Do you authorize the legislators to draft a new Constitution? Answer "*oui*" or "*non.*"
2. Do you approve the proposals of the Provisional Government on the duration and powers of the legislature?

For once the clichés of the songwriters proved to be an accurate description of the French, for, on October 21, 1945, in France they said, "*oui, oui.*" On the first question the vote was 18,585,000 in favor of a new constitution and only 700,000 against it. On the second question the affirmative also won out but the totals were significantly different: 12,795,000 "*oui*" and 6,500,000 "*non.*" On this second question the winning majority had been narrowed down to 60 per cent of the votes cast and only 50 per cent of the total electorate.

The reason for the big difference between the affirmative replies to the two questions was the opposition of the Communist party to the government proposal, which limited the duration of the constituent legislature to seven months. Communist opposition to this proposal was the first public breach in the ranks of the Resistance parties, the first warning sign that the still unborn Fourth Republic was going to suffer from the same internal divisions that had weakened its ancestors.

The Communists opposed the deadline on the powers and on the life of the Constituent Assembly because they were certain to win the greatest number of seats in the legislature. They wanted no brief seven-month tenure of office.

The elections were held simultaneously with the referendum. Communist expectations of victory were fully realized as their candidates rolled up the highest total of votes:

Communists	5,005,000
Socialists	4,561,000
Catholics (MRP)	4,780,000

The "Big Three" of the Constituent Assembly would thus be the parties which had been most active in the resistance movement. They won more than fourteen million of the nineteen million votes cast. The remainder was divided between two small groups, the Radicals and the Conservatives.

The Radicals had been France's most influential prewar party, but it was also the party of Daladier, the "man of Munich," which led to its early postliberation eclipse. The Conservatives, another influential group in the Third Republic, were equally handicapped by the memory of their part in the fall of France. Many individuals in the conservative groups of France had distinguished themselves in the Resistance but the great majority of the men of the Right had done business as usual under the occupation. They paid for their lack of patriotism at the polls.

The triumphant parties were all parties of the Left. The Catholic MRP particularly insisted upon being called a leftist party, to counter the anticlerical politicians who always branded the Church as rightist.

The embryo of the body politic of the Fourth Republic was thus a monster with a shriveled right wing, a shrunken middle, and a huge, swollen left wing. Most seriously, the body politic soon became separated from the head of the Republic when the Communists openly split with Charles de Gaulle.

༄

De Gaulle tried at first to effect a union and drape the misshapen embryo of the Republic in a tricolor flag.

On November 11, after placing a wreath on the tomb of the Unknown Soldier in the traditional Armistice Day celebration, de Gaulle delivered a speech calling on Frenchmen to "unite as brothers to heal the wounds of France. Fraternally we must try to silence the noise of our absurd quarrels."

There was, however, little fraternity in liberated France. The "absurd quarrels" were not ended, for the good reason that they were not so absurd as de Gaulle claimed.

The conflict that had developed between de Gaulle and the political parties went to the roots of the historic struggle between the legislative and executive powers in France. It was a classic conflict between the extremes of representative government and autocratic rule, between Communism and Caesarism. In addition, the political parties were competing among themselves, each seeking a dominant or a key position in the Republic they were mandated to create.

The Communists were striking for power as hard and as fast as they could. Since the referendum had given the deputies only seven months to draft a constitution, the Communists knew that every minute counted. This was their first, and might be their last, real chance to come to power legally. There was a Communist-Socialist majority in the Constituent Assembly resulting from the October 21 elections, so that for the first time in history the Marxist parties controlled the Parliament of France.

On November 13, 1945 the Constituent Assembly met to select a new chief executive. Catholic leader Pierre-Henri Teitgen and Socialist leader Vincent Auriol arose in turn to propose the name of Charles de Gaulle. All eyes were on the tiny, roly-poly Communist delegation leader in the Assembly, Jacques Duclos. Duclos knew the Socialist decision to back de Gaulle had halted for the moment the Communist drive for power. He spoke only briefly, saying that the Communists would of course vote with their "Resistance partners to preserve Republican unity." It was all over in one hour. De Gaulle was elected premier unanimously by the 555 deputies voting. It was, however, only the first round, and everyone knew it.

The next round began when Premier de Gaulle called in party leaders to discuss the formation of his cabinet.

De Gaulle told the Communists that he would be happy to

allocate cabinet posts to them but, he said, not one of the three key cabinet portfolios, Interior, Foreign Affairs and National Defense, which the Communists claimed they merited as the first party of France. De Gaulle told Thorez that, as chief executive, he had to exercise his mandate and appoint his cabinet ministers as he thought best.

Thorez rejected de Gaulle's offer angrily. The Communist party, he replied, demanded its fair share of responsibility on equitable, democratic terms, in accordance with the will of the French people, expressed at the polls.

Unable to form a government with the first party of France in opposition, but unwilling to entrust the police, the army and the diplomacy of France to a party that he considered an agent of a foreign power, de Gaulle decided to return his mandate as premier to the Constituent Assembly. He wrote a letter to that effect to Speaker of the House, Félix Gouin. Thus France had a cabinet crisis before it even had a constitution.

The political bureau of the Communist party promptly issued a communiqué saying the party was ready to assume its responsibilities, a very strong hint that the Communists were ready to name one of their own men to form a government in place of de Gaulle. The Catholic MRP just as promptly sent out a communiqué restating its loyalty to de Gaulle, insisting it would support nothing less than a government of national unity formed under the General's leadership. The Socialist executive committee met and decided that it would join a government without de Gaulle if necessary, but only a "three-party" coalition. The Socialists refused to be trapped into a Communist-Socialist merger in which they would be swallowed up and the country be torn by class warfare.

Vincent Auriol proposed that the party leaders go to see de Gaulle and try to find a compromise. The Communists refused and came out into the open demanding the premiership for one of their members. The Socialists again said they would only vote for a Communist if the Catholics joined them. The Catholic MRP again refused. The parties were spinning around in circles, getting nowhere, a preview of the next decade of French history as well as the specter of the past.

De Gaulle decided the time had come to make his position clear to the people of France. He delivered a nation-wide radio address explaining that he was ready to co-operate with the Communists, to seek their "valuable support" in solving economic and social problems but, he said bluntly, he would not confide in them "the three levers that control the foreign policy of a nation: the diplomacy that expresses it, the army that supports it, the police that covers it." The policy of France, said de Gaulle, must be that of a "balance between the two great political powers of the world in the interests of the nation and of peace itself."

Without specifying Russia and America by name, as the great powers to whom he had referred, de Gaulle made it clear that he was referring to those nations. He went on to say that France must not take sides for either of the two great powers, even in appearance, which was why he could not grant the pro-Soviet party direction of the three key ministries.

De Gaulle concluded by rejecting any compromise on that central issue: "As for myself, I would deem myself unworthy of being chief of government of France if I failed, for reasons of political expediency, to give full consideration to this issue of supreme national interest."

The Communists were furious. Their editorials screamed insults at de Gaulle, called him a dictator, a new Napoleon, an apprentice Caesar. They said the breach in the unity of the Resistance was final, could never be closed and that they would vote against de Gaulle if his name were again put forward for premier.

The Socialists were almost as critical of de Gaulle, of the contents as well as of the tone of his address, particularly the sensational hint he had given that war might be threatening between Russia and America. The Socialists were further alarmed and angry at de Gaulle's use of the national radio network to speak directly to the people, over the heads of their representatives, after he had already returned his mandate to the Assembly. This was to them a modern version of Louis-Napoleon's plebiscites. The Socialists too began to talk about demagogy and the threat of dictatorship.

The deadlock seemed unbreakable and tensions were high when the deputies began to convene on Monday afternoon, the nineteenth of November, to take action on de Gaulle's resignation. Strong police cordons were thrown around the Assembly building, from the public entrance on the Quai d'Orsay around to the deputies' entrance in the Place du Palais Bourbon. Army units were stationed on the Pont de la Concorde and the Pont Alexandre III.

Inside the Assembly the diplomatic galleries were packed. In their center boxes, overlooking the red-plush hemicycle of the House, sat the Ambassadors of the Soviet Union and the United States. It was more than six months before the rupture of the wartime alliance, before the cold war had officially begun, but de Gaulle, like Churchill, had a prophetic vision of the future.

Inside the Palais Bourbon, in the strange world of the French Parliament, nothing corresponds to the reality of the outer world. The meeting turned out to be one of the calmest ever held in a frequently stormy Assembly. There was no tension, no violence, no bitterness. A deal had already been made by the party bosses the night before. It was a signal of how political affairs would be conducted in the early years of the Republic: by the political party leaders, meeting outside Parliament.

The deputies of the Assembly had become agents of parties rather than representatives of constituencies. It was a result of two vital political changes that distinguished postliberation France from the Third Republic: the introduction of proportional representation and the growth of strong and disciplined political parties.

The deal was the result of an understanding between the Socialists and Catholics to refuse to throw their balance of power either to the Communists or to de Gaulle, but to force both of the conflicting parties to compose their differences. It was put in the form of a motion expressing confidence in de Gaulle, returning to him an imperative mandate, that he could not refuse as a patriot, and appealing to him to renew his negotiations with the Communists.

The motion was proposed and seconded by Socialist André Philip and Catholic Robert Schuman. It passed by a vote of 358 to 39, the Communists abstaining. That same evening de Gaulle bowed to the will of the Assembly and asked the leaders of the three majority parties to meet with him again the next morning to break the deadlock.

The debate had revealed two more significant signs of the future: there was no majority for a Communist government but there would be no carte blanche for de Gaulle. When forced to choose

between Thorez and de Gaulle, the parties chose de Gaulle but
with firm instructions to him to ease his inflexible position.

The deadlock was quickly broken. The Communists knew that an
all-or-nothing position would leave them with nothing. De Gaulle
knew he had to make some gesture of conciliation, without yielding
the principle involved. The solution was ingenious, as French political
solutions generally are. It was also meaningless, for it evaded, rather
than resolved, the issue.

It was a Solomon-like decision to split the Ministry of National
Defense into two departments: a Ministry of the Armed Forces and
a Ministry of Armaments. The Armed Forces portfolio was given
to Catholic Edmond Michelet, while Communist Charles Tillon was
named Minister of Armaments. Thus the Communists had a voice in
national defense but did not have their hands directly on the defense
forces. It solved nothing, satisfied no one for very long, but it saved
faces and provided time to prepare for the next round.

ᏯᏯ

The next and penultimate round was fought in December in the
Budget debate. It was almost the last round. It came in the course
of consideration of National Defense credits. As so often in Assembly
debates, the crisis erupted at three o'clock in the morning.

Without warning the Socialists suddenly proposed an amendment
to the National Defense Budget, reducing its credits automatically
by 20 per cent because of the "scandalous waste and disorder in the
defense establishment." Vice-Premier Vincent Auriol, de Gaulle's
righthand man in the cabinet, although himself a leading Socialist,
intervened immediately against his own party's amendment, demanding that it be withdrawn, or "the government would draw the necessary consequences from the Assembly's action," an unmistakable
threat of resignation.

The Communists, seeing a new opportunity to split the Socialists
from the other Resistance groups, promptly announced they would
vote for the Socialist amendment. The Assembly recessed at dawn
until the following afternoon, during which time moderate party
leaders tried to persuade the Socialists to withdraw their amendment,
without success.

When the Assembly reconvened the next afternoon de Gaulle stalked into the Chamber determined to lay down the law to the lawmakers.

At the first opportunity he arose from the government bench, faced the House and said: "Does this government have your confidence or doesn't it? It is your prerogative to say yes or no. You can vote or refuse to vote the credits the government says it needs." De Gaulle warned the deputies, however: "This will undoubtedly be the last time I will speak in this Chamber. Therefore I want to tell you now: if you do not respect the necessary conditions for responsible and dignified government, you are heading for a time when you will bitterly regret the path you have chosen."

The chief of government told the legislators in conclusion: "My conception of the presidency is the following: so long as the Assembly does not withdraw its confidence the government alone bears the responsibility of executive power. If this confidence is withdrawn, even partially, the government will resign."

De Gaulle's intransigence and his enormous personal prestige, particularly in military matters, carried the day and the credits were restored. However, by threatening to resign if the deputies limited, "even partially," their mandate to the government, de Gaulle had made a serious crisis seem inevitable, for the sovereign Assembly was jealous of its powers and resentful of de Gaulle's autocratic rule. The forces of history were at work, the specters of past autocrats haunted the Chamber.

However, there was no crisis. De Gaulle made it easy for the deputies. He simply quit in disgust, unable to stomach the daily quarrels of government life in France.

On the morning of January 20, 1946, Premier de Gaulle walked into the cabinet meeting room, sat down and announced: "I have decided to relinquish my post. My decision is irrevocable. I have asked Vincent Auriol to assume the direction of current affairs until a new government can be formed." De Gaulle thanked his colleagues for their past co-operation, got up and walked rapidly out, never to return again.

At nine-thirty that night his chief administrative assistant, Gaston

Palewski, delivered his official letter of resignation to Assembly Chairman Félix Gouin.

In the letter de Gaulle asked Gouin to inform the Assembly of his resignation as President of the Provisional Government. He explained that "from the day I assumed the charge of leading the country to its liberation, its victory and its sovereignty, I considered that my task must come to an end when the representatives and political parties of the nation would be able to assume their responsibilities." He said he had only consented to stay on beyond the elections because of the unanimous request of the Assembly, in order to see France through the transitional period.

Then de Gaulle made an astonishing statement: "Furthermore, after immense trials, France is no longer in a state of alarm. . . . The economy has become active again. Our territory is in our own control. We have set foot again in Indochina. The public peace is not troubled."

These "reasons," given by de Gaulle, were so patently untrue that the letter embarrassed his most fervent admirers.

France was not out of danger, not beyond the "state of alarm." Economic "activity" was barely crawling. If it was true that Frenchmen had set foot again in Indochina, it was equally true that Indochinese nationalists had trampled on their toes. They had declared their independence from France and set up their own government in Tonkin. As for the "public peace," it was profoundly troubled by strikes, demonstrations and by the general knowledge that Resistance networks, particularly the Communists, had built up a cache of arms, instead of turning them in as the Government had asked.

De Gaulle left his followers disorganized and dismayed, the country confused. His name will always be associated with the courage, vision and glory of June 18, 1940, of his refusal to accept military defeat, but the glory will always be tarnished by the memory of January 20, 1946, when he quit under fire at a moment in French history almost as crucial as the dark days of June, 1940.

De Gaulle's standing in French history might have been even further blackened had he not abandoned another project that he was considering just before deciding to quit his post as chief of government. De Gaulle, for many weeks, had been seriously considering a *coup d'état.* He admitted this publicly in his speech at the Vélodrome d'Hiver in February, 1950, and again two years later at the RPF National Council meeting at Saint Maur.[1]

It is to de Gaulle's credit that he finally rejected the idea of a *coup d'état* and that he abandoned power when he had it, thus disproving the charges that he was an apprentice dictator, but not, as his admirers insisted, proving that de Gaulle was a true democrat and patriot. True democrats and patriotic defenders of the Republic not only reject the idea of a *coup d'état*; they never even consider it, no matter how briefly, let alone for weeks.

De Gaulle had another alternative to the frustrating deadlocks of tripartite government than quitting in disgust, an alternative that he finally took a year later when he returned from his self-imposed exile to lead a new political movement. He could have done that in January, 1946. He could have resigned and called a news conference that day to state fully and frankly his real thoughts about the dangers menacing France.

De Gaulle was petulant and irresponsible when he sent his letter to Gouin. Had he stated his views immediately on the urgent necessity to create a balance between the legislative and executive powers he might have profoundly influenced the drafting of the Constitution in a constructive manner.

The General chose, instead, to steal off silently in the night, to sulk in his tent for a full year before returning, too late, to the political battleground. History is replete with crucial ifs and howevers but Charles de Gaulle has contributed one of the most tantalizing might-have-beens in all the conjectures of French history.

∾

For the Communists the de Gaulle resignation was a gift from the gods of politics. They could not have hoped to defeat the General in a direct attack. His voluntary retreat made a test of strength unnecessary, leaving the Communists the strongest force in the field. It was apparent that if they could find a way to drive a wedge in the Socialist and Catholic ranks, they could become masters of all France.

They found the wedge immediately: the religious school issue, the

[1] See Philip Williams, *Politics in Post-War France*, London, Longmans, 1954, page 17, footnote 7.

one issue on which the Social Democrats and the Christian Democrats divided.

As early as November, 1944, the Socialist party had held a National Congress at which a resolution was adopted recommending the strict neutrality of the State in matters of private school education. The resolution called for "cancellation of the Education Bill of 1942," which allocated an annual subsidy of some seven billion francs to Catholic schools.

The separation of Church and State, historic cornerstone of the "lay Republic," was an uncompromising principle for the Socialist party. The Socialists were staunch partisans of religious freedom but they refused to equate freedom to worship with state subsidies for religious schools. The Catholics, they said, were free to worship as they chose, free to have their own schools if they desired, but not entitled to get their education free from the taxes paid by other citizens.

The Catholics, in reply, argued that true freedom was based on education. How could they defend their faith, they asked, if they could not educate their children? They called their private schools *"écoles libres,"* free schools, to underline their case. The Catholic party leaders were particularly anxious to reassure the millions of devout citizens who were suspicious of the Christian-Socialist origins of the MRP and who could only be kept as electoral clients by a vigorous defense of Catholic schools.

The Socialists were equally anxious about their clients, the workers of France, who looked with suspicion on any project to support the Church. Once again the old ghosts of history loomed up in modern France: Cardinal Richelieu and Versailles frightening the Republicans, 1793 and the Terror frightening the Catholics. It was a tragedy that the Social Democratic and Christian Democratic parties should have been separated by this ancient quarrel but it was a live issue to them and not just a ghost.

Many liberals failed to appreciate the real problem of the Christian Democrats in France. The religious school issue was a matter of life or death at the polls for the MRP. Catholic leaders like Teitgen and many others were as socially conscious as any liberal or Social Democrat. They had no intention of violating the principle of separation of Church and State. Yet they were genuinely convinced, as well as politically persuaded, of the importance of Catholic school education.

It is easy for a non-Catholic, particularly a non-Catholic politician, to say that they should not have forced this issue, yet it was extremely difficult for the Catholic party politicians to do otherwise. Moreover, there were not enough public schools in France. If the Catholic schools had closed, hundreds of thousands of children would have been thrown into the streets.

As for the Socialists, they too were in a difficult position. They had to make many concessions on economic and social policies to the bourgeois parties in the name of democracy and the common front against Communism. These concessions cost them working-class support. They felt they had to draw the line somewhere, and for them it had to be drawn on the basic dividing line between Right and Left, the basic principle of the Republic, the separation of Church and State.

The Communists, always adept at drawing lines, helped draw this one for the Socialists. In a few weeks time they had realized their principal objective: a two-party Marxist alliance, controlling a majority vote in the Assembly. On April 19, 1946, the Socialists joined the Communists in voting for the draft Constitution of a Fourth Republic, which had mainly been written by Communists and left-wing Socialists. The draft created an all-powerful Assembly. Had it been adopted it might have wrecked French democracy for a long time, for the Communists could have made themselves masters of Parliament and then the country.

The draft Constitution was, however, rejected by an alerted and alarmed electorate in the second national referendum of May 5, 1946. The voters were anxious to end the provisional status of the Republic, but not at the price of delivering it to the Communists. This time the voters did not say, "*Oui, oui.*" They said, "*Non.*" The margin of defeat for the Communist- and Socialist-endorsed Constitution was one million votes. The official totals:

For	9,454,000
Against	10,585,000

The combined Communist and Socialist vote in the elections of October, 1945, had been nine and a half million, so the Left had not lost in absolute strength. However, the fact that the other groups had polled a million more than the Marxist parties indicated that the pendulum which had swung far left in October, 1945, had gone as far in that direction as it would and was beginning to swing back toward the Right.

The rejection of the draft Constitution meant that a new Constituent Assembly had to be elected to start in all over again. The elections were held on June 2 and the results further confirmed the swing away from the Left.

The Catholic party, which had led the opposition to the Marxist concept of a republic, polled 5,589,000 votes to win 169 seats in the new Constituent Assembly, displacing the Communists as the first party of France. The big jump was due largely to the Catholic campaign as the "party of General de Gaulle," a claim that the General did not repudiate.

The Communists lost only a little ground, with 153 seats, while actually increasing slightly their popular vote. The Socialists, apparently severely judged by their clients for their alliance with the Communists, lost almost 400,000 votes and were reduced to 129 seats. The Left, therefore, no longer had an absolute majority of the House; in fact, no homogeneous majority of any kind existed in the second Constituent Assembly.

The outlines of the Third Republic could already be discerned in the embryo of the Fourth.

ᏓᏇ

The new "first party," the Catholic MRP, took the lead in framing a new Constitution. However, having displaced the Communists as the most powerful party in the Assembly, the MRP was somewhat more inclined to favor the creation of an all-powerful Parliament. The MRP had one quality in common with the Marxist parties, and that was its group ambition and discipline. It was a monolithic party in the leftist style, and its group leader could snap the whip over its delegates in the Assembly, as pitilessly as any Communist commissar.

Party leader Georges Bidault, elected Premier of the new Provisional Government after the June elections, was more flexible than de Gaulle. He had been closely associated with the Communists and

Socialists as President of the National Council of the Resistance. Bidault was anxious to reconstitute the Resistance alliance.

The Communists and Socialists, shaken by the election results, less fearful of Bidault than of de Gaulle, were equally inclined to seek a coalition of interests. They agreed to let the Catholics take the lead.

The three parties worked rapidly together to produce the new draft Constitution. They succeeded in terminating it by the end of September, 1946. On the very day that the tripartite political alliance produced its draft Constitution in Parliament, Charles de Gaulle decided to intervene to prevent its adoption by the people. At a ceremony commemorating the second anniversary of the liberation of Epinal, the General addressed some sixty thousand people and called upon them to vote against the draft Constitution a second time.

De Gaulle called for a strong presidential system, based on a strict separation of powers. Above all, de Gaulle insisted that the chief executive should be independent of Parliament, "a Chief of State placed above the parties." The President of the Republic, for de Gaulle, should have the power to name the Premier and all the ministers, and also the power to dissolve Parliament. He said the President must be able to ask "the country to make known its sovereign decision by elections."

The Communists and Socialists launched an immediate counter-attack against de Gaulle. They accused him of Bonapartism, pointing out once again the parallel between his proposals and Louis Napoleon's use of the plebiscite. They also recalled Marshal Mac-Mahon's use of the power of dissolution as the horrible example of what happens when military men are made presidents.

The Catholics were in a terrible dilemma, caught completely off guard. They knew that a great part of their electoral clientele was "Gaullist." The millions of admirers that de Gaulle had in the country had no other party to join, since de Gaulle himself still refused to lead a political party. If the Catholics opposed de Gaulle, they might lose all their new-won strength. If, however, they followed de Gaulle's advice, they would have to reject a constitution they had drafted themselves, and prolong the dangerous, provisional status of the Republic.

It had been almost two years since all France had been liberated.

A vast task of reconstruction waited to be done. The legislation and planning needed to reconstruct French strength at home, and influence abroad, could not be accomplished by a Parliament whose members were constantly concerned with being re-elected every seven months.

After considerable soul-searching, the MRP decided to campaign for approval of the Constitution on the grounds that the country needed a permanent, effective regime. The contortions of party polemicist Maurice Schumann, in the official party paper, *l'Aube*, were extraordinary to behold. Schumann tried to prove that de Gaulle was actually counting on the MRP, "the party of fidelity," to attenuate the dangers of the Constitution by its vigilance in Parliament.

On October 9, just four days before the referendum, de Gaulle, angered by Schumann's sophistry, issued a communiqué to the press, making his opposition as precise as possible, "so that there cannot be the slightest doubt" of his opposition to the Constitution drafted and endorsed by the MRP.

On October 13, the country was called to the polling places for the third referendum in a year. This time, however, many millions failed to show up. Weary of the perpetual squabbles, unenthusiastic about a constitution that had been denounced by the country's liberator, yet concerned about political party warnings that another refusal might bring anarchy and chaos, more than eight million registered voters, one third of the electorate, stayed at home, either unable or unwilling to make up their mind. The final results:

Oui	9,296,419
Non	8,166,000
Abstentions	8,143,981

The Fourth Republic was born at last, but it was not a happy event. Only one-third of the people recognized the infant Republic as theirs. One-third rejected it outright. One-third of the nation was apparently indifferent, not even bothering to validate or annul its birth certificate.

∾

A French statesman of the nineteenth century, Jules Ferry, once said: "What France needs is weak government." This has been the creed of French democrats ever since. From Napoleon to Pétain, military dictators have used their powers to destroy democracy, whether power was given them freely as a trust or whether they seized it by force. The Fourth Republic was deliberately designed to make it impossible for that to happen again.

Article 13 of the Constitution expressly forbids the legislators to delegate their powers. Article 94 forbids revision of the Constitution if any part of France is under enemy occupation. Both clauses are clearly aimed at preventing a repetition of the surrender of authority by the deputies of the Third Republic in times of national crisis or, if a coup is engineered, of making certain that it has no legal sanction such as the vote of full powers to Pétain.

The majority in the Constituent Assembly was agreed on the necessity to vest all powers in Parliament. This was the central motivating force in the drafting of the Constitution. There was an equally large majority in agreement on the urgency of establishing ministerial responsibility to the legislature. The Catholics, the Communists and the Socialists all wanted a parliamentary regime, not a presidential system, as de Gaulle had demanded. The presidential system had been tried in 1848 and had led to the coronation of Emperor Napoleon III. Few French politicians would risk the system again.

To prevent even a premier from acquiring too much power, the Constitution vested almost all authority in the legislature. The executive was not only made responsible to the National Assembly, it was its prisoner, with almost no powers of its own. The right of dissolution, an important balance against the virtually unchecked legislative body, was so weak, even on paper, that it had little value.[2]

The real test of the Constitution would, however, only come in practice. The Constitution of the Third Republic had been no more popularly received than that of the Fourth. It had only been approved in the Constituent Assembly of 1875 by one vote. It had been drafted by royalists who were trying to design it as a transition back to a constitutional monarchy.

Yet the Third Republic grew very differently from the way its founding fathers had planned. It is the habit of fathers to plan the future of their children, instead of concentrating on making a child

[2] For further discussion of the Constitution, see Chapter 9, on Parliament; Chapter 10, "The Organs of State," and Chapter 13, on the French Union.

fit to face his own future. The future always belongs to the new generation, not the old, a simple, obvious truth many men forget. The same is true of political regimes and institutions.

The same political institution may be good or bad depending upon its place in time and space. What was good for eighteenth-century America is not necessarily good for twentieth-century America. The Constitution of the United States has had to be amended some two dozen times. A political regime can only be evaluated in terms of the society whose welfare it was designed to promote, and by the degree to which it faithfully reflects and respects the prevailing opinions of its own particular community.

More than a decade has passed since two out of every three French voters failed to endorse the Constitution, yet it has endured with very few revisions and the infant Republic has grown and prospered through one of the most trying periods of French and world history.

Constant criticism of the Constitution has not ceased, but it is now constructive criticism, reformist rather than revolutionary. The central issue ten years after the passing of the Constitution is the weakness, instability and consequent inefficiency of government and the utter inadequacy of the clauses regulating Overseas France. Most French democrats admit that a way must be found to increase the executive power and limit the legislative but few Frenchmen seriously propose changing the power equation sufficiently to make the executive stronger than or even equal to the legislative branch.

The Constitution, with all its faults, proved to be an adequate formula for raising the infant Republic. Or, if you prefer, did not prevent the Republic from developing. It could have certainly been a more perfect document. It can be, and is slowly being, perfected. However, it is no longer, if it ever was, the dominant factor in the functioning of the French political community. No constitution determines its society. The Soviet Constitution, on paper, is an intensely democratic document but Soviet society is a slave state. The British have virtually no constitution, yet enjoy life in one of the freest, most democratic societies in the world.

The place to look for an evaluation of French democracy is thus not in the written Constitution of the Fourth Republic but in the behavior and state of health of the living organism itself.

II A CLINICAL EXAMINATION

5 *The Body Politic*

The body politic of France is draped in as colorful and varied an assortment of political opinions as any of the mannequins in the most elegant salons of the *haute couture* of Paris.

The people of liberated France had a choice of some thirty-six political models to choose from in the first elections of 1945, with a color range from People's Red to Royal Blue, with all shades and mixtures in between. Red was a popular color in 1945. A royalist party even called itself the "Socialist Monarchists," selecting as its emblem a red fleur-de-lis. However, no one color or party could dominate in a country famed for the individualism of its citizens.

Frenchmen sought office under such original labels as "The Motorists' Defense Candidate," "The Party of National Discontent," "The Party of the Non-Parties." The quintessence of French individualism was achieved by Canon Kir when he campaigned in the Côte d'Or Department in 1951 as an "Independent Independent," after having quarreled with the leaders of the National Council of Independents. He was elected, thereby realizing the classic dream of a French politician: to head a party composed only of himself and just enough voters to put him in office.

Even after eliminating the eccentric individual cases, there are at least twelve tickets regularly competing in national elections put up by parties big enough to present candidates in several departmental districts. Curiously, and typical of the Fourth Republic, only one of the twenty in recent elections frankly called itself a "party." The others contrived with great ingenuity to find a wide variety of original synonyms.

The French Socialists refer to their party as the SFIO; the initials stand for the title "French Section of the Workers' International."

71

The Catholics chose to be known as the "Popular Republican Movement." The cells of the French body politic are apparently composed of sections, movements, rallies, councils and unions. The only cell that labels itself a political party is the "Parti Communiste Français."

༄

In practice, few of these names correspond to a political reality. It is almost as though each group had deliberately set out to choose a name that would be the opposite of what it was meant to represent. The French Communist party has demonstrated too many times its subservience to Moscow and its ecclesiastical insistence on obedience and faith, to be considered either French or a democratic political party in the Western sense of the term.

The "French Section of the Workers' International" is a highly inappropriate title for a Socialist party that is national-minded and composed mainly of functionaries and salaried employees rather than workers. The Workers' International, in any case, has been dead for a quarter of a century and more.

The Catholic MRP is no longer a "popular movement"; it has lost both popularity and motion in the ten years since it was founded at the liberation.

France's widely read political analyst, Jacques Fauvet of *Le Monde*, has suggested that the MRP, the SFIO, the RGR, ARS and URAS, prefer to use their initials instead of their full titles to hide the gap between the ideals invoked by their names and the reality of their political conduct. The Radical-Socialist party has not been radical nor Socialist since the First World War. The Action Républicaine et Sociale is an inactive, immobilist and conservative group, whose social program consists in opposing almost all social reforms.

The contrast between names, objectives and performances is only one of the many paradoxes that make French politics so incomprehensible to foreign observers and often to the French themselves. The confusion of labels is paralleled by a corresponding difficulty in classifying the party cells by structure and orientation.

The various political groups embrace entities as totally different in form and organization as the rigid, monolithic Communist party, the amorphous alliance of Independents and Peasants or the amoeba-like RGR that multiplies or divides itself at will.

Some parties, like the Socialists, have a doctrine, a political philosophy, a definable structure and discipline. The Socialist party has a party leader, democratically, if indirectly, elected by members, and supported by a corps of dues-paying members and militants. Others, like the Radicals and Independents, are political clubs, rather than parties, whose main function is to serve as campaign headquarters for its members during elections and to provide confidential back rooms for political strategy meetings between elections.

It has frequently been just as difficult to classify the parties by political orientation and there have been many angry disputes at the start of a parliamentary session in the course of assigning the groups seats to the right, in the center or to the left of the Speaker.

The successful Gaullist candidates for the Council of the Republic at first refused to sit on the right wing of the hemicycle in the Luxembourg Palace when they were assigned that position after the elections of 1948. They claimed they were not a "rightist party." The Gaullists were finally allowed to take seats in the center and on the left in the empty back rows of the Chamber, so as not to invade the territory of the Radicals, Catholics, Socialists and Communists, who occupy the front benches in those sections.

The same fight broke out more violently three years later when the Gaullists became the largest group in the National Assembly and wanted to dislodge the Radicals and the Catholics. One of the Radicals made the ingenious suggestion that the Communists and Gaullists ought to exchange places, since the traditional authoritarianism of the classic Right was best represented these days by the Communists.

The seating arrangement was finally put to a vote. All the parties between the two extremes of Gaullism and Communism banded together to vote the RPF deputies into the right-wing benches and keep the Communists where they have always been located, on the extreme left benches of the Chamber. This solved the seating arrangement of the Assembly but not the basic question of defining accurately the Right, Center and Left of the French body politic.

The classic political labels, Right, Left and Center, have, in fact, begun to lose their meanings in the mid-twentieth century.

The peasants and merchants descended from the revolutionaries of 1789 are on the Left in defense of the civil liberties won in that political revolution, but on the Right when it comes to the issues of the later Industrial Revolution and the economic and social liberties demanded by the workers.

The Christian Democrats are on the Left on issues emanating from the economic and social revolutions of the twentieth century but on the Right when it is a matter of defending the traditional interests of the Church.

In one and the same party, such as the Radicals, you find such men as Edouard Daladier, "the man of Munich," and Edouard Herriot, "the grand old man of the Republic." The "war of the two Edwards" was a constant feature of Third Republic politics. The traditional Radical schism has been preserved in the Fourth Republic by the war between Edgar Faure and Pierre Mendès-France.

As the French like to say, "The more things change, the more they stay the same."

ᖤ

Americans and Britons who profess their astonishment at the French multiparty system, overlook the fact that in their own countries the people are also greatly divided and the parties faction-ridden.

The British Labor party has suffered from internal disorders for years. Aneurin Bevan and Hugh Gaitskell have been fighting for control of the party since the end of the war.

In America, no one can pretend that the Republican or the Democratic parties are cohesive, homogeneous groupings. Southern Democrats are the political counterparts of the most reactionary wing of the Republican party. Right, Left and Center are also meaningless terms in American politics.

The difference is that the multiple American parties exist inside the cover of the two huge coalitions known as the Republican and Democratic parties. They have their fights and divisions at primaries and party conventions, not in the public square and only rarely in Congress. The French party system is exactly the same as the American at the primary level except that the primary and party levels in France are elevated to the national and parliamentary stage.

What it amounts to is the fact that the French political system puts its emphasis on political democracy whereas the Americans put their emphasis on the republican form of government, which, as the fathers of our nation believed, was the vital shield against the anarchistic nature of pure democracy.

Our American *philosophy* of government is democratic, but our *form* of government is republican. In France the contrary is true—the French Republic is a philosophical symbol but the actual functioning of the political system is that of a parliamentary democracy, a system that cannot work efficiently, for it does not provide the machinery to bring individual differences into gear.

The dilemma of the French derives from the attempt to preserve individual differences in their political and governmental systems, instead of using those systems to preserve human rights. It is impossible to make men think and act alike except under a dictatorship. The virtue of the two-party system is that it allows individual differences but prevents them from canceling each other out to the point of paralysis, as in France.

The British and Americans were fortunate in developing a two-party system, partly by design and partly by accident. The founders of our Republic and the British constitutional monarchy were conscious of the dangers of pure democracy and provided checks and balances against it. However, these checks and balances would not have by themselves assured orderly government.

The essential operating mechanism of government is the party system rather than the form of the State. If the Republican and Democratic parties in America split apart into their respective, heterogeneous elements, as they almost did in 1952, then our government and our congressional system would become as unmanageable as the French. This is a danger of which America's leaders are acutely aware but which is generally ignored by or unknown to the public. The two-party system, as much as the Constitution, should be credited with giving America free but orderly government.

The framers of the Constitution did not devise the two-party system. No one said, "Let there be a two-party system!" Its development came more than half a century later as a result of a complex of factors, geographic, economic and social as well as political.

The French multiparty system was also the result of design and accident. The philosophy of the revolutionaries of 1789, as we have noted, was principally responsible for casting France in the fragile mold of a political democracy. Long before 1789, however, the French people had been divided by other frictions. The religious wars played a decisive role in setting Frenchmen against Frenchmen, particularly the massacre of the Protestants on Saint Bartholomew's Day. Had not Catherine de Medici been a fanatic and Henri IV an unprincipled cynic much of France's political woes of today would have been avoided.

The gravest errors were made by the leaders of the Revolution in the "Civil Constitution of the Clergy" which alienated the Church from the Republic and turned the Revolution into a religious and civil war. The counterrevolution of the Catholic provinces of Brittany and the Vendée in turn alienated the democrats of France. The wounds on both sides have never healed. Ever since 1789 France has been the battleground of two warring religions: Catholicism and anti-clericalism.

This is one of the tragedies of contemporary France, for the religious conflict prevents the union of the liberals and Socialists with the Christian Democrats, a union urgently needed to reduce the fragmentations of France's multiparty system and restore the health of French democracy.

ᕳᕲ

The multiparty system in France has, however, already been greatly reduced in the Fourth Republic, in comparison with the Third. There are still too many parties in France to permit stable, orderly government, but the trend is toward a reduction of the number of the parties and a concentration into bigger political coalitions or groups of parties.

Six main groupings of parties have been dominant in Fourth Republic politics, reading roughly from Left to Right: the Communists, the Socialists, the Radicals, the Catholics, the conservatives and the reactionaries. The first four of these groups are organized in more or less cohesive and recognizable parties, although the Radicals tend to split apart and then come together again. At the moment they are split between the supporters of Mendès-France and Edgar Faure, but despite their internal differences they are both center, democratic groups.

The two forces that require a fuller explanation are the conservatives and the reactionaries on the right.

The conservatives are exactly what the word normally means: men who are trying to conserve their special privileges, to maintain the status quo by resisting all social change. In this group are such parties as the Independents, the Peasants and a variety of "moderates." What distinguishes them from the reactionaries is that, by and large, they are men who are at least political, if not economic and social, democrats. They are loyal to the Republic.

The reactionaries of the French Right, however, are not loyal to the Republic, nor do they wish to conserve the status quo. They are counterrevolutionaries, men who have never accepted the principle of the Republic of 1789 or the social revolution of our times. They are, in varying degrees, totalitarian in spirit if not in actual practice or doctrine.

This is an extremely disparate group of men, ranging from such giants and modern aristocrats as Charles de Gaulle to such pygmies and plebes as Pierre Poujade. They share one quality in common, however: they are all "against the regime," that is, dedicated to the destruction of the parliamentary system of government, and, in the case of Poujade, to the destruction of democracy itself.

The struggle for power among these six groups has been intense. In the course of the struggle the six have sometimes coalesced into three, as the center parties were forced into a common front of self-defense against the extremes. The democratic parties have been successful in their defense against Communism and Fascism. It is one of the encouraging aspects of French politics that is sometimes forgotten in the stress of more sensational, eye-catching crises.

A typical case of overestimating the strength of the extremes and underestimating the vitality of the Center occurred in the elections of January, 1956. Scare headlines in France and abroad announced: "Extremes Win Elections," while subheadlines explained: "Sweeping Red Gains; Poujade Triumph."

In point of fact these were highly tendentious headlines. The so-called "Red gains" were of parliamentary seats but the Communists had increased their seats for purely technical reasons, deriving from an electoral law, and not as a result of an electoral victory—a most important distinction.

The Communists, in fact, lost rather than gained votes, their total dropping by two hundred thousand. What had happened was that the electoral law of 1951, which had been loaded against the Communists and against General de Gaulle, had been revised. Had the same electoral law applied in both elections the Communists would have lost seats in 1956. The headlines were certainly not justified, and led to considerable misunderstanding and needless fears.

Poujade's "triumph" was closer to the truth but still highly controversial. Poujade's ticket won 11 per cent of the vote, a little more than two million ballots, and fifty-two parliamentary seats, a very considerable group of deputies for a party that did not exist in 1953 and for a man who was almost unknown only a year or two before elections.

His party, however, was in last position among the major groups, so that the word "triumph" is at least misleading. Many people abroad, and even some in France, thought that Poujade had won the elections, or at least had emerged as the major figure in France. This was simply untrue. Mendès-France won more votes than Poujade; Guy Mollet's Socialist party also won more votes than Poujade. All the traditional parties surpassed the Poujade ticket.

Moreover, there was nothing really new nor startling about the big Poujade vote. There have always been at least two million votes on the extreme Right in France; the same votes that had once gone to Colonel de la Rocque, then to Pétain, then to de Gaulle. There have always been at least two million reactionaries in search of a leader. When they discovered that de Gaulle was not a Fascist, not a dictator, they transferred their votes and affections to Poujade.

Thus Poujade was a new name but not a new phenomenon in France, nor was his voting strength any greater than others in his category had enjoyed before him.

The real story of the 1956 elections in France was not the "gains" of the extremes, headlined in the press, but the remarkable recovery of the democratic forces, which had been crushed by the extremes in 1951 only to come back very strong in 1956. In 1951 the Communists and the Gaullists won more than nine million votes, or 49 per cent of the total! In 1956, however, the Communists and Poujadists won six and a half million votes, or only 33 per cent of the total cast, against eleven million for the rejuvenated majority democratic parties.

The Republican conservatives increased their vote from 2,295,000 to 3,486,000, profiting from the retirement of de Gaulle and the fact that many of the former Gaullists refused to follow the rabble-rouser Poujade.

The Socialists picked up the two hundred thousand votes that the Communists had dropped, one of the most encouraging signs of a revival of French democracy in ten years.

The Radicals, led by Mendès-France, boosted their total by a half-million votes. Mendès-France and Socialist party leader Mollet campaigned together under the banner of a coalition they called the "Republic Front." It was their democratic coalition, if any, that triumphed, and that formed the new government after the elections.

The real tragedy of the 1956 elections was not extremist gains but democratic divisions, during and after the electoral campaign. Edgar Faure and Antoine Pinay offered Mendès-France and Mollet their hands in peace, proposing a "government of national union" to direct France through the crisis of Algeria. Mollet and Mendès-France turned down their offer.

Mendès-France considered Faure and Pinay to be even greater dangers to French democracy than Poujade or the Communists, because he considered them to be weak and inefficient, thus a discredit to French democracy. Mendès-France is a hard, bitter and angry man. He was also a disappointed man in 1956, for he had hoped to do much better in the elections than he did.

It was the peculiar personality of Mendès-France that split the democratic camp, for, after having spurned the friendship of Pinay and Faure, he then broke with his own partner, Guy Mollet. Mendès-France resigned from the cabinet in the spring of 1956 to return to the role in which he feels most comfortable: the opposition.

This is what is wrong with France today, these frictions and divisions of the democrats, this paralyzing cleavage of the Center of the body politic. The threat of Communism and Fascism would be greatly diminished if the democrats could form a union, compose their differences and support a program that would eliminate the conditions in which Communism and Fascism flourish.

The differences dividing the democrats are real and deep. Even the controversial character of a Mendès-France would not be enough to fracture the body politic if there were not other forces at work. The schisms derive from older, more intense ideological, social and economic conflicts among the peasants, workers, industrialists and intellectuals of France.

Thus an examination of the French body politic cannot be complete nor can its ills be diagnosed accurately, without probing under the surface and examining each of its parts individually, as well as in relationship to each other.

It is in any case more prudent and rewarding to determine the real forces that operate under the misleading labels of Left, Right and Center, for it can truly be said of the French body politic that its right hand does not know what its left is doing and that often it cannot even distinguish its right from its left.

6 Red Cells on the Left

"We are not a party like the others."

Communist leader Maurice Thorez, who has laid down the line for French Communists for more than a quarter of a century, is not a man like others, just as he decreed that his party must be unique in the French political community. Coal miner, farmhand, bargeman and house painter by turn in his early career, Maurice Thorez careened through a zigzag cycle of adventures that propelled him in and out of prison cells and parliamentary seats.

Thorez was indicted in Paris for desertion from the army in 1939, acclaimed as a hero in Moscow where he fled, and then returned to Paris in 1944 to be named to one of the highest offices in his country, as Vice-Premier to Charles de Gaulle.

More than once it seemed as though Thorez were through. Ten years after his flight to Moscow he was on his way back to Russia on a stretcher, paralyzed by a stroke, following a cerebral hemorrhage. But he came back to Paris again, leaning on a cane, to reassume leadership of the party and complete a purge of potential rivals, that had been begun for him by his ever-faithful lieutenant, Jacques Duclos.

Duclos, like Thorez, has been a Communist militant most of his life. The two men were among the first to leave the Socialist party and join the Bolshevik faction that created the Communist party after the schism at the Congress of Tours in 1920, on the issue of a French Socialist alliance with the Moscow-led Communist International. From the very first Thorez and Duclos pledged their allegiance to the motherland of Communism, Russia.

Thorez and Duclos are the personification of French Communism and the history of their careers spans the entire history of the

81

French Communist party from its creation to date. They are the Hammer and the Sickle of France, as dissimilar yet as inseparable as those twin symbols of Communism.

❧

Before his stroke in 1950 Thorez was a powerful man, packing one hundred and seventy pounds of muscle into a five-foot-ten-inch frame, hard as a lump of his native Pas-de-Calais coal. Product of the grim, smog-stained north, he was the very image of a proletarian. Bull-necked Thorez was in his element haranguing huge crowds. At one public rally I saw him knock a heckler sprawling with a ham-fisted slap that sent his victim's cap flying ten feet into the air. He has been involved in fist fights on the floor of Parliament as well as on the docks of Marseilles.

Thorez first acquired an international reputation and won control of the French party in October, 1934, when he laid down the French Communist line of supporting "A Popular Front of Work, Peace and Liberty," one full year before the Moscow Comintern realized that it was the correct strategy to meet the growing menace of Hitlerism, the spread of Fascism through Europe. The acknowledgment that Thorez was ahead of the Kremlin came at the Seventh Congress of the International in Moscow on August 2, 1935.

Dimitrov of Bulgaria, Secretary General of the Comintern, delivered a laudatory address, saying: "France is the country where the working class has shown the international proletariat how to fight Fascism." Old Bolshevik Dimitrov then turned to the council table, where Maurice Thorez was sitting, and raised his hand in a salute to the Frenchman. Every delegate arose in a standing ovation to the thirty-five-year-old chief of French Communism. It was one of the most extraordinary tributes ever paid a Western Communist in Moscow.

When Thorez returned to Paris he was the undisputed number one man of the French party.

❧

Jacques Duclos could never hope to be a number one man. He simply did not look the part. Barely five feet high and almost as wide, Duclos has the shoulders and chest of a heavyweight wrestler, the legs of a midget. Peering brightly behind enormous, black shell glasses, he looks half-owl, half-penguin as he waddles up the steps to the speaker's platform in the Assembly, balancing his top-heavy frame on foreshortened stems.

His comic appearance is quickly forgotten when he begins to speak. With caustic irony and stinging tongue, Duclos can rasp the nerves of the thickest-skinned deputy in the House.

When Parliament was debating the first Marshall Plan program, in 1948, Duclos waited for a quiet moment, saw his opportunity when Foreign Minister Georges Bidault paused to sip a glass of water on the speaker's stand. Duclos's voice, with his rich southern accent, could be heard distinctly through the Chamber, as he asked with exaggerated politeness: "Would the Honorable Foreign Minister not prefer a Coca-Cola?" When Bidault tried to reply Duclos shouted: "Oh, sit down, you've got delirium Trumans."

Duclos is viciously, cruelly insulting. I have heard him call Foreign Minister Robert Schuman "a Rhinelander who wore the German uniform in the First World War and is now bidding to be the batman for an American general in anticipation of a third world war."

No matter how insulting he dares to be he has an instinctive sense of timing and stress, just managing to keep within a hairline of going too far and setting off a grave incident. Only once that I can recall, listening to and reading some three hundred Duclos speeches, did I find an attempt at wit, in the worst possible taste, that boomeranged against him.

Speaking in Toulouse on April 28, 1946, he boasted that the Communist party electoral victory was not "an extraordinary miracle," adding, "We did not get any special blessing. Up to now I have not heard of God's joining the Communist party."

This crude offense to the thousands of Catholics present and the millions who had voted for the Communist party cost the Communists dearly. Never again did they dare to slur the Christian faith openly, confining their attacks after that to "church interference in politics."

❧

At the liberation of France in 1944 Thorez and Duclos could boast that they had built the largest, strongest Communist party in the West. They were certain that they had a good chance of coming to power legally at the polls and recommended the tactic of "co-operation with capitalism."

There was no more fervent nationalist in France from 1944 to 1946 than Thorez. He sent out a no-strike rule to the Communist trade-union leaders and ordered the maquis leaders to turn in their arms and allow their units to be broken up and integrated into the army when de Gaulle demanded it. He profited at the polls for his "good citizenship," whitewashing the memory of his wartime desertion and of the Communist collaboration with Vichy and the Germans in 1940 during the period of the Nazi-Soviet Pact.

Then the first split came over the issue of cabinet posts for Communist ministers. The final break in the policy of co-operation with capitalism came in the spring of 1947, just a month after the Big Four Conference in Moscow had broken up in failure, and a month before Marshall's speech at Harvard that was the diplomatic turning point of the postwar period.

The break with capitalism came about as a result of a strike at the big Renault automobile plant at the end of April. Communist labor leader Benoît-Frachon, chief of the General Confederation of Labor, CGT, told Thorez he could no longer hold the workers in check, and that the Communist party was being accused of betraying the working class. Thorez promptly demanded a wage increase. When Premier Paul Ramadier refused, on the grounds that it would wreck the government's anti-inflationary program, Thorez broke cabinet solidarity and voted against the government.

Ramadier expelled the Communists from his Cabinet on May 5, 1947. Communists have never gotten back to power since in France.

⁂

The spring and summer of 1947 were confused weeks for the Communists, who floundered around in search of a new policy. They had ended their "co-operation with capitalism" but the Soviets had not yet ended their wartime alliance with the capitalist powers.

The Soviet refusal to join the Marshall Plan was the signal that a new policy was in the making. It came in the creation of the Cominform.

Duclos was the French delegate to the secret meeting in Poland in August, 1947, when Zhdanov denounced the errors of the Western

Communist parties. He dutifully brought back the new line to Thorez. Both of them promptly and publicly confessed their "sins," in an analysis of strategical errors published in the official party magazine, *France Nouvelle*, November 1, 1947.

The sin was "failure to understand the real reason for our expulsion from government." The real reason, as Thorez wrote it: "We have failed to define clearly the nature and extent of the changed international situation, notably the regrouping of the imperialist, antidemocratic forces under the direction and for the benefit of the United States." Thorez "confessed" he had failed to realize that the Communists had been expelled from the Ramadier Cabinet "on orders from Washington" and not because of a conflict on the wage-price issue. He had forgotten, he said, that the class war was also an international war.

From then on the Communists fought on both fronts.

On the home front they launched a series of insurrectional strikes that had France teetering on the brink of revolution in the winter and spring of 1947-48. They called out the gas and electric workers, cut the water supply, stopped the railways. Paris looked like a city under siege when the Communists struck the municipal services in a walkout of subway men, bus conductors and, most unpleasantly, the garbage collectors, street cleaners and gravediggers.

The Minister of the Interior was a Socialist, Jules Moch, a tough and courageous man, whom the Communists feared and hated. He purged both the army and the police of Communist fifth columnists and called out the troops to break the coal-mine strike that threatened to deprive the country of fuel just before the onset of winter. The Communists called him Blackjack Moch—Moch-la-Matraque—accusing him of being "a capitalist goon."

Although Moch knew the political risks involved in a Socialist suppression of a strike, he told the workers that they were the dupes of agents of a foreign power and that he would use maximum force against any "illegitimate insurrectional strike." He called out three divisions of army troops, including the fearsome Senegalese colonials.

I was at Lens, in the heart of the coal fields, and saw the colonials charge the workers' barricades with drawn bayonets. Their strength was so formidable that resistance was hopeless. This was exactly what

Moch had planned, using Marshal Lyautey's tactic: "Show enough force so that you need not use it."

Moch broke the strikes and also broke the myth that had paralyzed political leaders for months: the belief that Thorez could seize power overnight by giving the signal for a working-class insurrection.

⌒〜〇

The strikes cost the Communists heavily, not only breaking their hold on labor but also on the electorate.

They suffered a beating at the polls, for the first time since the liberation. In the municipal elections of 1947 the newly formed RPF of General de Gaulle swept the country, won almost 40 per cent of the total votes and captured control of the most important municipal administrations. De Gaulle demonstrated in the field of politics what Moch had proved in labor, that the Communists could not come to power either legally or illegally.

A setback of the proportions suffered by the Communists in 1947-48 could have been disastrous to most parties, but the French Communist party "is not a party like the others." It is a church and an army, organized spiritually and militarily on the principles of blind faith and unquestioning obedience.

Thorez and Duclos set about reorganizing the party to meet a changed situation. They no longer needed, nor wanted, a very large membership. They had hit a peak of about a million members in 1946 at a time when they wanted to pose as a responsible "Republican party." Their ranks were swollen with opportunists, idealists and admirers of their Resistance record, many of them, however, not convinced, reliable Communists. For the return to a revolutionary policy, and in preparation for the need to go underground again, they began to weed out the unreliables and cut the party back to a manageable size.

The strikes had been useful for that purpose. It separated the men from the boys, the fighters from the fair-weather fellow travelers. Parallel with the strikes, Thorez also tested the faith of his followers on the second front of Communism, the international struggle.

With French troops fighting a desperate war in Indochina, Jacques Duclos sent an open telegram of congratulations to rebel leader Ho Chi Minh, congratulating him on the anniversary of his revolution.

Then the Central Committee of the party tested the loyalty of its members with a communiqué in October, 1948, proclaiming that "the people of France will never make war against the Soviet Union."

The storm of public protest that followed this made Communist spokesmen back down with an explanation that they meant the party would not support an *aggressive* war against Russia. This explanation did not hold up for long. All doubts about what they really meant were dispelled by Thorez himself, when he sent out a rallying cry for a fifth column in February, 1949, in a statement that was tantamount to an open declaration of treason.

The statement was published in the party paper, *Humanité*, on February 22, 1949, in the form of a report on a Central Committee discussion of "the urgency and necessity of union for the defense of peace." The report noted that

Maurice Thorez was led to make the following declaration: "The enemies of the people, thinking they can embarrass us, ask the following question: What would you do if the Red Army were to occupy Paris? This is our reply:
'If the common efforts of all freedom-loving and peace-loving Frenchmen do not succeed in bringing our country back into the camp of peace and democracy, if our people are then dragged, despite their will, into an anti-Soviet war, and if in these conditions the Soviet Army, defending the cause of the people, is led to pursue the aggressors on to our soil, then can the workers, the people of France, act toward the Soviet Army otherwise than the peoples of Poland, Rumania, Yugoslavia and others?' "

Although Thorez had phrased his declaration in the form of a rhetorical question, to avoid an immediate indictment for treason, the device fooled no one and was not meant to. Thorez had plainly stated, and wanted it to be known, that the Communists would act in France as they had in the Eastern countries, as a fifth column for Russia, that they would greet the Red Army not as an enemy but as a liberator.

More remarkable, perhaps, than the Thorez declaration of allegiance to class and ideology rather than to country—which might be expected of a Communist leader—was the reaction of the French people. County elections were scheduled to be held shortly after Thorez had raised the red flag of international Communism and the voters would have a chance to say what they thought of the traitorous

declaration he had pronounced. Many political observers were sure
that Thorez had committed political suicide deliberately, preferring
to convert the party into a small, hard-core clandestine organization.

No such result emerged from the elections. Instead, the Communist lists won almost 25 per cent of the popular vote.

This phenomenon of Communist electoral popularity, despite the
most flagrant lack of patriotism, the frequent exploitation of workers'
professional interests for Communist tactical purposes, above all, the
remarkable discipline and dedication of otherwise individualistic
Frenchmen once they become Communists, is one of the most
baffling of all the mysteries of French affairs.

How can one out of every four or five French voters cast his ballot
for a party that boasts it will not fight for his country? Why do
workers stay in Communist-led unions when they are brought out on
costly strikes for political protests against treaties instead of for
improvement of the workers' lot? How can they believe the electoral
programs of men like Thorez and Duclos who have changed their
policies every five years, who have been guilty of desertion, treason and
collaboration with enemies of the French Republic, and who have
never fought for French democracy except when defense of France
coincided with defense of Russia?

In the past ten years I have asked these questions of hundreds of
French Communists and non-Communists who vote for that party.
I have found that the answers almost always fall into one of three
categories, depending on the degree of Communism of the man I
questioned:

1. The confirmed Communist militant does not believe any of the
charges against his leaders or he has a ready-made answer for them.
They deny that Thorez deserted the army. They say he was forced to
flee because "the real traitors, the pro-Hitler capitalists" were planning to arrest and imprison all Communist leaders. The confirmed
Communist does not believe it possible to be guilty of treason because
"the bourgeois State is not the true motherland of patriots." Of the
five million Communist voters in France only about one hundred
thousand are Communist fanatics of this ilk.

2. The majority of the Communist party members are not fanatics
but they too have either been hypnotized by Communist propaganda
or have rationalized their position. They blame French leaders for

having entered into a Western European military alliance in 1948, allowing Marshal Montgomery to set up headquarters in Fontainebleau, thus "provoking" the Communists to declare their support for the Red Army.

The fellow travelers are emotional "neutralists." As for the abuse of strikes for political purposes they have a pat answer: the workers cannot gain their ends without political representation. "Pie-in-the-sky unionism alone cannot bring social progress," they say. There are about a million party members and fellow travelers of this nature in France.

3. The vast majority of French Communist voters, however, are not Communist at all. They are an army of four million malcontents who are fed up with the failures and broken promises of weak governments, bitter at being gouged by profiteering speculators and shopkeepers, weary of hot, cold and colonial wars.

As one devout Catholic and anti-communist voter told me: "Where else can I register my protest against the mess in my country? How else can I frighten the government into cleaning it up? If I thought there were any chance the Communists would come into power in France I would never vote for them. If they try a *coup d'état* here as in Prague I'll go out on the barricades to stop them. But, until conditions improve here, I'll vote for them."

This, I believe, is the principal motivation of most French voters for the Communist ticket. It is an encouraging sign, for it means that five million Frenchmen are not fanatic servants of a totalitarian power. They are not irrevocably lost to the democratic faith.

ᏀᏦᎧ

Although the Communists have been unable to win their way back to political power since 1947 and equally unable, despite riots, strikes and sabotage, to prevent France's participation in the Atlantic Alliance, they nonetheless have been successful in maintaining their position as the "first party of France." In every election of the Fourth Republic, from 1946 to 1956, the Communists have won at least 25 per cent of the votes cast.

Their total votes, however, have fallen from a high of 5.5 millions to a low, in 1956, of 4.7 millions. The Communist party press has lost most of its postliberation circulation and is now sold to and read mainly by party militants. Membership has fallen from a peak of more than a million to less than three hundred thousand and there are signs, at the close of 1956, that tens of thousands of people are quitting the Communist party and Communist-controlled trade unions in revulsion at the Soviet rape of Hungary and the total subservience of the French party to the Russians.

The French Communist party was the only major party in Europe to denounce the Budapest insurrection as "Fascist" and to approve the savage massacre of Hungarian patriots by the Red Army. Polish, Yugoslav and Italian Communist papers and spokesmen were contemptuous of the French Communist servility. The French Communists alone remained faithful to the memory of Stalin. And they paid heavily for their callousness and sterility. When an angry Parisian mob attacked party headquarters and set fire to it the Communist party called for a general protest strike throughout the country on November 13, 1956. The strike was the worst failure in French labor history. At the Renault Auto Works, for example, only 250 out of 39,000 workers came out on strike. The Communist grip on labor, which had been weakened by the unsuccessful strikes of 1948, seemed completely broken by the winter of 1956. At the same time the Communist party suffered a severe defection from its ranks, when their leading intellectual apologist, Jean-Paul Sartre, finally broke with them in a violent denunciation of the Hungarian slaughter.

French Communism thus is well past its peak and sliding downhill. It still remains a strong force, because of its large parliamentary delegation, but strong as it is in absolute terms it is much weaker relative to its postliberation strength and the trend is running against it. It certainly can no longer terrify and paralyze the body politic of France. It might therefore be said, in diagnostic terms, that France is still suffering from an excess of Red cells on the Left but that the danger of a hemorrhage is no longer acute. Communism is, however, a chronic malady and France will not be well politically until the democratic parties win back the great proportion of disgruntled citizens who register their protests with Communist ballots.

7 *Spasms on the Right*

France has never had a great, intelligent conservative party of the Right.

This harsh judgment of the French Right was not made by a man of the Left but by one of the most eminent conservative historians, André Siegfried, writing in one of the largest conservative papers of France, *Le Figaro*, of Paris. Siegfried's analysis of the inadequacies of French conservatism was published on July 23, 1951, shortly after national elections in which the Right had made an extraordinary comeback, winning control of one-third of the seats in Parliament, almost doubling its total in the previous election five years before.

If France's distinguished political historian was correct in his evaluation, then a most interesting question has to be asked: how could an unintelligent, discredited conservatism capture enough popular votes to win one-third of the seats in Parliament? A foreign observer, who has seen intelligent conservatism in Britain and in America, might also be permitted to wonder if it was conservatism in general or French conservatism in particular which was lacking in intelligence.

According to psychologists, one of the essential qualities of intelligence is ability to adapt to changing circumstances. By this standard of measurement Siegfried's judgment that the French Right is unintelligent is confirmed by history. The French conservatives have never completely reconciled themselves to modern democratic capitalism or to the republican form of government. They still yearn for the pre-1789 days of the *Ancien Régime*. France may not have a large, *intelligent* conservative party, but it is the only major Western democracy that has always had a large, *reactionary* conservatism in the true sense of the word. Ever since 1789 the Right has been reacting against the Revolution, against equality and fraternity and, on occasion, against liberty itself.

The majority of its leaders and its followers has had only one consistent loyalty: entrenched privilege. The Right has demonstrated its readiness to sacrifice not only the Republic, which it despises, but the nation itself in order to preserve its social and economic interests.

France is thus the only major Western democracy which suffers from a large, disloyal opposition on both the Right and on the Left. The disloyalty of the Left is of fairly recent origin, dating from the birth of Communism. The disloyalty of the Right, however, goes back to the birth of the Republic, Louis XVI's flight from Varennes and his fatal attempt to crush the Revolution with the aid of the émigrés and the Austrians.

In modern France the Right has duplicated Louis's betrayal. The Conservatives of France openly espoused treason in 1936 when they declared war on the Popular Front with the rallying cry: "Rather Hitler than Léon Blum." They proved that their battle cry was not mere propaganda when, after the fall of France, the conservative Vichy regime put Léon Blum in jail and allied itself with Hitler.

A few leaders of the Right, men like Paul Reynaud, Louis Marin and Joseph Laniel, resisted the foreign enemy and fought loyally for the Republic, but the Lavals, Darnands, Flandins, Maurras, followed by millions of merchants, farmers, industrialists and upper middle-class professionals, willingly, almost joyfully, betrayed both their country and the Republic. The Resistance was a pure, bright flame of courage, but it was a lonely torch in the wilderness of collaboration that blacked out most of the country.

The dishonored leaders of the Right were either imprisoned or declared ineligible for political activities after the liberation. A good many passive collaborationists and even some activists sought political refuge in the Communist party, whose objective was to become the first party of France and which consequently did not examine too rigidly the credentials of new adherents. Many conservatives also sought absolution in the ranks of the Resistance-born Catholic party, MRP. The postliberation Right was reduced to a small party of conservative resistants, called the Parti Républicain de la Liberté, which was lucky to win two dozen seats in the Constituent Assembly.

The regeneration of the Right in the next five years resulted from one of the most extraordinary of the many paradoxes of French political life. The moribund Right was resurrected by its two greatest wartime enemies, Charles de Gaulle and Maurice Thorez. Thorez proved that the extreme Left was a greater danger to the Republic than the Right. De Gaulle gave the Right a heroic leader for the first time. De Gaulle, who had saved the Republic, made anti-Republicanism respectable. At last the Right was able to identify its own selfish interests with the interests of the nation.

However, when de Gaulle and his chief lieutenants insisted a little too enthusiastically upon social justice as one of the principal aims of their "revolutionary" movement, they were deserted by a part of their troops. Many of the French conservatives feared de Gaulle's unorthodox ideas and resented his autocratic leadership.

They found a new and safer hero in Antoine Pinay, the personification of the "little man." The "Right" not only sensed where to butter its bread, but where to get it at the least cost and sell it at the best price. In the first six years of the new Republic the conservatives shifted allegiance from Christian-Democratic Bidault to autocratic de Gaulle to conservative Pinay, with an unerring instinct each time.

In general terms, therefore, it is possible to describe the Right, its tactics and reasons for its regeneration as a political force. What is more difficult to describe is its composition, clientele and ideology. De Gaulle and Pinay are both "men of the Right," but Charles de Gaulle is a big man, literally and figuratively, the symbol of *"la grande France,"* whereas Antoine Pinay is a little man, the symbol of *"la petite France."* Paul Reynaud and Pierre Poujade, both "Rightists," are as dissimilar as Eisenhower and McCarthy, both Republicans. The label rightist or conservative covers a wide variety of personalities and political philosophies.

Also on the Right are the peasants, the most anachronistic of all the conservative elements in French politics. Peasant conservatism is not only historic; it is prehistoric. The peasants are the spiritual descendants of the Druids, the pantheistic priests of ancient Gaul. The most important of the gods of Druidism was the sun. The modern Druids of France have substituted the symbol of the sun, gold, as their principal object of worship. The peasants bury it in their fields, in the laps of the other gods of nature that they revere.

The Right, therefore, is composed of four main tendencies, two of them conservative, two of them reactionary: the druidistic peasants and the Republican businessmen on the right of Center; the apprentice Bonapartes and Hitlers on the extreme Right of the body politic.

The peasants have no special hero; they worship gold. The hero of the Republican businessmen is Antoine Pinay. At the moment those who yearn for a new Bonaparte are without a candidate, since the retirement of de Gaulle. They have had some hopes for Marshal Alphonse Juin, which might materialize if the situation in Algeria worsens. De Gaulle himself is by no means out of the picture. The Fascists have a new superman: bully-boy Pierre Poujade, hero of the tax-evading little shopkeeper.

These are the groups and the men responsible for the spasms on the Right that have so often racked the French body politic. A brief examination of each may be useful to understand exactly what is behind the vague, inaccurate, appellation "Right," which is loosely applied to these disparate political groupings.

ᆖ

THE CONSULAR RIGHT

From Napoleon I to Napoleon III, from Marshal MacMahon through General Boulanger and Marshal Pétain, there has always been a military man or frustrated royalist to play the role of a Roman consul in France.

Charles de Gaulle played that role in the Fourth Republic, but only for a brief time. Despite deceptive external appearances de Gaulle was miscast and indeed in the wrong play. He was a Hamlet, not a Caesar. The tragedy of de Gaulle, "the gloomy hermit of Colombey," was essentially the tragedy of the gloomy Dane, the man who could not make up his mind.

De Gaulle could not decide whether it was his mission to save or destroy the French parliamentary regime after he had liberated the Republic. He resigned in disgust in 1946 but then changed his mind and came back to the political arena in 1947. Even then he could not make up his mind whether to play the game or break it up.

He organized the RPF, calling his movement a "gathering of the people" and not a party. Yet there is only one way to come to power democratically and that is to operate in the framework of the party system. The RPF had to go to the polls.

It did well, winning more than four million votes in the national elections of 1951 and the largest single parliamentary delegation. But it did not win a majority. Therefore de Gaulle had to co-operate with other parties if he wanted to govern. Consuls, however, do not co-operate, nor do they govern; they rule. Unable to rule, de Gaulle quit again. He sang his political swan song at a news conference in Paris in July, 1955, when he said to reporters: "It is my intention not to intervene again in what is conventionally called 'the public affairs of this country.' . . . I say farewell to you and perhaps for a long time to come."

Charles de Gaulle may have retired voluntarily from public life, but it is not certain that his retirement is any more final than his two earlier departures. Nor did it dispose of the problem of "Gaullism." There has been a de Gaulle in France in one form or another in every generation since the Revolution. There may well be another de Gaulle in the next. The latent Bonapartism of the French people is always there under the surface, always ready to erupt. Consular conservatism may not always have a consul to rally behind, but it is always ready when one comes along. It would be a rash historian and an incurable optimist who would assume that with de Gaulle's departure the counterrevolutionary forces of France will all become reconciled to the parliamentary regime.

ᄋᠰᢕ

THE DRUIDISTIC RIGHT

Every Frenchman is at heart a peasant, although not all Frenchmen actually till the soil. The "peasant" in every Frenchman is expressed in his fierce individualism, resistance to mass organization and discipline. Perhaps the one peasant quality that all Frenchmen share is the peasant's determination to elevate his children to a higher rank in the social hierarchy. More than a century ago French historian Michelet observed that the fondest hope of a peasant is that his son not be one.

One of the most passionately proud "peasants" I have met in

France is Jean Delcroix, a suave and urbane industrialist whose "peasant" activity consists in selling Diesel engines for tractors and publishing a farm journal, *La Terre Nouvelle*, in Paris.

If literate, progressive-minded men like Delcroix were really peasants, then there would at last be some hope of seeing a large, intelligent conservative party in France. Unfortunately, Delcroix and many like him are "peasants of Paris."

The true peasant of France is neither literate nor progressive-minded. His world is bounded by the fence around his property. On that piece of land he is a king; for his family he is an autocratic patriarch. He is apt to be a violent man. Quarrels between peasants can end with a blow, a kick or a duel with hunting guns.

Hardly a day goes by without some story in the Paris papers about brutality, violence and murder in the countryside. The quick-tempered, hard-drinking hillbilly of American folklore is a more picturesque, romantic version of a French peasant type, the main difference between them being that the Frenchman does not carry a guitar or sing.

The French peasant, like the hillbilly, brews his own "moonshine," generally potent "*alcool blanc*," which the American soldiers discovered during the war and labeled "white lightning." It was an excellent "antifreeze" in the winter campaign for both the soldier and his jeep. Unfortunately, it is also given even to school children in rural France when winter sets in. For the French peasant, unlike the hillbilly, home-brewing is legal. There are some four million "*bouilleurs de cru*" or legal moonshiners in France.

However, the French peasant does have a hated "Revenooer" to fight and he is always ready with pitchfork or gun to drive the government agent off his land. There is a tradition of peasant revolt, "*la Jacquerie*," that goes back to the peasant uprisings of 1358 when "Jacques Bonhomme" rebelled against the soldiers of the king living on his land and against the extortionate rentals and assessments of the nobles. The tradition is still alive in France today.

There were great peasant revolts in the Midi in 1907 and 1910, under the Third Republic. Under the Fourth, from 1950 to 1956 there were peasant revolts at least once a year, the most violent and widespread occurring in August, 1953, when the wine growers barricaded the roads and paralyzed communications in four departments.

The peasants not only armed themselves on the barricades, they launched an ingenious form of air offensive against the police. Local beekeepers, clothed in heavy masks and gloves, put a ring of hives around the barricades and sent out squadrons of angry bees to dive-bomb the forces of the law.

This is, of course, a caricature rather than a true portrait of the peasant. Not all peasants are violent, not all are rebels or retrograde. Nor are they politically united. There are Communist peasants, monarchist peasants and radical peasants. The socialistic peasants of the south have little in common politically with the Catholic peasants of the Vendée.

The peasants are almost as much sinned against as sinning. They refuse to pay taxes directly but they do pay heavy economic tribute in another form: in high prices for industrial commodities and low prices for their own produce. The net income of the peasant is very small.

Price supports, surplus-buying, crop subsidies of every kind imaginable, cost the State and the consumer a great deal of money without providing a decent life for the peasants of France, mainly because of the antiquated distribution system of the French economy, dominated by the Paris market and strangled by thick-fingered middlemen.

The political result is the peasant anarchist in open rebellion against the established order. The peasant, living in isolation in the dispersion of the countryside, tends to be a guerrilla fighter. It is not surprising therefore that there has never been a mass peasant party, but rather a number of individualistic peasant groups.

This dispersion of the peasant vote is, however, one of the main sources of its strength in France. Having no rigid organization, no political philosophy or doctrine, other than defense of its own economic interests, the peasant vote has always been a salable political commodity. It is the rule rather than the exception in Parliament to find Communist, Catholic, radical and conservative deputies of the same rural department all sponsoring the same or similar versions of a bill favoring agriculture.

Changes are, however, being effected in the French countryside, by a mechanization of the land, improved use of fertilizer and technical education projects. Inch by inch the peasant is plodding toward the twentieth century. It is one of the encouraging developments in contemporary France—for patient observers.

⌖

THE REPUBLICAN RIGHT

The Right only began to reconcile itself to the Republic at the turn of this century after the disastrous blunder of the Dreyfus case which discredited the royalist and militaristic Right.

Three conservative parties were born in the new century, the Alliance Démocratique, the Action Libérale and the Fédération Républicaine. It is significant that the qualifying adjective in each case —democratic, liberal, republican—were words borrowed from the vocabulary of the Center and of the Left. It was a recognition of the fact that the majority of the French people had accepted the Republic and would expect its political representatives to espouse its principles and be faithful to it.

The Center liberals began to form alliances with the conservative Right after the Russian Revolution. From then until the Second World War the Right played an important role and frequently took cabinet posts in Center governments.

The Fascist leagues of the thirties and the regime of Marshal Pétain discredited the Right again and there seemed little hope that a Republican conservatism could ever develop in France. The hope seemed even dimmer when General de Gaulle revived the traditions of the consular Right.

The failure of Gaullism and the intransigence of the General gave "Republican conservatism" its big chance at the turn of the mid-century. It came in 1952 when de Gaulle's RPF disintegrated. Conservative members of the RPF rebelled against de Gaulle's orders and voted to invest as premier an obscure leather manufacturer from central France, Antoine Pinay, who looked a bit like Charlie Chaplin playing the role of Landru.

Pinay turned out not to be a comedian or an ax murderer, although he did wield a big political hatchet when he split the RPF.

Pinay had been ineligible for election to the first Constituent Assembly after the liberation, because he had been a wartime delegate to the Vichy National Council. He was virtually unknown in the second Constituent, to which he was elected after having been cleared of charges of collaboration by an investigation that revealed his help to the Resistance as mayor of Saint Chamond during the occupation.

No one paid much attention to this mild, little man, whose record was neither very bad nor very good. A modest man, Pinay described himself in the biographical dictionary of the Assembly as: "Antoine Pinay, Master Tanner, Honorary President of the Syndicate of Leathers and Skins of the Rhône and the region of Lyons."

The miracle of Pinay was the power of the common man to stir millions of other common men. He is a kind of French Harry Truman, and he surprised all the experts, as Truman did, by demonstrating the vote-getting ability of a simple, honest man.

Pinay was exactly what he seemed to be: a laissez-faire, conservative businessman. He was loyal to the Republican State but opposed to state controls of business; he believed in the traditional virtues of the bourgeoisie: order, thrift and a balanced budget. He was as alarmed by inflation as any sound businessman ought to be, and unlike the many unsound businessmen of France, who see inflation as an opportunity for speculative profits.

Pinay refused to raise the tax rate. Instead he floated a loan, and on July 23, 1952, after only a few months in office, he announced triumphantly that his loan had brought 428 billion francs—a little more than a billion dollars—into the vaults of the Treasury. This was a remarkable financial success, particularly in view of the fact that during the same period of time savings deposits, postal check accounts and regular Treasury bond sales all increased.

The loan, however, did not balance the budget, nor did it unfreeze the hoarded gold of France. It brought in only thirty-four tons of gold out of an estimated cache of some two thousand tons buried in the gardens of the peasants and the socks of the shopkeepers. Meanwhile, in order to balance the budget, Pinay cut the investment program of the State. He sold short France's future for a present precarious stability, curing inflation by stagnation. In addition he had granted tax amnesty and special tax exemptions of various types to those who had subscribed to his loan, so that the net effect of his financial program was to have rewarded profiteering and tax evasion. This may not have been his purpose but this is what his policy brought about.

Nonetheless Pinay's popularity in the country rose as prices fell under his administration. The French people apparently did not mind the pinch of the tourniquet of stagnation that Pinay used to stop the hemorrhage of inflation. Pinay became a national personality in a few months' time, the apotheosis of the common-sensical common man who had solved a problem that had baffled the experts for years.

It was the worst thing that could have happened to Pinay politically, for he incited the fears and jealousies of the party bosses and his colleagues in Parliament. His popularity in the country was a threat to their own authority. The minute that Pinay became a national figure his days were numbered.

Pinay was guillotined in the Chamber, as all French premiers eventually are, after ten months in office, a bit better than the average term. He was not, however, forgotten by the people of France. A public opinion poll, early in 1955, just after Pinay returned to office as Foreign Minister in the Faure Government, showed that he was the second most popular man in France, just behind Mendès-France in public esteem. This was a remarkable achievement, coming two and a half years after having been out of office.

The *"expérience Pinay"* demonstrated that there is a potential for responsible conservative leadership in France. Pinay is certainly no "savior" of France. Yet he does fill the role of a savior of the Right, from the follies of autocracy and dictatorship. As for the Center and the Left, their record of leadership was no more brilliant than Pinay's and in many cases less successful.

The emergence of a Pinay on the Right is a sign that perhaps French conservatism is coming of age, that a responsible, loyal French Tory or Republican party is developing. In absolute terms, in comparison with the evolution of the entire national community, the Right remains retrograde, but in terms relative to their own past French conservatives today, with all their faults—and they are many and costly—have evolved far beyond the Right of the nineteenth century, or even the first half of the twentieth. This is the important and little-publicized role of a Pinay. It is one of the most encouraging developments in contemporary French affairs.

THE ROWDY RIGHT

Encouraging as is the advent of a Pinay on the political scene, it is equally discouraging to witness the atavistic appearance of a man like Poujade, a political Cro-Magnon man, out of the caves of central France.

Poujade is a lowbrow and a roughneck in every sense of the words. His thick black hair seems to grow out of the bridge of his nose. His muscular neck is always prominent in the spotlight as he goes through his peculiar political strip tease on the speaker's platform. He combines the worst features of Elvis Presley and Huey Long. When Poujade enters a meeting room his supporters cheer and women scream like enraptured bobby-soxers. The frenzy mounts as he warms up to his speech and begins to tear off his clothes. First he wrenches open his collar, then pulls down his tie and, for a grand finale, rolls up his shirt sleeves, baring his strong arms. I have never actually seen him bare his manly chest but some reporters swear he sometimes tears his shirts off as he reaches the climax of a fighting speech.

Poujade was unknown until 1953, when he achieved national prominence at the age of thirty-five as the leader of an antitax movement that sprang up spontaneously through the country. It all began in July of that year when Poujade received an appeal for help from a fellow municipal councilor in the village of Saint-Céré, where Poujade ran a small stationery store and bookshop. His friend, Freizac, a local cabinetmaker, who doubled in brass as a blacksmith, was notified that a tax inspector was coming to check his accounts. Freizac appealed for help, for he did not want his books checked and he could not afford to pay a fine. It was out of this incident that grew the Union for the Defense of Merchants and Artisans, the UDCA of Pierre Poujade.

The technique of the UDCA shock troops was to send a commando squad to any shop that was due for a tax inspection and to block the doors when the inspector arrived. If the police came and broke up the picket line Poujade and his men would then take up a collection to pay the fine or tell their fellow member to refuse to pay it. If he followed their advice and went on a tax strike the government would put a lien on his property and then put it up for sale at public auction, to pay the tax debt. Poujade's bully boys would then attend the auction, prevent anyone else from making a bid, buy back the property for a few cents and carry it triumphantly back to the shop.

In a year's time Poujade attracted almost a million shopkeepers and artisans to his movement. When he came to Paris for the first time a crowd of twenty thousand came to cheer him at the Vélodrome d'Hiver. His strip-tease technique made him colorful copy for reporters so he soon acquired a national and an international reputation, much greater than even his rapid rise merited.

His strategy has since shifted from the original tax-evasion campaign. Poujade, who has cunning and a natural political instinct, has seized upon the civil war in Algeria as an issue of greater value and wider interest than the narrow defense of lower-middle-class merchants and peasants. He has become more openly nationalistic, xenophobic and anti-Semitic, aping the Fascist leagues of the prewar period.

His greatest success came in the 1956 elections, as we have already noted. Since then, however, his movement has begun to lose steam. Four of his deputies in Parliament rebelled against his dictatorial methods and resigned from his group, just as de Gaulle's followers revolted against the General's high-handed leadership. Poujade went much further than de Gaulle in trying to control his men. He used the Communist technique of considering the deputies in Parliament as his soldiers in an army, rather than representatives of a constituency.

Poujade rented a hotel in Paris early in 1956 and insisted that all his deputies stay there so that he could keep an eye on them and call on them at any time. He also ordered them to have their parliamentary salaries sent directly to him instead of to them, and he then doled out to them a salary which he thought they ought to have.

The danger of the Poujade movement, like that of any other anti-Republican group in French history, is that a serious defeat for France in the outside world or an economic depression would give the Fascists the opportunity they need to seize power. It is a real danger but one that should not be exaggerated. A know-nothing like Poujade has never had real national support in France. The intellectual Fascism of a Maurras, the almost noble authoritarianism of a de Gaulle, or the paternalism of a Pétain, are much more native to

French soil and to the French temperament than the imitation-Hitler rabble-rousing of a Poujade.

The extreme Right like the extreme Left in France, while strong, is nonetheless a minority movement and has never been able to come to power alone or by its own means. From the restoration of the Bourbons by the allied coalition in 1815 to the short-lived Pétain corporate state of 1940, the Right has been a foreign imposition on the French and never lasted long beyond the departure of its foreign sponsors.

More important than the threat of Fascism is the failure of the democrats to create a socially just and economically efficient society in modern France.

The spasms on the Right make the body politic jittery, but what causes the paralysis of French affairs are the schisms in the Center.

8 *Schisms in the Center*

Ever since Caesar first commented that all Gaul was divided into three parts the development of French society seems to have followed a pattern of threes. Whatever symbols one might seek to describe the French Republic—its motto, the colors of its flag, the political and social groupings of its citizens—the magic number is always three: liberty, equality and fraternity; blue, white and red; peasants, workers and bourgeois; Left, Right and Center.

The political parties of the Center are faithful to the pattern, for they too are three in number: on the left of center, the Socialists; on the right of center, the Catholics; in dead center, the Radicals. These parties are occasionally united in a common front against the extremes of Right and Left in times of crisis but normally, if that adverb can be used at all in French politics, the parties of the Center are divided among themselves. They share only one ideal in common: they are all democratic parties. Instead of the titles Socialist, Catholic and Radical, they might be more appropriately designated as Social Democrats, Christian Democrats and Liberal Democrats.

These parties together form the democratic heart of the Republic. Each symbolizes one of the triple aims of French democracy: the Liberals stand for liberty, the Socialists for equality and the Christians for fraternity. This is the great trinity of French politics. In this respect, as in so many others, the French reflect the hopes and aspirations of all peoples everywhere, for social, economic and political democracy are variously stressed and imperfectly achieved in contemporary society.

The conflicts among the democratic parties of France, the differing emphases they put upon each of the democratic ideals, are not a peculiarly French phenomenon. Democracy means different things to different men throughout the world. By examining what it means to Frenchmen, the most articulate and least conformist of men, perhaps we can all learn a good deal more about what democracy means to us.

ᲙᕷᏉ

THE SOCIAL DEMOCRATS

The French Social Democrats have never been able to decide whether they were Socialists first or democrats first. From its birth in 1904 the French Socialist party has suffered from a split personality. Its founders, Jules Guesde and Jean Jaurès, represented the divergent tendencies of French Socialism. Guesde insisted that a Socialist party must never collaborate with capitalism and must, above all, never participate in a bourgeois government. Jaurès argued, on the contrary, that Social Democrats must collaborate with all other democrats to save the Republic from its enemies. He insisted that the Republic could only evolve safely to the higher form of the Socialist State after the enemies of democracy had been defeated.

The thesis and antithesis of Guesde and Jaurès have never been synthesized by French Socialists. First one school of thought, then the other, gains the ascendancy, as the party shuttles back and forth from the opposition to the governmental majority. It is one of the basic characteristics of the French Socialist party. The point of view of Jaurès prevails more often, and it was a protégé of his, Léon Blum, who became the first Socialist ever to head a French Government. Like Jaurès, Blum was a rationalist and a humanist more than a Marxist. One of the most brilliant French intellectuals of this century, Blum was the prototype of a Social Democrat, never certain at any moment whether to put the accent on "social" or "democrat."

Blum took the party into an electoral alliance with the Radicals in 1924 in the name of national unity. It was Blum again who led the Popular Front against Fascism in 1936. The Popular Front experiment was a historic example of how Socialism in France gets torn apart between forces on its left and right. Blum and the Socialist party bore the brunt of responsibility without being able to force their program upon their bourgeois Radical party and Marxist Communist party allies.

Blum was caught in a pincers between Daladier and Thorez,

neither one of whom had his sense of national responsibility and social justice. Daladier was an appeaser of Hitler and Fascism; Thorez was as dedicated to the eventual destruction of Blum and the Socialist party as of Hitlerism. Hitler and Mussolini thus had a field day during the Popular Front. Republican Spain was raped and thousands of German Jews were slaughtered while France's Republican Jewish Premier wrung his hands helplessly. Blum's own . party was riddled through with pacifists and appeasers. The secretary general of the Socialist party, Paul Faure, was supported by more than half the members in his advocacy of nonintervention. Three out of every four of the Socialist deputies in the Chamber voted full powers to Pétain in 1940.

ᘐᘗ

After the birth of the Fourth Republic the Socialists tried once again to synthesize social and political democracy in a new version of the Popular Front. They called it the "Third Force," an alliance of democratic parties against the extremes of Communism and Gaullism. Once again it was the Socialists who had to sacrifice their economic and social program to save the Republic in a time of national crisis.

The Indochinese War broke out during the term of office of an all-Socialist Government, headed by Léon Blum. Shortly after the outbreak of the war a Socialist, Vincent Auriol, was elected President of the Republic and another Socialist, Paul Ramadier, succeeded Blum as Prime Minister. It was Ramadier who then expelled the Communists from his cabinet. It was under his government that Socialist Jules Moch broke the strikes of 1947 by calling out the army to fight the workers. It was another Socialist, Léon Jouhaux, co-president of the General Confederation of Labor, who walked out of that body in 1947 to form a new trade union, the Force Ouvrière, and split the French labor movement wide open.

Only Socialists could have carried out such a program of colonial wars and strikebreaking without provoking a bitter class war. A Radical or a Catholic party leader could not have dared do what Moch and Ramadier had done, and, if he had, he would have been called a Fascist. No one outside the Communist party would call men like Blum, Ramadier, Moch, Auriol and Jouhaux totalitarians. The Socialists thus made anti-Communism and colonialism respectable in France. They saved the Fourth Republic from the double threat of Communism and Gaullism, but at the expense of almost every principle for which they stood.

The Socialists knew they were being exploited by their allies of the Third Force, who cheerfully gave them all the "dirty jobs" without compensation. However, the veteran party leaders and a majority of the Socialist deputies were convinced there was no alternative but to sacrifice immediate party interests to the higher interests of the Republic, and consequently, they believed, to serve the long-term interests of the party. They felt that if they were to do otherwise the extreme left revolutionaries or right reactionaries would seize power, destroy the Republic and end all hopes for eventual social democracy. They believed they had to fight first to save the Republic and then to make it a republic of social justice.

More than any other group in France the Socialists deserve the credit for leading the fight against Communism in the Fourth Republic. Had they stood aloof, or had they agreed to go ahead with the Communists in a "Marxist alliance," as they did briefly in 1945 in the drafting of the Constitution, France would have been ripped apart by class warfare. The Republic would have been wrecked, for the opposition to a Communist-Socialist front could only have come from a dictator. By accepting a break with the Communists, the Socialists assured democratic leadership of the fight against Communism. This was their great contribution to French democracy in the Fourth Republic and it cost them dearly. From 1945 to 1951, when the Socialists finally quit the Third Force to return to the opposition, they lost half of their voters and more than half of their membership.

ოↄ

The contribution of the Socialists to the defense of the Republic, important as it was, was basically a negative contribution. They prevented a catastrophe but did not succeed in furthering social progress. This failure was mainly attributable to the other democratic parties' inability or unwillingness to see that social democracy is as important an answer to Communism as political democracy. In one respect, however, the failure was due to the Socialists' own blindness on one of the most important issues of France: the religious issue.

Many of the Socialist leaders at the liberation were practicing Christians. André Philip was a devout Protestant. Many others were Catholics. The Socialists and Catholics in the underground had learned to know and respect each other, had begun to realize that the old stereotypes were caricatures. The Catholics discovered that Socialists were not all atheistic, church-burning Reds, getting their orders from an anti-Catholic International. The Socialists discovered that a man could be a devout Catholic and go to Mass every day, without plotting with his priest to "Romanize" the Republic. In the Resistance, the village priest and schoolteacher had fought side by side against the Germans and the French Fascists. There was a real hope that these Christian and Social Democrats could create a new Catholic, democratic Fourth Republic of France.

An early opportunity for a new unity presented itself in September, 1944, when François Moch, brother of Jules Moch, presented a resolution to the first postliberation congress of the Socialist party, calling for an end to the old quarrel with the Catholics. Moch's resolution stated that many Socialists had learned in the Resistance that there were "devout believers who were at the same time devout Republicans." It expressed the wish that "comradeship in the battle shall herald a Republic in which everyone works for social justice . . . in which none seeks to restrict the freedom of conscience of his neighbor."

The resolution passed the committee, and received applause from the congress when Moch brought it to the floor. However, Moch, in an excess of zeal, revealed that the Provisional Government had decided to amend the traditional secularist laws of the Republic and grant special privileges and benefits to Catholic schools. This decision was still secret and the decree implementing it was not scheduled for promulgation until after the Socialist Congress had passed the Moch resolution. The tactical plan of the government had been to proceed from the general principle of social-Christian reconciliation to its particular application on the religious school issue.

Moch's premature revelation killed that plan. A delegate arose and pointed out that a change in the secular laws of education would violate "the Republican principle of separating the Church from the State." He proposed an amendment to the Moch resolution. The amendment called for the repeal of the Pétain subsidies to Catholic schools and reaffirmed the principle that "nationalization of education is the necessary safeguard of Republican unity."

The amendment was passed by acclamation. There was no need to take a vote. A chance for democratic unity between Socialists and Catholics was lost. Once again France was a victim of her history. The passions and memories of 1789 were more potent, more alive than the still fresh events of 1944.

ᔕᕽᕽᐧ

Despite the Catholic school dispute the Socialists were forced to maintain a political coalition with the Catholics and Radicals against their common enemies, the Communists and the Gaullists. After the elections of 1951, when the Communist and Gaullist threats appeared to have passed their peaks, the Socialists decided that the time had come to go into the opposition. They had to close the gaps in their ranks and try to win back the members and voters they had lost because of their "collaboration with the bourgeois parties."

The Socialist opposition, from 1951 through 1955, was on the whole constructive, responsible and successful. The party won back many of its old members and increased its electoral strength. It narrowly averted a disaster in the debate on the European Defense Community Treaty which was a veritable *"crise de conscience"* for French Socialists. Twenty of the most able, loyal and nationally respected party members rebelled against the Executive Committee order to vote for EDC. However, the party survived the inner conflict, eventually pardoned the rebels and reformed its ranks. It did well in the 1956 elections, increasing its popular votes, and party leader Guy Mollet was invested as premier soon after the elections.

The cement of union in the Socialist party, each time a fissure appears, is, strangely, a product of the same forces that permit the gap to open in the first place: the democratic organization and procedure of the party. Disputes are not sins in that party because Socialism, unlike Communism, is not a political religion. Refusal to follow the majority is not insubordination, for the Socialist party is not an army. Opposition in the ranks is simply an infraction of the rules, which is sanctionable but eventually forgivable. Above all there is a sense of camaraderie among Socialists that is rarely found in other groups or parties. There is a kind of Quakerism about French Socialists. When they address each other as *"tu"*—the switchboard operator at party headquarters even uses this familiar form of address when talking to strangers on the phone—it has the quality of the Quaker use of "thou."

Socialism is a kind of Protestantism in France and there are many members and leaders of the party who are of the Protestant faith. The majority of Socialists, however, are freethinkers and agnostics, which is itself a phenomenon found more frequently in Protestant than in Catholic countries. This democratic agnosticism of the French Socialists is at one and the same time both the strength and the weakness of the Socialist party. It is a source of strength because it is flexible and does not crack under pressures. Yet it is a source of weakness because a democracy is always less "efficient" than an autocracy, less disciplined than a religion. This is even more true of a political party than of a society. The Socialists have no all-embracing explanation of society or of the soul to offer their followers as do the Communists and the Catholics. They preach neither revolution nor salvation, which puts them at a great disadvantage in revolutionary and Catholic France.

The Socialist appeal therefore must be aimed at attracting the citizen who is neither devout nor militant and who has no property interests to defend. There is only one group of Frenchmen that has all those particular qualities, the white-collar worker: the post office clerk and the ribbon clerk; the auditor and the customs agent; the legion of men and women who are neither workers, managers, bosses nor proprietors, who are neither desperate enough to revolt nor sufficiently privileged to accept their lot.

This has become the principal membership and electoral clientele of the French Socialist party. Only eight of the Socialist deputies in the National Assembly of 1951 had been industrial workers, as against sixty Communist deputies from the working class. One-half the delegates on the party's federal committees were civil servants or white-collar workers. Only 13 per cent of the federal committeemen were blue-jean workers. Edouard Herriot once said that the Socialist party reminded him of a little café-restaurant in his neighborhood which put up a sign that read: "RESTAURANT OUVRIER—CUISINE BOURGEOISE."

In this respect party leader Guy Mollet is a typical mélange of working-class origins and middle-class functions. A son of workers, he became a schoolteacher, an instructor of English language and literature. He wrote an English grammar and for many years after entering politics continued to contribute learned papers to philological reviews. Deputy and mayor of Arras, the city of Robespierre, Mollet is an intellectual Socialist revolutionary, but in practice a staunch defender of the bourgeois Republic.

Mollet was one of the leaders of the group Libération-Nord in the Resistance and won personal distinction for bravery. He became a major political figure in the Pas-de-Calais district. In 1946 he led a revolt of the young Socialists against the established leadership of the party, succeeding in ousting veteran Daniel Mayer from the chief executive post.

Mollet was forty-one years old when he led the "young Turks" revolt. Nothing could be more typical of a Socialist party leader than to be considered a young hothead at the age of forty-one. It is not only an old-fashioned party, it has become a party of old men. French Socialism is badly in need of rejuvenation but there is little effort made by the party to appeal to youth.

This is one of the notable weaknesses of French Socialism. It is not, however, the main weakness, which is the need to bring its doctrine up to date. The Marxism of Guesde and Jaurès does not apply to mid-twentieth-century France, or, if it does, it is no longer the real doctrine of the SFIO. The name SFIO itself is an anachronism and its survival symbolizes the nostalgia for the past that characterizes the Socialist party. The party is no longer a section of an International. It is no longer revolutionary, nor a workers' party. It has no unique commodity to offer in the political market.

This was seen many years ago by Léon Blum. I saw Blum shortly before his death in 1948, at his little office on the Boulevard Poissonière, in the editorial rooms of the Socialist paper, *Le Populaire*. I asked the venerable Socialist leader if he could tell me why his party had lost so many votes since its peak at the liberation. He sighed sadly and replied: "What have we to offer nowadays? The Communists are Socialists, the Catholics are Socialists, even the

Fascists call themselves 'National Socialists.' Everybody's a Socialist. We shall have to invent a new word or a new idea."

French Socialists are still waiting for the new word, the new idea.

ᏬᏉ

The Christian Democrats

The Catholics of France, too, have long been waiting for the word.

A prophetic French political analyst of the 1920's, Albert Thibaudet, once described Christian Socialism as one of the six great movements of the French democratic tradition, predicting that some day it might assume direction of French political affairs. Thibaudet believed that the great mass of Frenchmen was ready for Catholic leadership: "There is youth, waiting for a guide; there are empty frames waiting for the vision; there are men waiting for a man."

It seemed for a moment in 1941 as though youth had found its guide, the empty frame its vision and men their leader in the person of a young Catholic student, Gilbert Dru. Dru had gone into the maquis to fight the Germans in a Resistance network that he called the "Mouvement Républicain de la Libération." He issued a manifesto, *Youth Looks to Politics*, in which he wrote: "Tomorrow there will be a new political conception to inspire the necessary Revolution. . . . We want to do something new, healthy, clean and useful."

Young Dru was killed in the maquis but not before his call for leadership had been heard. Thousands of young Catholics followed him into the underground to fight for the Republic that the Church once regarded as the fortress of the anti-Christ. Not only students joined the Catholic Republican Movement of Dru. Politicians, parliamentarians, journalists and labor leaders of militant Catholic movements recognized in the appeal of Dru a messianic message, pointing out the road to a Christian democracy that would lead a new France out of the wilderness of political factionalism into a promised land of freedom and justice for all.

A young Jewish convert to Catholicism, Maurice Schumann, who had been active before the war in the Christian league, Jeune République, joined the Mouvement Républicain de la Libération, and restated Dru's objective for the future as "the continuation of an effort that dates back to 1789, not merely to reconcile the revolutionary tradition with Christian doctrine, but to link them tightly together." Many other young Catholic leaders rushed to join the movement, among them Georges Bidault, Robert Schuman, Pierre-Henri Teitgen and Robert Lecourt, leaders of the prewar Catholic political party, Parti Démocratique Populaire. Hundreds and thousands of young Catholics, from every social and professional milieu, heard the new word and rallied to the cause of Christian democracy.

At the liberation the movement changed its name to Mouvement Républicain Populaire, a logical and significant change. Since France was liberated a new word had to be substituted in the title for "liberation"; the decision to replace it by the word "populaire" symbolized the determination of the new Catholics to form a *people's* organization, a rallying point for workers as well as for peasants and the clergy. It was more than just a party or an electoral alliance, it was meant to be a spiritual family of all believers.

The MRP, as it soon became known, succeeded beyond the greatest expectations of its leaders. At the liberation the Catholic movement had almost a quarter of a million militant members and attracted, in the first elections of October, 1945, 4,700,000 votes, to make it the second party of France, just behind the Communists. By June, 1946, campaigning as the "party of fidelity" to General de Gaulle, the Popular Republican Movement reached its apogee as first party of France, with 5,589,000 votes. No other single party in French Republican history ever achieved this total before or since June, 1946.

Exactly five years later, however, in June, 1951, the MRP sank to its lowest point, losing more than 50 per cent of its membership and its electoral strength. It has been in decline ever since, slipping to fifth position among the six major parties in 1956, barely getting a larger vote than Poujade. By then the shining vision of Gilbert Dru had long been clouded over. Catholic youth had no guide, no man to lead it. The war coalition of Social and Christian Democrats was shattered. The future of French political Catholicism was dark.

The story of how that came about, of how the shining vision of a Christian democracy united with a social democracy was distorted into the old nightmare of the clerical-anticlerical, politico-religious war, is one of the keys to the mystery of what went wrong in the

Fourth Republic, of how it was trapped in the wilderness, just as it was in sight of the Promised Land.

ఆం

There were good reasons at the liberation of France to believe in the vision of Gilbert Dru and the creation of a pro-Republican Catholic party. The leader of the National Council of Resistance, Georges Bidault, was a Catholic of unquestioned loyalty to the Republic. His editorials for the paper, *l'Aube*, before the war, had denounced the policy of nonintervention in Spain. Bidault led the attack on Daladier for the appeasement at Munich. After the fall of France he had immediately gone into the Resistance. At the same time, his colleague Maurice Schumann had escaped to England where he was among the first to join de Gaulle's Free French. Schumann's was the voice that carried the news of the free world to occupied France in his radio program beamed from London, *"Les Français parlent aux Français."* Thus both among the resistants and the liberators there were strong, respected voices of Catholic Democrats.

Many of the militants who joined the ranks of the Popular Republican Movement were equally dedicated democrats. Gone were the anti-Semites, the royalists, the intolerant hate-mongers who had done disservice to French Catholicism in the past. By the hundreds of thousands French Catholic workers joined the Christian trade union CFTC, Confédération Française des Travailleurs Chrétiens, whose membership rose to 800,000 and promised to shoot up past the million mark.

Yet, under the surface, opposition forces were at work. The suspicions and hatreds of the past had not been liquidated overnight. They had simply gone underground. The hate-mongers, the fanatics, whose minds had been poisoned by men like Maurras, were still there. They were waiting for a chance to strike back at the feared and despised "Godless Republic." Just as the Socialists were still motivated by a traditional fear of the Church, so were many Catholics still fearful of the Republic.

Since there was no conservative party for them to join at the liberation they joined the MRP, even though its leaders were Republicans and Socialists. They had no other place to go. This was apparent in the first elections. Before the war no Catholic party had ever won more than fifty thousand votes. The MRP vote was in the millions. The conclusion was inescapable: the conservative voters and the traditional Right had gone underground in the MRP. Despite its leftist program they had seen in it a confessional party that could become their new home. Because of its Resistance record the MRP was the perfect refuge for the collaborator, who could whitewash his stained record by becoming a Christian Democrat. The Right, borrowing the technique of the extreme Left, was "boring from within" the MRP.

All went well at the start for the Christian Democrats, despite the infiltration of right-wing and anti-democratic elements. The fact that de Gaulle would not deign to head a party of his own permitted Bidault and Schumann to campaign under his name. De Gaulle, as every Frenchman knew, was a devout Catholic, and Bidault, his Foreign Minister, was one of his closest associates, as close as any independent man could get to de Gaulle. When the General resigned and the Socialists joined forces with the Communists, the Catholics led the opposition to the Marxist parties as the champions of liberal democracy. Their vote soared to new heights.

Then the balloon burst.

Bidault, increasingly alarmed by the perpetuation of a provisional regime and irked by de Gaulle's haughty, almost contemptuous treatment of the Christian Resistance leaders, decided to assume leadership on his own. The MRP took over the drafting of the Constitution, reconstituted the Resistance alliance with the Communists and Socialists and prepared for a fight with de Gaulle. De Gaulle struck back, denounced the draft Constitution, called on the people to reject it. Although the Constitution was adopted the MRP lost heavily at the polls.

The rout of the MRP was confirmed in the municipal elections when de Gaulle's newly formed RPF swept the country, rolling up almost 40 per cent of the votes, while the MRP was pulled down to less than 10 per cent. The traditional, conservative Catholic votes had deserted the MRP for de Gaulle. It was a serious setback for the Christian Democrats. The MRP total in the elections of November 11, 1946, had been just under five million votes. A year later it had fallen to less than two and a half millions. The loss of the Catholic party's electoral strength was not a progressive decline, as in the case of the Socialists. It came all at once in 1947 and the MRP never recovered its losses.

The effort to hold its followers and to win back some of those who had left the ranks inevitably forced the MRP leadership into a position of intransigence on the Catholic school issue, for exactly the same reasons that impelled the Socialists to an equal intransigence against educational subsidies for the Catholics. Thus the MRP moved slowly but steadily to the right of center, further and further away from the new, healthy vision of Gilbert Dru.

The MRP, however, cannot simply be dismissed as a reactionary, rightist party. It was the MRP that pushed for and voted for fiscal reforms in almost every government in which it participated. The Catholic deputies were mainly responsible for legislating the application of the labor code to the overseas territories of France. The MRP voted for the law on collective bargaining and the sliding scale for wages, a key provision that contributed greatly to stemming the hemorrhage of inflation in 1952. It is typical of the MRP that it led the fight inside the government for the sliding scale at exactly the same time that it was pushing through Parliament the Barangé law for subsidies to Catholic schools. It was MRP leader Robert Schuman who initiated the European Coal and Steel Community, the first historic step toward a Franco-German reconciliation. The "Schuman Plan" was bitterly opposed by the traditionally nationalistic Right.

The Christian Democrats, like the Social Democrats, have therefore made a great contribution to the Republic in many spheres. They have also been guilty of grave errors and, in some cases, of immoral and unchristian actions. We shall examine some of these tragic errors later in this study, particularly in the section on colonial developments. The wars in Indochina and Algeria, the massacres in Madagascar, the betrayal of promises in Tunisia and in Morocco, these disasters must be charged in great measure against the MRP and its leaders, men like Bidault, Letourneau, Coste-Floret and Pierre de Chévigné. The Socialist party shares the blame for these bloody wars and counterrevolutions with the MRP. From Ramadier in 1947 to Mollet in 1956 the Socialists bore a heavy responsibility for the wars and counterrevolutions in the Union of Overseas France. Naegelen and Lacoste played as decisive a role in the rebellion of Algeria as did Letourneau and Coste-Floret in Indochina.

It is therefore difficult, if not impossible, to be categorical about the place in contemporary France of the Socialists and the Catholics. Neither one is "good" or "bad." Both have alternately saved and sabotaged the democratic structure of the Fourth Republic and the French Union. Both have agonized through soul-searching crises of conscience. Both have survived those crises.

From the perspective of history the Christian Democrats, like the Social Democrats, are a stronger, more vital force in the Fourth Republic than they were in the Third. In terms of the present they are still fighting for their lives in this transitional mid-century in which France herself is fighting for survival. The two struggles are not unrelated.

France will not survive as a great nation if its Christian Democrats and its Social Democrats lose their battle for existence. The Catholics and the Socialists will lose that battle if they do not some day, and soon, end their fratricidal wars. The menace of the antidemocratic forces in the world and in France is too great to permit the luxury of internecine quarrels of another century.

ᘒ

The Liberal Democrats

The term "liberal," when applied to the Radical-Socialist party of France, can only be used in the European and not the American sense of the word. In America, a liberal is progressive-minded. He wants to change the existing order of things for the better. An American liberal is a reformer, a "do-gooder." In Europe, however, a liberal, although broad-minded and liberty-loving, is suspicious of hasty change or radical reforms. He is tolerant and egalitarian in principle, but moderate and even conservative in action. The French liberal is easy to describe but difficult to define, for he has no doctrine and no distinct political coloration. He is opportunistic and favors parties with the same characteristics. The party most closely identified with and frequented by the laissez-faire liberal is the Radical-Socialist party.

The Radical-Socialist party is a perfect expression of the liberal temperament. It is neither radical, nor Socialist, nor even a party. It is more a political club or league, something of a cross between Tammany Hall and the Daughters of the American Revolution. The Radicals consider themselves to be the guardians of the principles of 1789, just as the DAR members are sure they alone are faithful to 1776, but the "party's" main function is to provide its members with meeting rooms and a central machinery for the purpose of collective political propaganda during election campaigns.

The skill of the Radical party in forming electoral alliances during campaigns is extraordinary. In four elections, from 1945 through 1951, the Radical popular vote hardly varied at all, but the number of Radical candidates elected to Parliament increased steadily from twenty-eight to thirty-two to forty-three to seventy-eight. They were able to do this by running on joint tickets with other parties. In 1951, the Radicals outdid themselves: of their seventy-eight successful candidates for office, fifty-eight ran on a Third Force ticket, three ran on a de Gaulle ticket and seventeen ran on a ticket opposed to both the Third Force and de Gaulle. Never has political cynicism reached such heights. It paid off for the Radicals in government as well as in Parliament. They were the only party in France to participate in every government of the Fourth Republic from 1946 through 1956.

The Radical-Socialist leaders are personalities rather than party members. The gamut of their temperaments and talents extends through the entire range of French characters, from the amiable, plodding Dr. Queuille to the tough, hard-driving Pierre Mendès-France.

Dr. Queuille is a country doctor turned politician who set several records for longevity. One of his cabinets stayed in office more than a year, which is a miracle in France. From September 9, 1948, to October 10, 1949, Dr. Queuille held on to the post of premier by the simple expedient of doing nothing at all. He set new standards for do-nothingness in a regime where immobilism had been raised to the level of a fine art. Dr. Queuille not only broke the long-sitting record for prime ministers, he also won the blue ribbon for elections to the premiership. He was invested three times by Parliament. His prescription for government, in his own words, was "The art of politics is not to settle questions but to silence those who raise them."

Queuille was able to set his records because everyone trusted him not to do anything that might upset anyone and also because of the position that the Radical Party occupied in the first legislature of the Fourth Republic: center of the Center. The right and left wings could only meet through the Radical link between them. On the Catholic school issue the anticlerical Radicals were spiritual brothers of the Socialists; on economic policy they joined forces with the Christian Democrats and the moderates against the Marxists. Since they could be all things to all men but really represented almost nothing themselves the Radicals were the perfect compromise party. This has been their classic position in French politics.

The Radicals were always able to find flexible leaders who managed to bend with every force. Edouard Daladier was the most skilled whirling dervish of the party in the Third Republic. He was an enthusiastic supporter of Blum's Popular Front against Fascism and he was later a partner of Chamberlain in appeasing Hitler at Munich. Unlike Dr. Queuille, who excelled at doing nothing, Daladier excelled at doing anything. With men like that among its leaders the party was never at a loss for exercising power, under any circumstances at any time.

The Radicals, however, had more to offer the Republic than immobilists and opportunists. Clemenceau, the Tiger of France, was a Radical-Socialist. So is Edouard Herriot, who was a highly respected leader of Europe as well as of France in the decade 1920-30. Herriot was a rival and an enemy of Daladier inside the Radical party and fought him for a quarter of a century.

In the Fourth Republic "the two Edwards" are old and tired men but their act has found a successor in the fight between Pierre Mendès-France and Edgar Faure. Once a Damon and Pythias, Mendès-France and Faure became a political Cain and Abel. Faure did nothing to help Mendès-France in the critical confidence vote that brought his government down. Mendès-France retaliated by capturing control of the Radical party and throwing Faure out.

It is one of the tragic features of contemporary French politics that Faure and Mendès-France should have split apart and added to the already dangerous divisions of the democratic center. Their relationship to each other may be that of Daladier and Herriot, but Faure is no Daladier nor Mendès-France an Herriot. Both are bigger, more brilliant men than their predecessors. They are also young men who, barring accident, will play a major role in French affairs and perhaps world affairs for many years to come. Their careers to date are an integral part of the history of the Fourth Republic and began with its birth.

ᕙᏉ

Whenever political reporters gathered around a café table in Algiers, in 1943, the conversation would eventually turn into a guessing game, whose object was to pick the names of the future premiers of liberated France. One name more than any other invariably appeared on everyone's list: the name of a thirty-six-year-old lawyer, Edgar Faure. Faure was considered a sure bet, not only because he was brilliant, eloquent and witty but because he so obviously wanted to become a prime minister. And, since so many politicians, brilliant and otherwise, eventually do become Premier of France, Faure could not miss.

Faure's colleagues on the National Liberation Committee used to joke about his ambitions. They composed a political catechism about him: "Who is Edgar Faure? Nobody. What is Edgar Faure? Everything. What does Edgar Faure want to be? Prime Minister." Faure laughed as much as anyone at these jokes. He told me once: "I don't care much what they say about me so long as they keep talking about me." Faure is a disenchanted and very French Frenchman.

From his earliest youth Faure had been the sort of person people talk about. At the age of nineteen he became the youngest lawyer ever admitted to the Paris bar. At twenty-five he was chairman of the Bar Association. At thirty-four he was secretary general of de Gaulle's legal department and two years later was France's deputy chief prosecutor at the Nuremberg Trials. At thirty-seven Faure made his debut in politics, when he was elected to the National Assembly in June, 1946. Three years later the freshman legislator was appointed Undersecretary of the Treasury. In 1952, at the age of forty-three, Edgar Faure realized his ambition when Parliament elected him premier, the youngest French prime minister of this century. Only one other man, Gambetta, in 1881, reached the top that young.

Faure's precocity is a rare distinction in a country like France where youth is not particularly encouraged nor admired. Faure said of his meteoric rise: "Luckily, I was born old and aged rapidly." This comment is typical of Faure's personality. There is nothing he enjoys so much as a witty *"mot."* His inability to resist an opportunity for an aphorism has made him many enemies among the victims of his sharp tongue, and has given him a reputation for being superficial and irresponsible.

Edgar Faure is certainly not superficial. His is a first-class brain. He is, however, a sort of intellectual dandy, who dresses up his ideas in lacy curlicues of perfumed prose, which earn him both admiration and criticism—admiration for the sheer pyrotechnical skill of his performance, severe criticism for the lack of responsibility that puts performance ahead of achievement. For Edgar Faure is more concerned about the way to do things than the need to get them done.

This is both the strength and the weakness of Edgar Faure. The way things are done is important, sometimes as important as the doing. However, the important test for a statesman is to find the dividing line between the essential goal and the useful manner. Faure failed to find that line of distinction in his handling of the Moroccan issue in the summer of 1955, and missed the opportunity of stopping the degeneration of France's North African positions. Yet, earlier that year, Faure completed the Tunisian negotiations for home rule which Mendès-France had begun and had failed to finish. And it was Faure who completed the difficult process of ratifying the bill for German rearmament in NATO. Commenting on that ratification, Faure told me: "Only Mendès-France could have bulled this bill through the Assembly. Only I could have maneuvered it through the Senate." This, in Faure's own words, is an essential difference between the actions of the two men. Mendès-France is a bull, Faure a maneuverer. Mendès-France batters down obstacles. Faure goes around them.

Edgar Faure is conscious of the differences between himself and Mendès-France. He knows he can never be as popular a national figure. This does not bother him. He is much too vain and too big to suffer from an inferiority complex. No longer a boy prodigy, Faure is nonetheless a very young political leader. For most men national leadership rarely begins before fifty-five. Faure's most bitter critics would not deny his intellectual force and his technical skill. He is a formidable man. His faults are as formidable as his skills, however, and he has much to live down. He has been branded as a tool of the *"patronat,"* the French big-business lobby, and although no one has ever published any damning evidence of this charge it is widespread and believed to be true by many of his colleagues. Foreign diplomats are also suspicious of Faure because of his opportunism and his frequent flirtations with the Communists and neutralists of France. Faure is angry and wounded by these charges but he has failed to convince his allies that he is a thoroughly reliable man.

It is difficult to predict the future of a relatively young political leader in any country, but above all in France. It is particularly difficult when he is so complex an individual as an Edgar Faure. A man with his extraordinary gifts but mercurial character can go in any direction. Faure has already, in a short time, made common cause with such diverse men as Mendès-France, Laniel, Bidault and Pinay. There is only one certainty about Edgar Faure: in whatever direction he may go you can be sure that he will go far.

ᘐᕉ

People put down their drinks, stopped their conversations and turned to the radio as the deep, big voice said "Good evening" and entered the room.

It was as though Pierre Mendès-France, or, as the French call him, "Mendès," had actually walked in to speak with us in person. We were expecting him. Every Saturday night at eight the people of France had a "rendezvous with Mendès." Not since the wartime speeches of Winston Churchill and the fireside chats of Franklin Roosevelt had any man been able to project his personality through the air to millions of people with such intimacy and authority.

This night Mendès had a special message for us. He had just flown back to Paris from Geneva, where he had successfully concluded a peace treaty ending the Indochinese War. The treaty had been signed in the very last minutes of a thirty-day deadline, just when it seemed that all hope of peace had been lost. Mendès had come to tell us what had happened and what it meant to each and every one of us.

"Believe me, on that night of the twentieth of July, within an hour of the end of our negotiations, when unforeseen difficulties arose to imperil our efforts, suddenly we felt a presence among us, commanding and imperious, a presence which dominated us, which forced us to conclude because no one could ignore or resist it."

Mendès paused for a long second and then continued more slowly, his voice heavy with emotion. "That force was yours. It was the profound feeling, among both our friends and our adversaries, that there could be no possible doubt about the determination of the French people to make peace or to take whatever measures were necessary to face the alternative. There could be no mistake about it that night. I have seen with my own eyes how overwhelming is the will of a great people, when it is clearly expressed and deeply felt. Yes, I have seen destiny bend to that will."

I looked around the room at my French friends. A usually voluble, sophisticated group, always ready with a sharp or witty comment, it was now a silent group of serious men and women. They were straining forward to the radio, looking intently at it, as though it were Mendès himself. For French men and women, weary of the tired clichés of professional politicians, despairing of progress after a decade of "do nothing" governments, cynical of promises never kept, the voice of Mendès-France was a voice from the wilderness, calling on the people to have faith in him, and, through him, in themselves.

ᕲᕗ

In the summer of 1954 the people of France were ready to believe any man who believed in himself. They were hungry, desperate for leadership and honesty. They wanted the truth, no matter how unpleasant. It was Mendès who offered them honesty and action, who represented the true alternative to the glib but bankrupt professionals who had administered postwar France. The contrast between the true nature and false promises of these men had become apparent to the entire nation. Little men, they had talked of grandeur; weak men, they had played at power politics; democrats at home they were despots in the colonies; personally thrifty they squandered the money of the State. Mendès-France, almost alone among the politicians of France, had refused to play their dreary game.

Only one other man had stood aloof and denounced the "stagnant, stinking swamps of French politics": Charles de Gaulle. Unlike de Gaulle. however, Mendès remained faithful to the ideal of a parliamentary democracy, despite its travesty in Parliament. He directed his scorn and wrath at the men who had perverted the system and not, as de Gaulle did, at parliamentary democracy itself. Mendès believed in the democratic system of France and believed in the people of France. When he pronounced the sacred, revolutionary phrase of 1789, "the will of the people," he spoke with all the mystic fervor of an Abbé Siéyès, who had declared that will to be supreme and divine. When Mendès denounced the corruption of the petty politicians he was the reincarnation of Robespierre, "The Incorruptible." Mendès consciously felt the fervor of the revolutionaries within himself. A full year before coming to power he had stood before the Congress of the Radical party and had solemnly warned the delegates: "Gentlemen, take heed, for we are living in 1788!"

This was the strength and this was the weakness of Pierre Mendès-France, the most complex, contradictory man in that most complex and contradictory country of France. His revolutionary ardor, his sense of identification with 1789, corresponded with a moment in history when the people yearned for ardor and for change. But Mendès is not a true revolutionary. He is a reformer. The change he seeks is a change of style and of method, not of structures and philosophies. Above all, his is a personal exaltation, not a true sense of identification with other men. This is the tragedy of Mendès-France, as it was the tragedy of Charles de Gaulle, whom he resembles in so many respects. These men, while completely dissimilar in physical appearance, religious, social and ethnic origins, are spiritual and psychological twins, and both played precisely the same role in the first decade of the Fourth Republic.

Charles de Gaulle, son of a Catholic professor of history at a Jesuit school, descended from Teutonic stock, tall, thin, cold and morose, reveres France but holds his fellow Frenchmen in contempt. Pierre Mendès-France, son of a middle-class dress manufacturer, descended from Sephardic Jews, short, broad, intense and dedicated, loves "the people" but dislikes people. The sense of intimacy that Mendès conveys is as ethereal as the radio waves that carried his presence into the homes and hearts of the French. In person this illusion of communion is destroyed, for Mendès shrinks from human contacts. His love for the people is an adoration of an abstract ideal. Thus Mendès, like de Gaulle, is a lonely man. He is a chief rather than a leader, for a leader does not stand apart from his troops, as did Mendès and de Gaulle in their terms of office. Their ministers were not their colleagues; they were disciples and devoted slaves. These disciples worshiped Mendès and de Gaulle, despite their despotic, intolerant personalities. Close associates of Mendès used to tell me, with the glaze of adoration in their eyes: *"Oui, Mendès est insupportable. C'est un grand homme."*

Great men are often insupportable. Yet there is a fundamental difference between the majestic rudeness of a Churchill and the cold, impersonal bad manners of a de Gaulle and a Mendès-France. Perhaps the most frightening quality of these men is that they often do not know they are being rude or cruel. Other people just do not exist for them. They are that rarest of the human species, genuine misanthropists. They are also an even rarer type of man: they are ascetics. They do not smoke or drink; they eat only sparingly of simple foods; they do not gamble, play games or sports. These are the qualities of a hermit or a monk but not of a leader of men. To lead men one must first understand men, their hopes, their fears, their earthy vulgarities, yet their capacity for selfless heroism. Neither de Gaulle nor Mendès fully understands his fellow Frenchmen, for neither is of a kind with them. Perhaps this is one of the reasons why they both were magnificent in adversity, inspiring in the opposition, but failures as Prime Ministers of France.

〰

The great failure of Mendès-France came on one of the most controversial issues of French and Western affairs: the "Treaty Instituting a European Defense Community." In the course of the debate on EDC Mendès revealed his inner complexes and destroyed the myth of his uncompromising political honesty and courage. On EDC Mendès was as tricky as a Faure, as weak and indecisive as a Queuille. Mendès, above all, was untrue to his own famous precept, the political formula that was his personal motto: "To govern is to choose." On EDC Mendès did not choose and thus failed to govern France. It was not his stand for or against EDC that marked his failure; it was his failure to take a stand that marked him as a less responsible leader than he had purported to be. His appearance before Parliament in the climactic debate on that issue was the low point of his career. He had insisted upon holding that debate, had insisted that France must make up her mind, but he himself failed to make up his own.

Mendès was nervous and unsure of himself as he stood before a tense, expectant Chamber on August 23, 1954. The man who had once taunted other premiers with political cowardice, who had said, "To govern is to choose, no matter how difficult the choice may be," this time began with an apology: "I cannot conceal the fact that I am embarrassed and ill at ease about the explanations I am going to present to you." Mendès admitted that a government, worthy of the name, ought to take an unequivocal stand on a matter of the highest national and international interest. Yet, he confessed, his government would not take such a stand in this debate. Mendès fumbled through a long, confused explanation of his dilemma. He reminded the deputies that he had promised them in his investiture speech of June 18 that he would try to reconcile Frenchmen on the divisive issue of an alliance with a rearmed Germany. He said he had tried hard to effect such a reconciliation but had failed. Therefore, in all conscience, he could not submit the EDC Treaty to the Assembly in the form of a confidence motion, or even as a government-supported bill. It would be a "free vote," permitting each man to make his decision according to the dictates of his own conscience, without political considerations. It was a humiliating abdication of authority by a man who had diagnosed exactly such indecisiveness as the major political ill of France.

His speech was the death knell for EDC. No controversial bill could possibly win a majority in the divided Parliament of France if the government itself refused to support it. Perhaps, as Mendès claimed in an interview with me a week later, EDC would have been defeated anyway, and by an even greater margin, if he had made it a confidence vote. Whether this was true or not is not relevant to an evaluation of Mendès himself. By letting EDC be destroyed, while remaining neutral, Mendès destroyed himself. Never again could he wield the same authority, never again could he point an accusing finger at weaker men, for his own hand had trembled at a decisive moment in history. Mendès may not have been the "assassin of Europe," as his enemies charged, but it might be said that he was one of the gravediggers of Europe, or, at the very best, a dry-eyed pall-bearer. He certainly was not a courageous champion of responsible government. Mendès, after August, 1954, remained an important, even a powerful political personality in France, but he was no longer a giant towering above lesser men.

What happened after that historic debate of August, 1954, was almost an anticlimax, although at the time it seemed to be the most critical moment in the postwar history of the Western alliance. The rejection of EDC had wrecked one of the pillars of Western policy and threatened to wreck the Atlantic Alliance itself. The alliance was saved, but not by Mendès-France. It was rescued by Sir Anthony Eden, who went on a flying tour of Europe and then convened the Conference of London, where he proposed the rearmament of Germany in NATO.

The acceptance of the Eden Plan by Mendès-France revealed the truth about his position on EDC: it was not the rearmament of Germany that had been troubling his conscience; what tortured Mendès was the thought of fusing France into a superstate of Europe. Mendès showed himself to be a French nationalist, not necessarily in the narrow, nationalistic sense of the word, but in the emotional context of the French Revolution and its concept of *"la nation."* This kind of nationalism was consistent with his character. Robespierre would certainly have voted against EDC. For all his talk of modernism, change and progress, Mendès-France is not a man with a vision of the future, he is a man still motivated by the precepts of the past. The main difference, on this score, between a Mendès-France and a Bidault is that Bidault lives in a dream world of the past, whereas for Mendès history is an example and an inspiration for the present. Mendès once told Parliament that no nation could expect to be treated as a great power because it once was great. France, he said, had to go to work, to make herself strong and powerful again. Yet Mendès did not see what a truly big man like Jean Monnet saw clearly: that work as hard as she could, France was no longer a great power in the world of the twentieth-century continent-nations. I feel certain that Mendès knew this but could not bring himself to admit it. Torn between reason and sentiment, he was paralyzed on this issue of Europe.

The last major act of Mendès as premier was the ratification of the German rearmament bill during Christmas week, 1954. By then he had lost the respect of many of his friends without winning the support of his enemies. Within five weeks he was voted out of office. It had taken exactly seven months and seventeen days, just about average for the course, for Mendès to suffer the fate of all French premiers.

On the bare facts of his legislative record it could be argued that Mendès was one of the least successful premiers of the Fourth Republic. His positive accomplishments were few in number and the major success of his administration—France's economic recovery in 1954—was due to the technical skill of his Minister of Finance, Edgar Faure, to whom Mendès entrusted the drafting and execution of the economic program. The personal accomplishments of Mendès himself were those of a surgeon rather than a creator. Mendès lanced abscesses that had been poisoning France and paralyzing the body politic for years. The end of the Indochinese War, however, was not a successful operation; it was an amputation. The dramatic flight to Tunis, where Mendès personally and publicly pledged home rule, earned him the reputation as champion of freedom for colonial peoples, but it obscured the fact that Mendès never did speak of independence but only of home rule, and that the phrase "*la présence française*" was as often on his lips as in the mouth of Bidault. Moreover, the promise of home rule was still in the stage of niggling negotiations seven months after Mendès had made his pledge. Edgar Faure, who succeeded Mendès as premier, made good the pledge.

It was also during the term of office of Mendès-France that the Algerian revolt broke out, in November, 1954. Mendès failed to appreciate the gravity or significance of that rebellion in the Aurès Mountains and it was more than a year before he developed even a vague outline of an Algerian policy. Nor did Mendès appreciate the urgency of one of the basic reforms needed in France: revision of the Constitution to give the executive more stability and authority. Instead of using his own great personal authority and popularity to force through such a reform Mendès dissipated his energies on a campaign against alcoholism. Alcoholism is certainly one of the ills plaguing France but it was well down on the list of urgent priorities in 1954. Mendès, the milk-drinking premier, made himself popular in the United States but somewhat ridiculous in France with his anti-alcoholism campaign. This was a specific case of his failure to understand his fellow Frenchmen.

Now that a full year has gone by, however, and Mendès can be seen from the perspective of time, the bare facts of his term in office are not enough to give the full measure of the man. Mendès was more than just a surgeon. He was, above all, a Messiah. This was his greatest contribution to French life, the one for which he is remembered and which makes him still a major personality. Mendès did what no surgeon can do. He breathed life into the soul as well as the body of France. He gave people hope, faith and, above all, self-respect. Mendès made Frenchmen proud to be French. He showed that power and prestige were not measured only in terms of brute strength and numbers. By the sheer force of his spirit he galvanized millions of men into action and made the world respect France and the French. He may have made the mistake of thinking that a man alone was bigger than the system of government but this is a mistake that can be corrected in the future and Mendès is still a young man.

He was only forty-seven years old when he was premier. His career is ahead of him. Millions of people still have faith in him and Mendès has supreme faith in himself.

ᖍ

After Mendès captured control of the Radical party machinery in May, 1955, he set out to make himself absolute master. He expelled Edgar Faure, René Mayer and other leaders of the anti-Mendès wing, who then formed a dissident Radical splinter party. It is curious to note that Mendès, who rails against "party bossism," is the highest-handed party boss of them all. It is also significant to note that Mendès, the democrat, is loyal to the system of parliamentary democracy, but Mendès, the man, is apparently incapable of accepting the basic rule of democracy: toleration of a minority and co-operation among men of different opinions.

The conflict between Mendès-France and Edgar Faure is typical of the schisms in the Center of French democracy. Both sides are guilty of putting personal quarrels, ambitions and doctrines above the need for national unity. The minority is as guilty as the majority. Where the majority is intolerant the minority is irresponsible. The system itself encourages irresponsibility. Minority groups are given a premium for irresponsible opposition: they can always hope to be in the new majority coalition when they bring down a cabinet. This is the basic, double weakness of the French body politic: multiplicity of parties and instability of the executive.

The real affliction of the French body politic is, thus, not so much the disease of its parts but the fact that the parts do not work together.

It is a case of disarticulation rather than degeneration. The effect of such a disarticulation of the political parties is that it paralyzes Parliament, which is serious, for Parliament is the central nervous system of the Republic. It controls both the legislative and executive powers in France. It is through Parliament that the parties themselves function. It is to Parliament, therefore, that we now turn in our examination of the state of health of French democracy, for there one can see the ultimate effects of the schisms in the Center, the spasms on the Right and the excess of Red cells on the Left that are so characteristic of the ailing body politic of France.

III   *A FUNCTIONAL EXAMINATION*

9 *The Nervous System of Parliament*

"The eyes of France are upon us, gentlemen. Let us proceed with a dignity befitting the free institutions of a democratic society."

The speaker, stern-faced, his jaw set stiffly above a wing collar and white tie, was Socialist André Le Trocquer, chairman of the Congress of Versailles, the joint session of France's two Houses of Parliament. Members of the National Assembly and Council of the Republic were about to elect a new President of the Republic, the sole occasion on which the bicameral legislature of France meets as one body. For the first time in French history the entire nation would watch its first magistrate be chosen and, at the same time, observe its representatives in action. The national television network had a battery of cameras spaced around the red plush hemicycle in the Palace of Versailles. Everything that took place in that Chamber would be seen across the country.

It was a historic setting. The forefathers of the parliamentarians present had gathered in that Palace of Versailles in May, 1789, when Louis XVI convoked a States General at a time of financial crisis in the kingdom. They had taken power into their own hands in the course of that meeting, had proclaimed themselves to be a National Assembly, representing the popular will rather than the royal pleasure. It was the first act of the Revolution. Ever since then the assembly of a Congress at Versailles was an occasion to rededicate the Revolution and demonstrate the unity of the people. No Congress of Versailles had ever needed more than two ballots to choose a President of the Republic, a unanimity rarely seen in the regular, separate sessions of the Houses.

There was no such unanimity in the Congress of Versailles of 1953. All traditions were broken when the deputies quarreled,

133

bargained and traded for votes day and night for a full week, setting the unprecedented record of thirteen ballots before electing an obscure Independent from Normandy, René Coty, as President of the Republic.

The people of France were profoundly shocked. They had witnessed the whole spectacle on television—an experience which they would not soon enjoy again, for the legislators realized they had made an error in letting the television eye of the people follow their antics. The newspapers of France, and foreign correspondents, reported the anger of the public and began talking about the "shadow of revolution" once again over Versailles.

What had happened to French democratic institutions? Was the Fourth Republic disintegrating even before it was a decade old? Was France really reliving the events of 1789? Were ghosts walking through the marble halls of Versailles? The Congress of Versailles certainly reflected a crisis of French parliamentary democracy. What caused this crisis? What was the future of parliamentary democracy in France, judged both on its performance in the past and its role in the present life of French society?

❧

The word *"parlements"* had been used since the fourteenth century to describe a series of assemblies or councils, called from time to time by the king, generally in time of crisis in his kingdom. The modern Parliament of France derives not so much from those medieval *parlements* as from the National Assembly created by the States General. This National Assembly, formed by the commoners when they broke away from the two privileged estates, the nobles and the clergy, was the first expression of a general popular will. The word "national" in its title symbolized the difference between the French, British and American concepts of a representative government. The French, in an excess of revolutionary zeal, declared that the people's representatives were the fountainhead of the State. Abbé Siéyès declaimed that "the Third Estate is everything." Neither the British nor the American representatives pretended to be the emanation of the nation itself. British parliamentarians and American Congressmen functioned as one element in a unity of powers. In Britain, the Revolution of 1689 had produced a parliamentary sovereignty that assumed the powers of an existing royal sovereignty, but with the king's consent and co-operation. The unity of the crown and the people was formalized in the typically British phrase, "the King, in His Parliament." The British Revolution was thus institutionalized in a functional unity of the king, his ministers and his subjects. The House of Commons was the place for the people's representatives, the House of Lords for the nobles, the Palace for the king, in a trinity of union. As for the clergy, the Reformation in England, by freeing the State Church from the Church of Rome, had produced a religious unity inside the kingdom. Britain was an island of its own and its revolution evolved in insular harmony.

The United States, too, was an island in the early years of the young Republic and its Revolution was able to take root in the country in a period of relative tranquillity. The roots were the clauses of the Constitution, which became the symbol of unity in the federal Republic. The Constitution was to endure as the very heart of American democracy and representative government. The will of the free people of America was expressed and safeguarded by the Constitution, not by the Congress, which was only an instrument of the popular will. The Congress of the United States was not even the principal instrument. A system of checks and balances had been devised to keep any one branch of government from dominating the others. The legislative body took its place as an equal and co-operating partner with the executive and judicial organs of state. They were unified in and limited by the Constitution, guardian of the revolutionary principles.

The very opposite occurred in France, not only because the French deliberately planned it that way, but because of many cultural, social and geographical factors that influenced the political shape of parliamentary democracy in France. The Church in France, unlike the clergy in Britain and America, was Roman Catholic, and the king was the loyal servant and protector of the "Prince of Rome." In practice, many French kings were, on the contrary, jealous of the political influence of Rome, but when it came to purely religious questions the kings, and particularly Louis XVI, were often devout defenders of the faith. The privileges of the clergy, protected by the king, were deeply resented by the Commons. The nationalism of the Revolution manifested itself partly in outbursts against the "foreign Church," partly in grumbling about Queen Marie Antoinette, "the Austrian bitch." Had there been a French State Church, as in England, had the Queen been French, or the King as devoted to his nation as to his church, France might have remained a parliamentary monarchy, as England did.

Speculation is, in any case, idle, for Catholic France, living on the crossroads of Europe, did not and could not evolve as Britain, nor as the United States. Religious conflicts, foreign influence, geography, as well as history, all combined to produce an unstable parliamentary Republic in France. The pressures on parliamentary democracy in France were irresistible from the start. The Revolution was menaced from within by counterrevolutionaries and surrounded by foreign enemies on all of its frontiers.

The 1789 experiment in constitutional monarchy ended on the guillotine, in 1793. When Louis's head was lopped off, the blade took with it the only unifying element of the French body politic. What remained was a rowdy, disorganized, debating society called the National Assembly, in which rival claimants for the role of "true spokesman" of the will of the people tried to shout each other down. It only took a year for self-appointed "Committees of Public Safety" to take command and for popular democracy to degenerate into tyranny, more oppressive than anything France had suffered under the kings.

French democrats never solved the problem of ministerial responsibility or separation of powers. The parliamentary history of France is a history of conflict between the legislature and the executive, with no king to act as arbiter, no constitutional machinery to provide a balance, and, above all, no period of peace and security long enough to permit a synthesis to evolve.

ᏇᏇᎧ

At the liberation of France in 1944 the framers of the new Constitution went back in history to seek symbolic inspiration for the Parliament of the Fourth Republic. They found the name in the National Assembly of 1789 and the principle in the Revolutionary Convention of 1793. The principle was the same one that caused all the trouble in the past: the investment of all power in the Assembly. No people are so learned in history and so willfully defiant of its lessons as the French. No group of legislators in modern democratic history has ever enjoyed the virtually unlimited powers of a deputy in the National Assembly of the Fourth Republic.

The deputies alone have the right to initiate and make laws. The Constitution protects them further by stipulating that they may not delegate this legislative authority. Once the deputies pass a law no one else may veto it, neither the executive nor the Council of the Republic, which can only request amendments. The deputies alone may initiate state expenditures, pass the budget, control the accounts of the nation, approve or disapprove a declaration of war, ratify important international treaties, investigate any aspect of national life that they feel like investigating. They may impeach cabinet ministers and try the President of the Republic for treason. The deputies, however, are responsible only to themselves, and eventually to their constituents, but they alone decide the electoral system under which they will go to the polls.

The President of the National Assembly (Speaker of the House) is, without actually having a title, virtually Vice President of the Republic, substituting for the President if ever the post becomes prematurely vacant. The President of the Republic may only communicate with the Assembly through its Speaker; he is not permitted to enter the Chamber. In the event of a dissolution of Parliament the President of the Assembly becomes the premier if the incumbent has been defeated by a vote of censure.

The deputies may appoint or dismiss governments at will. The President of the Republic designates the premier, but his nominee does not take office until endorsed by the National Assembly. A designate premier is only "invested" if he can obtain a majority vote in the Chamber. Under the original constitutional procedure this majority had to be an absolute majority of the Assembly. This was changed to a simple majority by amendments voted in November, 1954. However, to put a government out of office an absolute majority of "no confidence" is required.

This change was pushed through by Mendès-France who thought it might give the executive a bit more stability, by making it harder to put a premier out of office than into office. It is not at all certain that it will have that effect. In fact, it may have the contrary effect. One of the reasons, in the past, that some cabinets have endured longer than their popularity was the difficulty in finding an absolute majority for a replacement. Because of the 1954 change to a simple majority for investiture it is that much easier to agree on a new man and thus a greater temptation to oust an incumbent.

The Council of the Republic, the second House of Parliament, has only a consultative role to play. If a member wants to propose a bill it must first be considered by the National Assembly. The Council may not, by itself, alter an Assembly bill. It may propose amendments to an Assembly project but the Assembly, in a second reading, may reject all the suggestions of the Council.

Under the orginal provisions of the Constitution, the Council had a slight suspensive power, in a clause requiring the Assembly to override the Council's amendments by an absolute majority if they had been voted by an absolute majority in the Council. This had some potential veto value, since an absolute majority was often hard to find in the Assembly. On occasions the deputies used this clause as a pretext to let the Council "force" them into taking an unpopular measure.

Nevertheless the Council remains essentially a consultative chamber with no real powers. It has neither the first nor the last word in legislation. Its suspensive power was slightly increased by another constitutional revision in November, 1954, re-establishing in part the prewar practice of the shuttle of bills between the two chambers. The Council may now discuss a bill twice and take as many as one hundred days to complete its debate. Thus it can slow down the parliamentary machine a little longer, impose a bit more reflection on its parliamentary "partner" but, in the end, all the basic powers still reside in the almost omnipotent deputies of the National Assembly.

The number of paragons to whom this enormous power is entrusted totals 626 members, to be elected by direct, universal suffrage. Of this total, 544 represent districts in metropolitan France, including Corsica, 30 are from the political collectivities of Algeria and 52 from other territories of the French Union.

The omnipotent deputy must be at least twenty-three years of age, in possession of all his or her civic rights. The deputy must be free of any obligations to universal military training. In addition, a candidate-deputy must resign, within six months of the election, from any administrative post that gives him special influence in his constituency.

Deputies may be unseated by their peers for certain civil or criminal offenses, among them bankruptcy, theft, violation of public morals. A right-wing deputy, de Récy, lost his right to exercise his mandate when he was convicted of fraud, but his name was kept on the rolls of the Assembly for the purpose of calculating the absolute majority. The same procedure was followed in the case of the three Malagasy deputies convicted of treason after the Madagascar riots of 1947.

The case of the Malagasy caused considerable friction between the legislative and executive branches. Deputies normally enjoy the privilege of immunity from arrest and prosecution. The immunity can only be lifted by the consent of the Assembly or in cases of *"flagrant délit,"* when the deputy is caught in the act of violating the law. The deputies consented to lift the immunity of the men from Madagascar but only on condition that the accused members would not be charged with a capital offense. When the Malagasy were indicted for treason after their immunity had been lifted the deputies were furious, considering the indictment a breach of faith by the government. The Assembly thereupon created an Immunity Committee to safeguard the deputies' constitutional rights and also to establish an organized procedure for the future. The deputies, like most representatives, were reluctant to permit prosecution of fellow members, except under extreme provocation.

The number of executive applications for lifting of parliamentary immunity has reached a new high under the Fourth Republic, mainly because of the presence in Parliament of large Communist delegations who constantly stretch the immunity privilege to the breaking point. The abrogation of immunity by *"flagrant délit"* generally occurred in the course of Communist strikes and riots. Deputies were arrested in the Marseilles riots of 1947, in the coal mine strikes that same fall, at Saint-Etienne in the spring of 1948 and in the riots at Brest in 1950.

One of the most extraordinary cases in parliamentary annals was the celebrated *"Affaire des Pigeons"* involving none other than the group leader of the Communist delegation in the Assembly, Jacques Duclos. Duclos, veteran revolutionary, had made his career as the party parliamentarian. Under the cover of immunity he had published the party's revolutionary pamphlets and papers. He had successfully defied civil authorities for years, until one balmy June day in the summer of 1952, when Jacques Duclos was caught red-handed, so to speak, *"en flagrant délit."*

It was the day that the Communists were rioting to prevent American General Ridgway from succeeding to the post of Supreme Commander of Allied Forces in Europe, vacated in May by General Eisenhower. Communist "action squads" roved through the streets of Paris, building roadblocks along the route Ridgway would take. Helmeted police riot squads sought them out and Paris was the scene of pitched battles. One security squad suddenly came upon a suspicious-looking group of cars which were parked with their motors running. A police net closed in on them and armed inspectors ordered the men out. One of them was Duclos and, inside his car, the police found a series of pamphlets, posters and two dead pigeons. The pigeons' necks were wrung, the bodies still warm.

Duclos was promptly arrested, charged with inciting to riot. The police claimed the birds were carrier pigeons, that the cars were Communist riot headquarters, from which Duclos was directing operations, sending out orders via the carrier pigeons, and that he had killed the last two to destroy the evidence when the police closed in. The Minister of the Interior insisted that Duclos had forfeited parliamentary immunity by being caught in the act. The Communist parliamentary group leader was thrown into jail, protesting his innocence. Duclos swore to the examining magistrate that "the pigeons were for my dinner. They had just been given to me by a friend."

The magistrate appointed an impartial commission of experts to submit its findings to the court. Three men were named, one the President of the National Pigeon Raisers Federation, the second an Army Signal Corps expert on communications by carrier pigeon, and the third a distinguished professor of ornithology. The commission deliberated for three days, examined the evidence, conducted an autopsy on the pigeons and delivered its verdict to the court: the pigeons could possibly have been used for communications but they were indubitably and demonstrably eating pigeons, and if

Mr. Duclos said they were for his dinner he had missed a succulent dish.

The slapstick-comedy affair had its serious side. It demonstrated the role of an independent judiciary in French life, serving as a reminder to the government and police that justice was impartial and would defend alike the supporters and opponents of the regime, even if one was a political outlaw plotting the regime's destruction. It was a salutary reminder in the troubled mid-century era that freedom and justice are indivisible. There cannot be two standards, one for the supporters of the regime, one for its opponents. So long as the Communist party is not outlawed its members cannot be denied impartial process of law. And it cannot easily be outlawed in France, where one out of every four Frenchmen votes Communist. The "affair of the pigeons" was also a salutary lesson to the deputies, to tighten their own self-disciplinary controls. An abuse of immunity privileges might so anger the public that eventually it would lead to an abrogation of the privilege, for the rights of a sovereign are not immutable; they repose upon the consent of the governed and also impose upon the sovereign the responsibility of using his rights with restraint and dignity.

The only constitutional check on the deputies is enforced dissolution of Parliament. The Constitution empowers the Premier to dissolve Parliament if two governments are voted down by the National Assembly in a consecutive eighteen-month period. Even this minimum check is limited by other restricting qualifications, particularly by the fact that it becomes operative only if the governments are overthrown by formal votes of confidence. Since government ministers and premiers are all, with few exceptions, themselves members of the Assembly and leaders of the political parties of the majority, they connive with the Assembly to avoid falling on a confidence vote. The power of executive dissolution was used only once in the first decade of the Fourth Republic, by Edgar Faure, in the fall of 1955, but in that period of time the National Assembly had overthrown twenty-one cabinets.

Many deputies, particularly on the Right benches, are alarmed by the weakness of the executive and the irresponsibility of the sovereign Assembly. They are constantly preoccupied with projects for constitutional revision to apply some sort of automatic brake upon the Chamber. Paul Reynaud, a leader of the Independents, is the foremost advocate of an automatic dissolution any time a cabinet is overthrown, as is the case in England. In the summer of 1953, when the President designated him to form a new government, Reynaud told the Assembly with extraordinary frankness that he would not accept investiture unless the Assembly first agreed to revise the Constitution, to grant the premier discretion to dissolve Parliament. Needless to say, he was not invested. In the spring of 1955 Reynaud again pressed for revision of the Constitution, but this time in a more moderate project of dissolution. His project has not yet been adopted but a demand for stronger powers of dissolution gained considerable public support in the course of debate and is still under discussion.

There is, however, one brake on the sovereign Parliament that is not to be found in any article of the Constitution or any statute in law. It is rarely considered in that light, but perhaps the most effective limitation on the power of the National Assembly is the multiparty system in France. The fact that the legislature is divided into six almost equal groups has made the business of legislation complicated, confused and sometimes almost hopeless, but it has also been a most effective safeguard against the all-powerful body being kidnaped by a single group of men who could then make themselves the masters of the nation. Anarchy seems to be the French answer to dictatorship.

But this is a self-defeating answer. Major projects, vital to the health and security of the nation, are long delayed and rarely endorsed without a series of crippling amendments. It puts a premium on demagogy, since the legislators of every group always have a minority complex, are always seeking favors, and rarely feel strong enough to risk legislation that might be unpopular in the constituency. This is not, of course, peculiar to French democracy. "Pork-barrel politics" is a well-known phenomenon in other countries but it is particularly marked in France where the legislators have so many more responsibilities to discharge. Having kept most of the powers for themselves the legislators must take many more unpopular decisions than they would if there were a real executive in existence.

To solve their problem the legislators have revived a Third Republic practice of giving "emergency decree" powers to the premier, as they did in 1954-56 for Laniel, Mendès-France, Faure and Mollet, in turn. It is a most ingenious device, a sort of mad logic that illustrates the extreme subtleties of French political practice. The syllogism runs something like this: the basis of parliamentary democracy in France is a sovereign legislature to protect the people from a despotic executive; the sovereign legislature is paralyzed by internal divisions; therefore the legislators must transfer their powers to the executive. The theory is that the legislature is only "lending" the decree-power to the executive who, in any case, can be overthrown by the Assembly at will. Thus it is not really dangerous to give the executive emergency powers to do what the deputies are unable or unwilling to do themselves. Such are the Byzantine devices to which French parliamentarians are reduced in an attempt to bring some order into their chaotic parliamentary regime.

A principal factor producing chaos in the Assembly of the Fourth Republic is the existence of a large Communist group. American and British critics of French parliamentary democracy often tend to overlook the fact that a basic difference between their systems and the French is the presence, inside the French Parliament, of a large group of men dedicated to the destruction of parliamentary democracy. Most of the criticisms directed against the French Parliament, while largely justified, fail to appreciate the enormous handicap it labors under. The Assembly is faced with the insoluble problem of respecting the equal rights of all deputies, including Communists, and at the same time holding confidential committee hearings at which government officials are expected to discuss vital secrets of national security in the presence of disloyal men. Absolute equality is simply not possible when dealing with the enemies of the regime. Yet it is equally impossible to disenfranchise one out of every four citizens of the Republic by excluding their representatives from the business of legislation. The Frenchman is a highly civilized being, one of the most adult and most tolerant of all men, and there is almost no hatred between the Communist and non-Communist deputies in Parliament, with only a few personal exceptions. Yet the most tolerant, most dedicated of the democrats in Parliament are forced to reject their Communist colleagues, even at the risk of violating the spirit of the Constitution. This was the stand taken by Mendès-France in his investiture of June 18, 1954.

Mendès scorned Communist support, calling their votes "a poisoned gift," and saying that he would not accept Assembly endorsement as premier if his majority depended upon the Communist ballots. Mendès insisted that he must have a "Republican majority," indicating that in his opinion the Communists were not to be considered as members of the Assembly. The attitude of Mendès-France may have been morally praiseworthy but it posed an anguishing question of Republican legality, for he was, in effect, canceling out the ballots of some five million citizens who had sent the Communists to the Assembly.

❦

It might be expected that a multiparty system would result in a divided Parliament and that a divided, but powerful Parliament, would produce an unstable executive. This has certainly been the record of the Fourth Republic. From 1946 through July, 1951, the first legislature overthrew twelve cabinets, just about twice the executive instability of the Third Republic. The parliamentary calendar ran so far behind that, at times, there was no money to pay the public services and the government had to borrow from the Bank of France until the Assembly got around to voting the budget. The nation's defense forces could not place contracts for armaments with any certainty that the funds would be made available. Budgets were voted by "*douzième provisoire*," that is, a provisional monthly advance against an eventual annual appropriation.

What was most remarkable, however, about the record of that first legislature of the Fourth Republic was not its paralysis, its inefficiency, its frustrations and passions, all of which were predictable in so fragmented a Chamber. What was truly remarkable were the accomplishments of that legislature, the number and quality of the decisions it did take rather than the decisions it did not take.

The legislature of 1946-51 registered 12,000 bills, as against 7,000 for the Chamber of 1936 and 3,900 in the Parliament of 1914. Despite this increase of burdens and its own internal divisions some vital decisions were taken by the National Assembly. In each year of its life the so-called "do nothing" legislature of France did at least one thing of utmost importance, with full knowledge of the consequences, and each one of these decisions affected a key area of national security.

In 1947 Premier Paul Ramadier dismissed the Communists from his government and was supported by the majority of the Assembly, despite a very real danger of civil war. The Communists were thought to be so strong at that time that, as an official put it: "All Thorez has to do to take over the country is to make a few phone calls." Thorez made those phone calls in the fall of 1947, when he called out his shock troops in insurrectional strikes, but he did not take over the country. The democrats fought back with the full support of a majority of the deputies, and they defeated the Communists. They followed that fight by taking on another contest of strength with General de Gaulle's equally insurrectional movement. It took courage and determination, as anyone who lived in France during those anxious days knew, to fight a two-front war with the Communists and the Gaullists.

In 1948 the National Assembly endorsed an executive decision to link the destiny of France with its allies of Western Europe and America. The split with Russia that had begun in the summer of 1947 when Molotov walked out of the Marshall Plan conference in Paris, had by then hardened into a permanent breach between the wartime allies. Just as it had once been said that Thorez only had to make a few phone calls to take over France, it was then said that all that Stalin's legions needed to march to the Channel was shoe leather. The Russians had the shoe leather and the deputies could not be sure they would not march, yet they ratified the Marshall Plan, despite the threats, and began to draft a self-aid program in a European Economic Union. Even more daring in view of the Russian military threat was the agreement to join forces with Britain and the democratic Continental neighbors of France in a military Western European Union. This, too, took courage and determination for a "do nothing" Assembly.

In 1949 an even greater test faced the Assembly, when European Union was superseded by a broader, more dangerous coalition, the North Atlantic Pact—more dangerous because infinitely more provocative to the Russians. France burned the last bridge to the East when the deputies voted to ratify the North Atlantic Treaty, although they were obviously chilled by the fear of a Soviet aggression. As so often happens, those who observed the Assembly debates commented more extensively on the shivers and chills of the men on the parliamentary benches than on the more remarkable fact that the shivering men did not give way to panic. Frightened men who do their duty might be commended for their action rather than condemned for having been frightened. The "do nothing" Assembly did something important and, in the circumstances, heroic, on that morning of July 26, 1949, when it rejected in turn a Communist prejudicial motion and a Gaullist crippling amendment to ratify, by a vote of 420 to 183, the entry of France into the armed Atlantic Alliance.

In 1950, the Assembly took one of the most far-reaching and controversial decisions in French history when it voted to join with Germany in a European Coal and Steel Community. The country that had created the first "nation-state," the country par excellence of nationalism, agreed to try a new road to the future and to end, forever it hoped, the fratricidal wars of Western Europe by merging the basic industries which feed war machines. If those of us who lived through the years 1947 to 1949 in France knew the meaning of national fear, those who stayed on in the year 1950 also lived through the exhilarating birth of hope. The consequences of that decision will not be clearly judged for many generations to come, but it can already be seen that it set the French nation on a new course, rocky and devious, but a course which is still being pursued. There are certainly more efficient, more dignified legislatures than the National Assembly of the Fourth Republic, but there are not many anywhere that can boast of having taken so many historic decisions under such trying circumstances.

∽

In its political composition, in the social and professional origins of its deputies, the National Assembly is, I believe, a true portrait of France itself. This is an important fact to establish, for if the Assembly faithfully reflects the nation and its people then an attempt to correct its weaknesses cannot be limited to the mechanics of the Constitution or of the institution itself, but must also take into account the divisions among the people of France. I doubt that there is a "false France" in Parliament betraying a "real France" in the country, as some French, as well as foreign, historians claim. There is only one France, tortured by its divisions in private as well as public life, with worker against peasant, town against country, radical against clerical, producer against distributor against consumer, and all of them against the tax collector and the State. The motto of France is not "All for one and one for all," but rather "Every man for himself," interest against interest, in a dissension-torn country whose divisions have been hardened by centuries of conflict. Parliament is as much a victim as a cause of these divisions, and is much less irresponsible than some of the private organisms of French life.

In Parliament, the divisive elements are finally forced to work together, to compose their differences, no matter how painfully or inefficiently. There is little compromise or harmony in the private wars among the special interests of France. Indeed, they carry their wars into Parliament through lobbies and pressure groups that the deputies have a difficult time fighting off. Since every deputy is a minority deputy in the divided Assembly he is forced to defend every marginal electoral client. Thus the deputy has few votes to spare and only a thin armor of independence against the pressures of private interests.

Public pressure cuts right across party lines. A deputy from the Hérault must defend the vineyards, whether he is a Communist, Catholic or Gaullist. As Joseph Barthélemy admitted in the 1930's: "Every deputy from Normandy votes apples. Every deputy from the Hérault votes grapes. I have voted for eight years for Armagnac's wheat and brandy." Paul Reynaud, deputy from Dunkirk, told me: "The first concern of any deputy from Dunkirk is improvement of the port. National defense comes second." When an American contest winner, one of the innumerable traveling "Queens," came to Paris in 1954 to deliver a canister of American milk to Mendès-France, the only milk-drinking premier, he gave her in return a case of French champagne to bring back to America. Even Mendès had to support a major industry of his country despite his hatred of alcoholism.

Mendès once told me about the life of a committee chairman, at a time when he presided over the Finance Committee. "I open my mail at breakfast. There are at least two to three hundred letters every morning, three-fourths of which are requests for special favors, not limited by any means to my own constituents. At least half come from party colleagues and other deputies, forwarding requests they have received. If I help them it is understood that they will help me. It's very much the same kind of horse-trading that your American representatives are required to do, but in France we have a dozen political groups, not just two as you have.

"My morning is taken up with correspondence, reading of legislative documents and at least once a week by committee hearings. I am a rapid reader and an experienced lawyer, but it takes me all morning to wade through only a small part of the documents piled high on my desk. The afternoons are taken up again by committee hearings, when there is no public session of the Assembly. Between correspondence and hearings I must receive a stream of visitors, from single favor-seekers to official delegations anywhere from five to twenty men: trade-union delegates, political unions, farm groups, delegates of tax leagues, North African nationalists, North African colonists, every conceivable private interest. Requests for anything up to forty or fifty audiences a day are quite normal.

"I can't possibly see more than a dozen separate groups on any one day, so I automatically risk making three dozen enemies. I try to put them off, answer them by letter, promise a meeting later. I do what I can to dam the tide but nothing helps. We have a fifteen- or sixteen-hour day, a seven-day week, and on top of that the Assembly seems unable to reach a decision before four o'clock in the morning, after an exhausting all-night debate. Modern political life chews up legislators and executives. There must be a reform of the procedure, a defense against pressure groups and endless debates."

The greatest pressures on Parliament come from the organized lobbies rather than the individual favor-seeker. The most influential of the many pressure groups in France are the vine and beet-root farmers, the home brewers of alcohol, the trade unions, the Church, the schoolteachers, the trucking companies and the North African colonists.

There is an effective but very discreet "Big Business" lobby operating in the French Parliament—discreet because the "*Patronat*" is unpopular with the people. It functions through its association, the French equivalent of the N.A.M., called the Conseil National du Patronat Français, led by its president, Georges Villiers. It is reputed to have a political "war chest" of a billion francs (roughly three million dollars) "for public propaganda" in favor of its objectives, but actually, it has been charged, for direct cash payments to political groups and influential deputies.

A Communist deputy, Jean Pronteau, stated in Parliament in 1953 that investigations had revealed direct subsidies by the Patronat to the Radical party. He alleged the Radicals got a half-million francs for every deputy elected in 1951, and a million francs for every Radical minister in government. His accusations were never denied. Furthermore, a full-blown scandal followed the formation of Radical Premier René Mayer's Cabinet in 1953. He appointed as Minister of Health André Boutémy, alleged to have been the "pay-off" man of the Patronat's electoral subsidies. Boutémy was forced to resign from Mayer's cabinet, ostensibly because he had been a prefect under the Pétain regime, but many observers were convinced that the real reason was his identification with the Big Business lobby. "Big Business" tends to exert pressures on the "big" levers of control rather than on the individual deputies, concentrating its demands directly on government ministers and on the *"grands commis"* of the Republic, the directors of the nationalized banks, the *"inspecteurs des finances"* and the Finance Ministry itself.

The small and medium businessmen, more numerous and more typical of the small-scale French economy than the industrialists, have a very active lobby, the Petites et Moyennes Entreprises, headed by Léon Gingembre, as "go-getting" a lobbyist as the meaning of his name would indicate. "Mr. Ginger" is a familiar figure on the Paris political scene and he is received promptly when he seeks an appointment. There are more than two million shopkeeper votes in France and, one might say, that is a lot of ginger.

Perhaps the most effective of all the lobbies is the agricultural lobby. The peasants form a very large group in French life, comprising 36 per cent of the total working population. In the legislature of '51 the farm associations managed to have eighty-one of their own officials elected to the Assembly. More subsidies are voted to the producers of alcohol than to any other sector of French life.

French peasants are protected from foreign competition, bad weather and market variations. That does not mean that the French peasant is as prosperous as his American counterpart. With all the devices to help him, the lot of the French peasant is not an enviable one, but he is one of the most constantly courted sectors of the voting public. This is a political phenomenon that should not surprise Americans whose farm lobby is one of the strongest in the Republic.

The deputy is thus the target of public criticism and private pressures from his constituents, colleagues, party bosses and lobbyists. He must keep his local fences mended and at the same time find a compromise with fellow members of the Assembly to form a majority government, knowing that every compromise may hurt him in his constituency. It is not surprising to find the Assembly so often in crisis, but rather it is astonishing that it is ever out of crisis. A French deputy needs the slipperiness of a Houdini, the wisdom of a Solomon, the logic of a Sophocles and the patience of a Penelope. On paper he may be the most powerful politician in the democratic world, but in practice he is a weak and harassed man, underpaid, overworked and generally held in ridicule or contempt by his fellows. I have often wondered what motivation impels a talented, intelligent man to become a deputy in the National Assembly of France.

Yet hundreds of brilliant, dedicated men have devoted their careers and lives to the public service in the National Assembly. This is the strength of French democracy, the ultimate answer to those who believe that France is a decadent nation and that its Parliament is a cross between a lunatic asylum and a music hall. There have been madmen and comedians on the benches of the Palais Bourbon —what assembly in the world has not had its demagogues and clowns?—but the great majority of the deputies of France is neither lunatic nor comic. Bad men and good men, weak men and strong men, rich men, poor men, a few thieves and a few genuinely great men have taken their places on the red plush seats of the house of the people on the left banks of the Seine. They have demonstrated that the French democratic tradition is strong and healthy.

The shortcomings and mechanical defects of the parliamentary system are well known and corrigible. Some of them have been corrected, others are in the process of improvement. Progress has been slow, costly and painful but the legislature elected in 1956 was considerably stronger than the first legislature of 1946. Its greatest weakness, indeed, is its strength, for Parliament has too much authority, too many functions, to execute them all efficiently. The burden of executive responsibility is more than any legislature should assume.

Until the National Assembly relinquishes some of its excessive powers and grants the executive more independence and durability it will never be a completely sound institution. It has, however, proved to be more durable and flexible itself than anyone could have believed ten years ago. In their successful resistance to the challenge from powerful enemies of the Right and the Left the democrats of France have given good reason to believe that parliamentary democracy will continue to be the ruling force of French society.

10 The Organs of State

Of the many complexities and paradoxes of French affairs, the one that most bewilders foreign observers and does most injury to the prestige of France, is the cabinet crisis.

A country that has had twenty-two governments in eleven years does not, to say the least, give the impression of being a serious, reliable world power. Furthermore, some evil spirit seems to be operating in France to bring about a government crisis just at a moment when the entire world is watching. France is always getting caught with her cabinet down right in the middle of an international conference. Every one of the twenty-odd crises from 1946 through 1956 coincided with an important world event.

When de Gaulle resigned on January 20, 1946, the United Nations Assembly was having its first meeting across the Channel in London. Foreign Minister Bidault, French representative on the Security Council, was there fighting to prevent the French colonies of Togo and the Cameroons from being put under an international trusteeship. He had to excuse himself and rush back to Paris.

In June that year, Bidault, again Foreign Minister, was host in Paris to Russia's Molotov, Britain's Bevin and America's Byrnes, in a Big Four meeting to prepare a European Peace Conference, to settle the status of the former Nazi satellite countries. Down went the cabinet of Premier Gouin, and out of the conference rushed Bidault. He came back a few days later, breathless but happy. He had settled the crisis by forming a cabinet himself. Bidault became Premier as well as Foreign Minister in his own cabinet. However, it did not help him. Premier Bidault embarrassed Foreign Minister Bidault by resigning right in the middle of the Big Four Conference in New York in November, 1946. The subject of the conference was fairly important to France: the occupation policies in Germany and Austria.

One of the greatest disasters in French history then occurred before a new government could be formed. On December 10, 1946, the Indochinese War broke out with the Vietminh attack in Hanoi. On that same day, in Paris, the party leaders informed President Auriol that they could not reach agreement on a minimum program for a new government. It is typical of French politics that France was again without a government almost four years later when the Korean War broke out. The second Bidault government fell the night before the North Koreans crossed the Forty-eighth Parallel.

The cabinet crisis that most attracted world attention was the downfall of the Laniel government in the middle of the Geneva Conference on the Indochinese War. Once again it was Bidault who got caught short at the conference table. No diplomat in history has had to suffer the many indignities that have been Bidault's lot. The man who replaced him was Mendès-France.

Mendès himself did not escape the fate of all French premiers. He was right in the middle of vital negotiations with the Tunisian premier, on home rule for the Protectorate, when his cabinet came down. A member of the Tunisian delegation whom I saw the next day, made the appropriate and inevitable comment: "How can France pretend to judge our capacity for self-government when the French are apparently incapable of governing themselves?"

༺

It is, indeed, difficult for the friends of France to have faith in a country that repudiates its best men and that seems incapable of governing itself. It is even more difficult for foreigners to understand why cabinets fall and what happens in France when they do. In more than a decade of reporting French affairs I have been asked hundreds of times to explain the phenomenon of government instability. My compatriots cannot understand—and who can blame them—just how a nation can function without a government.

After one CBS news analysis in which I pointed out that France had been without a government for a cumulative total of 241 days, in the decade from de Gaulle to Mendès-France, I received a letter from a listener who wanted to know why a dictator had not seized power during the frequent absences of authority. "Who commands the army and the police when there is no government?" he asked. My correspondent wanted to know how the civil servants were paid, whether contracts were carried out, how international commitments were met, who ran the national railways and all the other state-owned industries when no one was running the state. Finally he ended the letter on a note of exasperated bewilderment: "And please tell me, if you can, why otherwise intelligent, educated, logical Frenchmen seem as incapable of governing themselves as the inmates of a lunatic asylum?"

These are valid and intelligent questions. They betray, however, a fundamental misconception of the nature of executive power in France and the mechanism of a cabinet crisis. It is a misconception that we reporters have undoubtedly helped spread, by insisting upon the more sensational aspects of government instability. Government instability is damaging enough without exaggeration. The reasons are grave enough without attributing them to lunacy, mad as they may appear.

To judge French affairs from an examination of the agitated surface of government is as incomplete and thereby as inaccurate as a study of ocean life based only upon a description of the waves. Just as the deep sea is calm when storms lash the surface of the water, so is France normally untroubled during a cabinet crisis. The trains still run, faster than any trains in any other European country, and with a better record of time consistency, for France has the best railroad system in Europe. The miners who work for the state continue to work and to get paid, and continue to break production records every year as they have since the liberation. During the crises of 1951-55 the French franc rose steadily in value on world money markets, French stocks doubled in market value, and production throughout the country increased by more than 20 per cent. The army calls recruits to the colors, the police maintains law and order, contracts are carried out and international commitments respected during so-called cabinet crises.

One of the most important international agreements concluded by the French in the postwar decade occurred when France was without a government. On July 10, 1951, Dr. Queuille's cabinet fell, but two days later, before a new government had been formed, a joint Franco-

American communiqué announced the granting of strategic bases in Morocco and tactical air bases in France to the United States Air Force. Thus the first important answer to the question, what happens to authority in France when a government falls, is: nothing. For governments do not really "fall." Their members do not flee into exile or get clapped in jail if they fail to escape, as in some South American revolutions. The "defeated" premier stays in office, along with his department heads, until a new government is formed. The only authority he loses, and it is an important one, is the power to initiate new programs or take new commitments. A "fallen" government is thus more accurately described as a "caretaker" government.

Dr. Queuille's caretaker cabinet concluded the air bases deal with the United States after his "resignation" of July 10 because the air-base program had been approved and negotiations started before July 10. On the other hand, Dr. Queuille was unable to approve another American proposition made during the same cabinet crisis: the proposal to invite Greece and Turkey to join the Atlantic Pact. This involved a new diplomatic commitment beyond the authority of a caretaker government. The crises of France thus make progress slow and costly for France and France's allies, but progress is made, just enough and just in time to prevent a real crisis from breaking out.

The second misconception about a French cabinet crisis is implicit in the word "crisis" itself. This is the most overused and misused word in the political vocabulary. Government instability is a chronic not an acute disease and the *"crises gouvernementales"* are more often symptomatic of the patient's bad temper than bad health. The French Parliament often prefers to change doctors rather than swallow bitter pills that an incumbent physician has prescribed. This is often the principal function of a crisis: either to avoid taking a difficult decision, or, sometimes, to make unpopular measures acceptable in order to "save the regime."

A classic example of this special function of the crisis was provided by the Socialists in the summer of 1950. After four men had tried and failed to form a new government, mainly because of Socialist opposition, the Socialist party finally voted for René Pleven, whose program was not notably different from those previously rejected. The reason was frankly stated by Socialist spokesman Edouard Depreux: "It is better to have an imperfect government than to permit the crisis to continue."

Most so-called crises are merely reshuffles of executive posts. A simple listing of consecutive premiers illustrates the stable rather than unstable nature of French cabinets. The eighth, ninth and tenth cabinets after the liberation were formed by Schuman, Marie and Schuman again. The men who formed the eleventh through sixteenth cabinets were: Queuille, Bidault, Queuille, Pleven, Queuille, Pleven. The twenty-two cabinets from 1945 to 1955 were headed by only thirteen different men: de Gaulle, Bidault, Ramadier, Schuman, Marie, Pleven and Faure were each premier twice, whereas the marathon champion Dr. Queuille was premier three times. Thus even the surface instability of cabinets is more apparent than real.

Departmental offices are even more remarkably stable. From January, 1946, to June, 1954, eight truly critical years in French and world affairs, only two men[1] alternated as Foreign Minister of France: Robert Schuman and Georges Bidault, both members of the Catholic party, MRP, both officially committed to the same foreign policy. This was an even more consistent record of stability in a key ministry than in the United States during the same period. Stettinius, Byrnes, Marshall, Acheson and Dulles succeeded each other in turn in America during the stable Bidault-Schuman stewardship of French foreign affairs. The real trouble with France, it might be said, is not its instability but its excessive stability.

The troubles in France mainly stem from a failure to modernize both the economy and the diplomacy of the Republic and to bring them into line with the realities of France's position as a world power. This has not been caused by cabinet instability alone or even primarily. Cabinet instability, like a high fever, is a symptom of a disease but not the disease itself. Like a fever, however, it is also painful, debilitating and dangerous, for fevers, although symptoms, can kill before the disease that causes them can be cured.

French political leaders have been searching for a long time for a way to make a cabinet more durable, less agitated. This is one of the most important of the many reforms urgently needed in France, but, when examining the nature of executive power and the reasons for

[1] There was a third French Foreign Minister, Leon Blum, in December, 1946, but he only held office for a month and hardly counted.

its instability, it is helpful to see it as it really is and not as it seems. It is only one of many and not the most important of France's troubles and considerably less critical than the frequency of the "crises" would suggest.

☙

There are signs that the trend is beginning to move slowly toward more durable cabinets and even toward a reduction of multiple parties. During the life of the first legislature, between the general elections of June, 1946, and June, 1951, there were twelve cabinets invested. From June, 1951, to January, 1956, there were seven new governments. The average life of cabinets in the 1951-56 period was considerably higher than during the previous legislature. Pinay stayed in office ten months, Laniel twelve months, Mendès-France seven and a half months and Edgar Faure ten months, a very high average for French cabinets. Guy Mollet was Premier for the entire year 1956 following the January national elections.

On the party level, the existence under the Fourth Republic of six major, more or less cohesive, political parties is a great step forward from the factionalism of the interwar years. Political parties only began functioning in France just before the First World War, a very short time ago in history. The fact that three of the six parties in existence today—the Communists, Socialists and Catholics—are nationally organized and correspond to a definition of a political party in Anglo-American terms, is another indication of the evolution of the party system in France, despite the divisions and temperamental obstacles to the development of mass parties.

Such a development, however, is necessarily slow and unspectacular. Government instability is thus likely to be the main feature of French political life for some time to come. It should be neither exaggerated nor minimized. Extreme views on governmental instability in France are likely to lead to false conclusions. The administration, as we have seen, is a good deal more stable than it appears to be. The French are not lunatics, nor are they incapable of self-government. On the other hand, governmental instability is a real and grave weakness of French democracy. It makes the process of government costly and inefficient. One of its most dangerous and least publicized effects is to leave too much authority in the hands of too many irresponsible individuals, to civil and military bureaucrats, who have upon occasion successfully defied their ministers and even plunged France into war in the course of a cabinet crisis.

∽

One of the most persistent and misleading clichés about France is the statement that the civil service is a state within a state, whose motto is: "The ministers pass; the ministries remain." Like the mandarinate of ancient China, the French civil service is said to live in a world of its own, unconcerned with the quarrels of the political war lords, who are fighting only for nominal control of the state; the civil servants feel that they exercise the real control. Ministers lay down policy but it is the bureaucracy that carries it out in practice. The policy itself is based upon facts supplied by the bureaucrats, who thus have a primary influence on its drafting, and it is the bureaucrat who decides how the policy is to be applied after it is proclaimed.

This is the classic description of the role of the French bureaucracy. Historian Crane Brinton, in his *Decade of Revolution*, pointed out that the royal engineers of the Ponts et Chaussées administration continued to function throughout the Revolution. Apparently it made little difference to the engineers whether France's bridges and roads were being used by the king's soldiers or the revolutionary troops just so long as they were kept in good repair. Republics, empires, kingdoms, fought their battles up and down the roads of France, but as fast as their cannon balls tore up the surface or brought down a bridge, the Ponts et Chaussées moved in to fill the holes and prop up the palings.

Some of the new generation of historians have seized upon this phenomenon as the "key to the riddle of France." They would have us believe that the civil service is a secret dictatorship of the bureaucracy. One recent writer went so far as to claim that ninety men of the Interior Ministry are the "real rulers of France."

I believe that this is an exaggeration and an oversimplification. Like any other country, France is a living organism, not a mechanism, and its life cannot be explained by such rigid analyses. Even the bureaucracy is composed of people. It is not some mysterious abstract thing. It can be described, its officials have faces and names. If they are "self-perpetuating," like a self-winding Swiss watch, this can be demonstrated, proved or disproved by citing specific cases.

Who are these anonymous "ninety agents of the Ministry of the Interior" who are the real rulers of France? Who appointed them if no government or minister did? What happens when one of the ninety masterminds dies? Who chooses a replacement? If the Conseil d'État is the real Parliament, then who elects, selects or otherwise invests a member of this Council? If the key to the riddle of France is the secret power of the bureaucracy then what is the key to the riddle of the bureaucracy?

In fact, there is no "riddle of France," nor of the bureaucracy. "Riddle," "mystery," these are dramatic words, used by writers to heighten interest in their analysis or, sometimes, to explain the unexplainable. France is not a mystery, it is a very old complex society, difficult to analyze and clarify, abounding in puzzling contradictions. There is no single "key" to France. France is not a locked door any more than it is a watch. France, as Pierre Daninos had his character, Major Thomson, say, "is a country divided up among forty million people." Some of these people are peasants, some are workers, some are politicians, some, indeed a great many, are bureaucrats. The "key to the riddle" is not the secret dominance of one of these groups of people; it is the interplay among all of them. It is the conflict among the human forces and not the mechanisms of the French State.

Even in a society of forty million individuals this interplay is conducted according to a book of rules. In France the book of rules is the Constitution. The rules may often be violated or circumvented—and we shall examine such violations—but first it is important to know what the rules are. What does the Constitution say about the Conseil d'Etat, the prefects, the civil service?

Article 30 of the Constitution is specific: "The President of the Republic appoints, in Council of Ministers, the members of the Conseil d'Etat, the Grand Chancellor of the Légion d'Honneur, ambassadors, envoys extraordinary, prefects, the directors of the Civil Service, generals, the representatives of the government in overseas territories." Article 47 further grants to the prime minister the power to make key appointments: "He makes appointments to all civilian and military posts, excepting those mentioned in Articles 30, 46 and 84." Article 46 refers to the appointment of the prime minister himself, which is made by the president. Article 84 lays down the procedure for the appointment of magistrates by the president on the recommendation of the Supreme Council of Justice.

There is thus no room for doubt, no mystification about the origins of the bureaucracy. The members of the Conseil d'Etat, and all the top officials of France, whether administrative, colonial, military or judicial, are selected and appointed by the supreme executive agent of the people, responsible to the elected representatives of the people. France is a state with a democratic structure. The Republic may be rotted through with termites but it is not a Potemkin village.

This has been demonstrated in practice many times under the Fourth Republic.

When Mendès-France was premier, his Minister of the Interior, François Mitterrand, clashed with the powerful Paris Prefect of Police, Jean Baylot. Mitterrand fired Baylot and replaced him with André Dubois. It is true that Baylot was not dismissed from the service. He was put on an inactive list. It is fitting that this be so. Political enmity should not deprive a man of promotions and pensions in the civil service. The civil servants should be protected from undue political pressures. It is equally true, however, that a government minister should be in a position to remove a senior official who refuses to carry out his policy.

The Baylot case is only one of many that could be cited. Pierre Bertaux was removed by political enemies as Director of the powerful Sûreté Nationale, the French equivalent of the FBI. Boniface, the brutal police chief of Casablanca, was fired, along with dozens of other police inspectors who were found guilty of obstructing administration reforms and encouraging French colonial "counterterrorism." When Jules Moch was Minister of the Interior and later Minister of Defense he conducted a sweeping purge of the police and the army on every bureaucratic level.

What then is the truth about the state within the state? If the bureaucracy is not all-powerful, just how powerful is it?

It is very powerful indeed. It is very difficult, and often impossible, for embattled politicians to keep effective supervision upon the vast departments under their control. This is particularly true in times of political crisis, but it is also true at all times. The complications of modern government, following upon the great increase of state properties and responsibilities, have made supervision of the bureaucracy difficult in all countries, and above all in France, where the administrative services are so vast and well entrenched.

The classic phrase "a state within a state" is, however, a misnomer. The bureaucracy would be more accurately described, I feel, as a powerful lobby rather than a "state." It is one of the many lobbies operating in France and not the strongest. The trade unions, the Church, the political pressure groups are just as powerful as the civil service. When it comes down to the basic decisions of the state, the economic and social programs and foreign policy, the bureaucrats have only a negative, obstructive power. It is not that they are master puppeteers, but rather they are spiders, spinning a vast, sticky net of procedures and statutes around the legislative and executive powers.

A brilliant administrator, like an Edgar Faure, whose extraordinary energy and mental powers enable him to amass all the vital information about his department in a short time, cannot be easily trapped in the web of the bureaucracy. When he was Undersecretary of State for the Budget, and then Finance Minister, Faure controlled his ministry and saw to it that the essentials of his policy were carried out. Less able men are, however, prisoners of the elite corps of senior officials, the Inspecteurs des Finances and other graduates of the *"grandes écoles"* that turn out the superbly trained men who are the administrative chiefs of the French bureaucracy.

This elite corps of men trained in the Ecole Polytechnique, the Ecole Normale and the Ecole des Mines, are not power-mad conspirators. They regard themselves as servants of France, of the nation rather than the particular form of state. They are often devoted, self-sacrificing civil priests. They are miserably underpaid. The salary of a Conseiller d'Etat in 1956 was roughly six thousand dollars a year. Many of the top civil servants could earn three times that much in private industry, and some eventually yield to the temptation and leave the service. Most of them, however, are dedicated men who spend their lives in the service of an ungrateful state. The French civil service on the top level is perhaps the finest in the world. If they exercise more power than they should, if they are sometimes contemptuous of and insubordinate to their nominal political superiors, it is frequently the fault of the politicians themselves who invite contempt and insubordination by their own lack of dignity, courage and authority.

The most striking illustrations of the power of the civil servants and their contempt for the government are found in the administration of overseas territories. For one thing they are further removed from the direct supervision of Paris. For another, French overseas policy was itself so undemocratic that it encouraged the most undemocratic elements in the administrative services to manifest themselves.

In Morocco, which was supposed to be a "protectorate," that is, a free state within its own borders, under the protection of France for military security and foreign affairs only, the French bureaucrats simply moved in and took over the direct administration of the country. I have seen French inspectors in Moroccan post offices who could not even speak the language of the people whose communications they were supposed to be facilitating. This direct usurpation of power by the bureaucrats was carried out with the tacit consent of the political authorities in Paris.

The most impressive testimony to the power of the proconsuls came from one of France's most distinguished statesmen, Robert Schuman, a veteran Foreign Minister and twice Prime Minister of the Fourth Republic. Schuman, writing in the March, 1953 issue of the magazine *La Nef*, frankly confessed that as Foreign Minister he had been powerless to control the colonial administration. Referring to the two Protectorates of Tunisia and Morocco, he wrote:

Before defining a policy to adopt we must first ask whose choice it is to speak in the name of France. The two Resident Generals are the highest in the hierarchy of responsible officials. They are on the spot, they receive and supply all information; the area of their initiative is vast and varied, quite apart from their own inclination to widen it . . . *they interpret instructions from Paris and determine the way to carry them out.*

Furthermore, Schuman admitted that the Foreign Minister did not really have a control over the colonial service. He wrote: "This is one of the fictions on which the democratic system is based . . . this fiction does not take into account the fact that in Paris, as I have just pointed out, we have only a limited control on the facts and the men who represent us."

This is an astonishing confession from one of the leaders of French democratic government, a confession of the bankruptcy of French Union policy and, indeed, a bankruptcy of government itself. Why did Schuman allow a Resident General, whom he appointed and whom he could dismiss, to "interpret" his instructions, and, even worse, "to determine the way to carry them out"? Who was really to blame: high-handed General Juin or Schuman himself?

That, it seems to me, is the basic question. There is nothing in the French system of state that gives power to the bureaucracy. It is the men who are empowered to govern the state who abdicate their power, partly because they are weak men and mainly because of political instability, which permanent civil servants exploit.

The kind of disaster to which such an abdication of authority could lead occurred in August, 1953, less than six months after Schuman's public confession of impotence. The colonial officials in Rabat carried out a *coup d'état* against the reigning sovereign, Sultan Sidi Mohammed ben Youssef. He was replaced on the throne of Morocco by a sultan more amenable to French rule. This was a purely administrative *coup d'état*, a conspiracy of the colonial officials, carried out without the knowledge of the government in Paris.

What did the then Foreign Minister Georges Bidault do about it? He simply bowed to the *fait accompli* and recognized the new puppet as the Sultan of Morocco. Nothing in the Constitution forced Bidault to yield to the civil servants. He chose to do so, apparently because he did not feel strong enough to impose his own policy.

The war in Vietnam was provoked by the same kind of administrative coup, as we shall report in our chapter on Indochina. Hundreds of thousands of people have died, billions of dollars have been drained out of the French Treasury, the Union of Overseas France has been wrecked, all because of actions taken without authorization, by irresponsible bureaucrats.

These irresponsible bureaucrats are not, however, dictators; they are receivers in bankruptcy, keeping the state functioning while the elected governors are quarreling among themselves. French society is kept in a state of suspended animation by its internal divisions. The disunity of the political parties and the people makes for weak government and strong lobbies but each of the pressure groups is a brake upon its rival. One force cancels out the other and the result is social and economic stability under the agitated surface of political instability. That, if anything, is the "key to the riddle of France."

⁓

The organs of state, like the nervous system of Parliament and the body politic, are basically healthy. There is no inherent paralysis of government. The disease afflicting the functioning of the state is disarticulation. The government reflects the disunity of Parliament, which reflects the disunity of the electorate, which in turn encourages the civil service, the lobbies, the unions, the Church and pressure groups of all kinds, to challenge the authority of the state and fight for a bigger share of the spoils. It is a vicious circle and results in vicious practices.

This may prove to be an incurable disease. France has been suffering from it for two centuries. It is my guess that France will continue to suffer for centuries to come and still survive. I do not know whether France will ever achieve a politically stable society in Anglo-American terms or whether the socioeconomic stability, which is the equivalent of stagnation, will ever become dynamic. I am persuaded, however, by the evidence already available, that the long-term trend is toward a more stable political structure. I am also convinced from evidence that we shall turn to next that France is also developing a dynamic economy. Underneath the surface crises of French life positive change is in progress. Like the Constitution, books on the death of the French Republic might be classified in the category of periodic literature.

11 *Fat Around the Middle Classes*

By any standard of measurement, France is the country of the golden mean, neither too big nor too small, too rich nor too poor. It is a middle-size, middle-class country, whose only extreme is a surplus of blessings by nature. France has more than enough of practically everything.

There is almost no wasteland in France. One-fifth of the land is verdant with forests and woods. Eight out of ten of France's hundred million acres are "useful" in the economic sense. The arable surface—wheat, grains, fruits, vegetables—represents 40 per cent of the total territory of France, that is, twice as much cultivable land as in Italy and four times as much as in the United Kingdom, both of which must feed populations slightly larger than that of France. There are only 125 inhabitants per square kilometer of agricultural surface in France, as against 260 in England, 350 in West Germany and 450 in Holland. In general, the fields on which the 125 Frenchmen live are more fertile than those that must support 350 Germans or 450 Dutchmen.

The subsoil is as rich in treasures as the soil. The iron ore reserves of France are estimated to be larger than those of the rest of non-Soviet Europe together. There is potash in Alsace and bauxite, of course, in Baux where that precious ingredient of aluminum was first discovered and christened. Since 1950, the French have begun to find oil and natural gas deposits in the southwest, where a miniature Texas is being born in the sandy soil between Bordeaux and the Pyrenees. Recent prospection in the Sahara indicates that there is a vast sea of oil flowing below the desert sands. The most serious shortages, besides oil, are high-quality coking coal and

165

cotton. But those raw materials can easily be bought abroad and, theoretically at least, paid for by France's exports of her own surplus wealth.

Relatively unpopulated in proportion to size and resources, France should have no trouble in exporting her surpluses. In order to pay for the materials that France must buy from the outside world, Frenchmen need only export 15 per cent of their total production compared with an export burden of 25 per cent in England, Germany and Sweden, and 50 per cent in tiny, overpopulated Holland. In contrast to other European countries France is a self-sufficient garden of Eden.

⚬↜⚬

With all her natural bounty, France for centuries has behaved like a grasshopper in a continent of ant nations, apparently unmindful of the wisdom of her own beloved La Fontaine. While other, less fortunate nations, worked hard and economized in times of plenty, ever fearful of hard times ahead, the bountiful French wasted and squandered their natural wealth in wars, revolutions and imperial ventures, while preserving archaic systems of farming, industry and distribution, and almost willfully ignoring economic trends in the outside world. France, until the mid-twentieth century, had so much fat to draw upon that it could survive disasters of war or blight that would have destroyed a less favored nation.

France was once the richest, strongest nation in the world, when wealth and strength were measured in terms of minerals and men instead of atoms and machines. Only 150 years ago, in the Age of Iron, France profited from its huge deposits in Lorraine and was the leading industrial world power. France had the largest, best-fed population in the Western world, at a time when manpower was equivalent to military power.

At the close of the eighteenth century there were twenty-five million Frenchmen, twenty million Germans, ten million Englishmen and only four million Americans. Giant Russia, a continent by itself, had only the same population as France but with virtually no industry. France at that time produced 135,000 tons of pig iron and almost 100,000 tons of iron ingots, as against only 68,000 tons of pig iron and 33,000 ingots produced by Britain. As for the infant United States, the newly born democracy in America was largely a farm country with few manufacturing or urban centers. The biggest city in America was Philadelphia, with 45,000 inhabitants, while New York City was a small port of 33,000 inhabitants. At that time a million people lived in Paris.

Mighty France helped tiny America to win its Revolution against Britain. The armies of the French Revolution defeated the combined armies of Europe. General Napoleon turned the entire continent into a province of France. It took a coalition of every major power in Europe, including Russia, to defeat Napoleon's Grand Army. All that less than 150 years ago, only yesterday in the perspective of history.

What has happened to France? What is wrong with France? What made the richest, strongest nation in the world descend to the status of a weak, dependent nation in so short a period of time? What has turned the Garden of Eden into an economic snakepit?

The sweet land of France is as fertile as ever and its human resources are as great as its natural treasures. No nation can boast of more, and few can count as many hard-working, thrifty peasants, industrious skilled workers, educated and talented managers, legislators, writers and artists. Why is it that the whole of this precious wealth in men and in materials adds up to less than the sum of its parts?

Why does France have a chronic deficit in its balance of trade with less favored countries? Why is the country with the strongest potential in Europe one of the weakest members of the European community? Why, in short, does the French economy seem as hopelessly muddled as French politics?

ოჯა

Since France was the strongest nation in the world in the eighteenth century it is at that period of history that a search for clues to the decline of France should logically start.

The France of Louis XIV was a growing, self-confident nation. Up to and immediately after Waterloo, France was still pre-eminent in population, two and a half times bigger than England. Yet at that very moment, at the height of French power, the decline of France began to set in, slowly and imperceptibly. Napoleon's victorious armies were winning Pyrrhic victories, destroying the source of French strength, the nation's manhood. The losses of the Napoleonic Wars added to the great losses of the revolutionary wars. Far more serious, although not immediately apparent, was the fact that France, at the dawn of the nineteenth century, began to stop growing.

The decline in the French birth rate began early in the 1800's. With the brief exceptions of the postwar years of 1816-18 and 1871-73, the French birth rate was virtually stagnant for more than a century, during a period of unprecedented growth in other countries. France, at the time of Louis-Philippe, represented one-seventh of the total population of Europe. At the turn of the twentieth century France had fallen to a position of one-fourteenth. Thus one of the primary causes of the decline of France was a relative decline in population, caused by war and sterility.

The decline in French power was speeded by many factors other than demographic. The nineteenth century found the world emerging from the Age of Iron to the Age of Steel. This transition from iron to steel cut down a great French advantage over other nations, for France's coal and iron ore were of poor quality for steel-making. The average iron content of French ore is not more than 30 per cent. French coal, moreover, is not suitable for the production of coke, particularly metallurgical coke. The best ore for steel was found in Sweden and the best-quality coking coal in Germany and Britain.

While industry was converting from iron to steel production the world system of economic organization was at the same time being completely transformed by the Industrial Revolution, from a guild and artisanal system to that of large, collective units of production and distribution. The effect of this revolution was to draw manpower away from agriculture and to create a new industrial society. This followed a natural course in Britain and Germany, corresponding both to the presence in these countries of basic industrial minerals and to the smaller proportion of land available for agriculture.

In France, on the contrary, the Industrial Revolution did not follow a natural course, but rather ran directly counter to the characteristics of French society. France had a very old, deeply rooted guild economy as far back as the twelfth century. When the feudal system began breaking down in France, a new class, the urban middle class, emerged to take the place of the obsolescent feudal lords. These bourgeois property owners, tradesmen, merchants and small factory owners of France were revolutionary only in their politics, only in their desire to complete the economic power, which they had already achieved, with political freedom. This they succeeded in doing in 1789. From then on the middle classes concentrated their energies on preserving their favored position in French society and preventing economic or social change.

There was no other class to challenge the bourgeoisie and force change. A precapitalist economy, with small units of production, France did not have a large working class. As for the peasants, the land reforms of the Revolution largely satisfied their major needs. Although there was constant grumbling and a serious financial crisis due to the cost of the revolutionary wars in France and in the United States, the peasants had their land and were content to let the bourgeois control the political levers of state. The little-man, middle-man society that evolved is the socioeconomic translation of the political "individualism" of the French. Property is sacred, self-interest is king. The State is regarded alternately as an enemy and a provider, depending upon whether the citizen is being taxed or subsidized. Government is supposed to provide floors under, but not put ceilings over, prices.

The proportion of peasants, merchants and workers in the Fourth Republic is changing in favor of the workers but not yet enough to change the basic balance of power of the bourgeois. Therefore socioeconomic legislation has not been radically different, except for an extension of subsidies to the workers in the form of social security benefits.

The census of 1954 revealed the strength of the bourgeois property owners in France. In agriculture, for example, four out of five million peasants own the land they till. In the field of commerce there are 1,453,000 owners of business or self-employed artisans, as against 1,301,000 commercial employees. France is probably the only country in the world where there are more self-employed than employed citizens in business. The industrial workers barely equal in numbers the total proprietors of land, shops and professions. However, the decisive political factor that assures the rule of the "haves" over the "have-nots" is the diversity, diffusion and tenacity of the property-owning citizens, who defend their self-interests more consistently and more determinedly than the industrial wage earners. The opportunistic, middle-class individualists reign supreme today as they did in the eighteenth and nineteenth centuries, and have successfully prevented France from entering the world of the twentieth century, except in isolated sectors of national life.

⤳

The years 1910-20 were the turning-point years of the French decline in power. Until then France, living off her fat, still large and powerful, could live in a private dream world of her own. The declining birth rate could be ignored, for in its early stages it was highly favorable to the French. There were less mouths to feed, more of everything for those fortunate to live in that blessed land. The defeat of 1871 by the Prussians was a severe blow, of course, but France, still vital, came back stronger than ever, conquered a huge empire abroad and girded for a return match with the Germans. It was then that the French were shaken out of their dream world, never again to return.

The First World War, fought for four years on French soil, shattered the thin core of prosperity and revealed the hollow shell of France. The full effects of the demographic and industrial decline came into play. France had no broad base of children to replace the men killed or maimed in the trenches, as other countries had. There was no broad base of industry with which the French could rebuild the destroyed homes, farms and factories, as other countries could. For in the previous fifty years, while France had been slowly declining, her neighbors had been growing slowly and were on the verge of the greatest expansion in their histories.

Great Britain, an unfertile island compared with flourishing France, could not grow enough food or raise enough materials to feed and clothe the ever-greater numbers of Englishmen, so Britain had had to gear itself to industry and world trade. Germany, a young nation, born in the Napoleonic wars, became a politico-economic community during the Industrial Revolution, and had grown with it. Both Germany and Britain built their industrial systems on a strong base of hard necessity and hard coal and both escaped the terrible destruction of the world war.

The economic and technological superiority of Britain and Germany were not, as is popularly believed, due to an Anglo-Saxon and Teutonic affinity for machinery as contrasted with a Latin incapacity for mechanics. This is one of the most absurd of all the clichés about France. The French, in any case, are not "Latins," nor is there any demonstrable proof that the ethnic origin of people has anything to do with their capacity for engineering and science. On the contrary, as we have already noted, France is not exclusively inhabited by poets, painters and pastrycooks. Frenchmen are just as adept at mixing cement as they are deft in mixing cake batter, whereas the British and the Germans sometimes confuse the two operations.

The real difference between the technological growth of Britain and Germany on the one hand and France on the other derives from sociological, political, historical, geographical and geological phenomena. France, it might be said, has suffered from a surfeit of natural advantages which made change and adjustments unnecessary until history and the rest of the world caught up with France and then left France far behind.

In the process of resisting change in a changing world the French sapped what should have been the strongest economy in Europe. The French were forced to make adjustments, but slowly, grudgingly and haphazardly, until the economy became a patchwork of self-defeating correctives. There are today six major defects in the French economic system, any one of which might wreck a less favored nation. They are: 1. protectionism; 2. agricultural backwardness; 3. regional disequilibrium; 4. inefficient distribution and production; 5. inequitable taxation; 6. high prices and low wages. Each one of these defects affects the others in a self-contaminating vicious circle. These economic sores are further aggravated by the irritations of social injustice and political instability. If the French had put their best minds to work to figure out a scheme for wrecking the soundest economy in Europe they could not have succeeded more brilliantly.

The most fascinating aspect of the patchwork economy of France, however, is that it does work. At the turn of the mid-century

European economists were saying that Britain was marching in perfect order toward inevitable bankruptcy while France was recovering rapidly in utter chaos. Of all the paradoxes of French life the health of its sick economy is the most extraordinary. Economics is usually a dry, dull field of exploration but a search for clues to the mystery of the French economy is, for me, as exciting as a crime thriller. Suspected murderers are legion, clues abound, but there is one baffling question: "Why is there no corpse?" Let us first examine the six principal clues and then see if we can solve the mystery.

ᕈᕈᕈ

1. PROTECTIONISM

The "free enterprise" system, so sacred to French laissez-faire businessmen, is neither free nor enterprising. The timid little producers and merchants of France live like mice inside the walls of the economy and rarely venture out into the market place. Customs tariffs, import quotas, cartel agreements, every traditional device for smothering initiative and stifling competition are practiced in France, plus a few tricks the French have devised themselves.

Almost every industry in France is trustified to the point of suffocation. One example among hundreds that could be chosen is the sugar trust, whose grandiloquent title is typical of the pompous nature of these organizations. It calls itself the "National Interprofessional Group of Planters, Manufacturers and Distillers of Sugar Cane and Beet Root," or, as abbreviated in French, the GNIPCBFD. Let us call them, for short, the Gnips.

The Gnips recently presented the government with a six-year plan for "improvement" of their industry. The Gnips proposed to take over the administration of the sugar-alcohol trade and set up norms for production and for government subsidies. The "plan" laid down the following procedures: each sugar refinery in France would get a fixed allotment of its share in the market, based upon its average production of its two best years up to 1956; for refineries that were also distilleries the share would be increased by their alcohol production figures for the base years; each manufacturer would, at the same time, be assigned a specific cane planter or beet farmer to furnish his raw materials—there could be no free play, no "shopping around" for supplies; prices for supplies and for sale of the finished products would be set by the central committee of the Gnips. Free enterprise, indeed! Compared with the French Gnips the Soviets are liberal descendants of Adam Smith.

This sugar plan is by no means exceptional. This is simply the way the French market place operates. It affects almost every sector of the economy. Take the business of baking bread, one that eventually concerns every citizen in the land. In 1955 the Ministry of Economic Affairs made a study of the bread industry and discovered that the wheat-grinding capacity of French mills had attained the incredible figure of 130 million quintals whereas the wheat-consumption capacity of the French people was only 49 million quintals. There was, thus, an excess capacity of 81 millions or enough to feed almost double the population. Obviously the mills were running at half-capacity; obviously, per-unit costs must have been high. Obviously, one would conclude, half the mills ought to convert to some other manufacture. Not at all. Parliament, under pressure from the millers' lobby, did just the opposite; it passed a law setting up a quota system for flour-grinding, assigning each mill a maximum tonnage based upon its capacity in 1935! Each mill, no matter how old-fashioned and uneconomic, was guaranteed a minimum of orders for survival and state subsidies were provided for those millers who could not produce their quota.

This kind of protectionism against both domestic and foreign competition is the primordial cause of France's decline. It is the economic negation of the Darwinian theory, for in France everything is geared to the survival of the least fit.

෨෬

2. AGRICULTURAL BACKWARDNESS

Too many Frenchmen earn too little on too many small farms. Seven out of ten French farms are less than twenty acres. They are family-owned and worked by one or two people. Only one out of a hundred French farms are "industrial farms," and only 2 per cent are larger than two hundred acres, that is, suitable for large-scale mechanized farming. This pattern of ownership is essentially democratic and healthy in the social sense, for the family-sized farm is the backbone of a sound agricultural system. But the French family-sized farm is too small for efficiency.

More serious is the fact that the ownership pattern physically resembles a crazy quilt. A farmer may own as many as ten strips of land, each separate from the others and each miles apart. This uneconomic and irrational fragmentation of farmland resulted from the "laws of succession," which gave each of the peasant's children an equal right to inherit a share of the estate. The division of land among the children after a farmer's death soon led to the breaking up of the estate. A girl would marry a man from another town but retain title to her strip of land; a son might leave for the city and sell his strip outside the family. This procedure over the years spread ownership in a random manner and broke up the farms into a million splinters.

The French have been trying for the past decade to bring back some order out of this chaos, through a program called *"remembrement,"* literally a "putting together of the limbs." This is, however, a slow, difficult process for it is not easy to persuade peasants to exchange strips of land. This man-made defect of the French economy is as hard to correct as it is to change the nature of man, particularly of so suspicious and obstinate a man as the peasant. He is high on the list of suspects. If the French economy is ever found dead some day, it is likely to be found with a pitchfork through its heart.

ᕦᕤ

3. REGIONAL DISEQUILIBRIUM

Geography, like history, has always been an important factor in fashioning both the French state and the French state of mind. The regional structure of the French economy is an essential clue to the mystery of a rich-poor France. Is France really a backward country agriculturally and industrially? Mediterranean and southern France are; northern and northeastern France are not. The wheatfields of the Beauce are not only rich in soil but are as efficiently farmed as any in Europe, just as the steel mills of Lorraine are as modern and productive as those of the German Ruhr. Yet Provence is almost as poor and primitive as Spain and the Massif Central is a Magdalenian survival in the world of the twentieth century.

It was long assumed by economists that it was the rocky, mountainous and sandy regions of France which pulled down the national average and were a brake upon progress. It has only recently been discovered that this is not the cause of agricultural difficulties. The main defect of French agriculture is the fact that the rural regions, even those with good soil and plenty of water, are underindustrialized and cut off from the progressive industrial regions. This results in a low productivity for agriculture and thus a low living standard for the entire country, since agriculture is the occupation of so many Frenchmen. The UN Economic Commission for Europe pointed out in its 1956 report that "the real handicap of French agriculture is not physical, it is social. It is paying the price of smallness of French industry and its uneven distribution around the country." Agriculture cannot flourish in an industrial desert and at least half of France, industrially speaking, is dotted with deserted villages.

This compartmentalization of France into rich and poor, rural and urban regions is totally unnecessary. Of all the countries in Europe France enjoys the best natural internal communications and the best network of roads, rivers and railways. The unnatural barriers separating the regions of France developed over the years partly by accident, partly by design. France's railway system, for example, was the first and the best in the world, but it was, unfortunately, developed too early, preceding the peak period of industrial expansion, whereas in other countries the rail net grew with and because of the industrial boom. The difference in timing was vital, for other countries developed regional rail lines as industry mushroomed, whereas the French developed a national network only, centered on Paris.

The French railways were conceived and financed by Parisian industrialists when Paris was not only the dominant city—as it is today—but virtually the only big industrial city of France. If you look at a communications map of France you will see a huge, nation-wide cobweb of rail lines and roads, with Paris sitting in the middle like a giant spider. Into the maw of the Paris market place pours the produce of the nation. A farmer in Bordeaux does not ship his crop to near-by Toulouse or Marseilles but sends it north to the commissionaires of Les Halles de Paris, who then reship it south, with all the added costs of freight and commissions.

This originally accidental pattern of growth has been perpetuated both by the growth in importance of Paris, as the financial heart of France, and by the traditional centralism of French society. From the

Capetian kings to the absolute, political monarchs of the National Assembly France has been governed by centrifugal force. All the brains, talents and energies of the nation are concentrated in and around Paris. Germany has its Berlin, Munich, Hamburg, Frankfort and Essen; Italy its Rome, Venice, Florence and Milan; but France has Paris, incomparable, magnificent and destructive in its pride and glory. Paris is high on the list of suspects in the crimes against the French economy. Its role is that of a beautiful vampire, sucking the lifeblood out of the nation, or, as economists put it: regional disequilibrium has impoverished French agriculture and weakened the structure of the economy.

ᕼᕯᕲ

4. Inefficient Distribution and Production

My daughter once had whooping cough in Paris and I learned a lot about the French economy thanks to her.

The doctor told me that there was a new drug that would calm her cough overnight and sent me off to a pharmacy near the Etoile to procure it. On my way over in the taxi I began wondering just why I had to go to this one particular drugstore. If the drug were so good why could I not buy it in my neighborhood pharmacy? My curiosity grew, when, on arriving at the pharmacy I saw a queue of more than a hundred anxious fathers and mothers lined up along the avenue.

When my turn finally came I found myself inside a small, dark room, redolent with the bittersweet fragrance of herbs and roots. Porcelain pots with Latin inscriptions lined the shelves, from floor to ceiling. Behind the counter, wearing a white surgeon's robe, was a middle-aged man, red-eyed and haggard from overwork. Without even asking for my order he reached under the counter, came up with a paper-wrapped package, said, "One hundred and seventy-five francs," and handed it over. I gave him the money, he rang up the cash register, made change himself. There was no assistant in the shop and a long line still waited behind me.

As the pharmacist was making change I asked him why he had not patented his wonderful new formula, to distribute through every drugstore in the land. He looked at me as though I were either a

lunatic or a foreign spy and said: "What! and lose my monopoly?
Look at the business I am doing. Everybody has to come to my
pharmacy." I pointed out to him that nobody was buying anything
other than the whooping-cough cure, so I did not see the advantage
of making people come to his pharmacy, whereas if he patented it
there was no limit to the sales possibilities in France and in the
world.

The little pharmacist brushed aside my arguments with eloquent
gestures: "I don't have the capital to build my own plant and besides
it doesn't make sense to build a plant for one drug alone. Therefore
I would have to sell my patent to the big companies. I don't trust
the big companies. Anyway I love my little pharmacy. I want to stay
here and be left in peace. I do not want to be big."

He had pronounced the fatal phrase, the secret password of the
millions of little French shopkeepers who do not want to be big.
France is a land of Lilliputs, inhabited by a few Gullivers. The
timorous Lilliputs are choking the life out of the country. There
are almost a million small retail shops in France and six out of ten
of them do less than $250 a month total business. Even the President
of the Chamber of Commerce of Paris, Fernand Dreux, once admitted in an address to the body that "individual enterprise has been
excessively developed in our country." In that speech of February,
1954, President Dreux deplored the fact that "in France today there is
one merchant for every four wage-earners, the highest proportion of
any country in the world."

This overburdened distributive system parallels a similarly clogged-
up productive apparatus. There is almost no big industry in American
terms in France. French production is small-unit and artisanal in
structure. Seven out of ten French factories employ less than twenty
workers. Thus productivity is low and prices are high. Yet the merchants and producers individually are not prospering simply because
there are too many of them, which is why so many of the little
shopkeepers and artisans join extremist movements like Poujade's
antitax league. Thus you have the absurd situation of distributive
and manufacturing systems that cheat the consumer without enrich-
ing the manufacturers and distributors.

The little French merchant-producer is not so much a criminal as he is a sick pygmy, suffering from undernourishment. The fat around his middle is not a sign of surplus profits but rather the typical distension of poor diet and a congested system.

5. INEQUITABLE TAXATION

Has there ever been a reporter or writer on French affairs who has not at least once in his career observed that "Frenchmen will die for their country but will not pay for it"? This is the truest of all the standard clichés about France. It is almost impossible to get Frenchmen to pay direct taxes. Only 27 per cent of all the taxes collected in France are direct. This truism, however, has produced one of the great myths about France: that the French do not pay taxes. They do, and heavy ones. The fact that the taxes are indirect makes them less obviously painful but no less heavy and costly in the end. The tax burden of France is almost exactly, to the fraction of a decimal point, equivalent to the tax burden in the United States: 21.8 per cent of gross national product in France, 21.9 per cent in the U.S.A. The fault in the French tax system is that it is inefficient, clumsy and socially unjust. Indirect taxes hit the poor rather than the rich. There is a physical limit to the amount of tobacco, alcohol, gasoline and other consumption commodities that the rich can consume, therefore the per cent of taxes to income, for a rich Frenchman, is much smaller than for a poor man, whose tobacco and alcohol tax is a considerable part of his weekly paycheck.

The French tax system has several iniquitous features, the most harmful of which is that it puts a premium on smallness, thus encouraging, if not actually being responsible for, the pygmyophilia of French businessmen. The operative mechanism is a tax-evaluation system called *"signes extérieurs de la richesse."* It is a method of computing income by symbols of wealth. Since the Internal Revenue Department takes it for granted that every return is false the collectors judge a man's real income by "exterior signs." For example, if a Frenchman employs a servant at a weekly salary of five thousand francs then it is assumed that he himself must earn at least fifty thousand a week. Similar ratios are established for cars and household goods.

This absurd and psychologically unsound reasoning assumes that the spendthrift earns more money than the miser, whereas the contrary is more often true. The effect of this standard of evaluation is to discourage the purchase of automobiles, television sets, refrigerators or anything that might excite the interest of the tax collector or the envy of one's neighbors. This is why you see French millionaires riding around in tiny cars and living in homes whose exterior façade is dirty, chipped and weather-beaten. Some of the most beautiful mansions in Paris, with an interior collection of lovely paintings and rugs, have the exterior façade of a slum.

This insane tax system came into being as a result of the stagnation of French business over a century of decline. It is a perfect example of the vicious circle of economic defects. The process began with the decline in the birth rate. Since the population was shrinking, or at best stationary, the productive apparatus was geared to a static demand. There was no incentive for a producer to invest in new plants or to expand production since he would have exactly the same number of potential customers next year or in fifty years. Thus the French invested in Russian railroads and the Suez Canal but not in France. Since industry was not expanding, while the cost of running the state was, the Treasury could only get its needed revenue by increasing taxes on the individual rather than the corporation. However, there was a limit to the amount of direct taxation that could be imposed on an individual, and it was politically unpopular to press that limit too hard. So, inevitably, the system of indirect taxation was developed.

From 1945 through 1955 no less than twenty tax reform plans were drawn up by successive governments and parliamentary commissions but none got beyond the debating stage. This tax system has given the working class a sense of being discriminated against, which has tended to accentuate the split among workers, producers, farmers and merchants, therefore widening the political divisions which prevent the durable majority in Parliament which is needed to break the vicious circle. It is like the old chain of disasters, "For want of a horseshoe a kingdom was lost." If the French economy collapses some day it might be said that "for want of a tax reform an economy was wrecked."

ᕕᕗ

6. HIGH PRICES AND LOW WAGES

The same curious chain of events that led from a decline in the birth rate to an inequitable tax system was responsible for the ruinous price structure of the French economy. French producers and merchants almost instinctively prefer a small-turnover, big-profit system to the mass-turnover, low-profit-per-unit system of the American producer. For a century and a half a French producer has known that his market for sales in the years ahead would be precisely the same or less than his current capacity could handle. So, why expand and why cut prices to encourage sales?

There is one other influence, preying on the mind of the producer, a nightmare that haunts every Frenchman: inflation. Why sell out your stock when new raw materials will cost so much more? Isn't it better, producers ask, to hold a big inventory and release the stock slowly at high prices? This psychology has developed over the years of petrification of the French productive apparatus. The inelastic supply of commodities, due to the lack of expansion, meant that in any period of prosperity and increased income supply could not keep up with demand. This is the basic and little understood cause of the chronic inflation which is the cruelest feature of the French economy. Inflation is one of the most unfair and destructive forms of exploitation and taxation. It wipes out savings, makes a mockery of wage increases, destroys confidence in the nation's currency, wrecks the nation's credit and prices its commodities out of world markets.

This process has been going on in France throughout most of the twentieth century. Inflation is the cancer of the French economy. It would have been better had France suffered a violent fever of inflation as Germany did, leading to a complete overhaul of the system, and a brand-new departure with new correctives.

The combination of inflation, high prices and low wages has given French workers the certainty that they are the victims of a deliberate plot to impoverish them. Some sixteen million French workers earn less than thirty dollars a week and some thirteen million earn less than twenty dollars weekly.[1] What makes this even more intolerable for the

[1] *Statistiques et Études Financières*, Supplement No. 85-86, table V, January-February, 1956, Ministère de l'Économie Nationale, Imprimerie Nationale.

workers is that they pay the highest proportion of the direct taxes since their salaries are declared on the books and cannot be falsified. The official breakdown on the payment of direct taxes by social categories of citizens is one of the most closely guarded secrets of state. However, many accurate estimates have been made by economists and the figures usually accepted as close to the truth are 75 per cent of direct taxes from wage earners, compared with 19 per cent from commerce and industry, and only 6 per cent from the farmers. The corresponding proportions of the active population are: wage earners 60 per cent, commerce and industry owners 15 per cent, and farmers 25 per cent.

This clearly inequitable distribution of national income and the national tax burden would have become completely intolerable and have led to revolutionary class warfare if it had not been slightly mitigated by social benefits to the workers. The welfare program in France is, however, economically unsound for it treats the symptoms of the disease instead of the disease itself. It is a state-directed relief program, compensating but not correcting the injustices of a distorted economy and creating new injustices of its own. It is manifestly unfair to pay two men different wages for doing exactly the same job side by side. Yet, in effect, this is the result of the family allocations system, for a man with four children has a total weekly income in wages and benefits almost double that of a bachelor on the same assembly line. This is socially praiseworthy but economically absurd. The costs of this program are also an important element of the high-price structure of the economy and one of the reasons why the French producer cannot compete on equal terms with a German or Belgian manufacturer.

The most negative effect of the social welfare system of France was its influence in the housing industry, which is a classic example of how good intentions pave the way to a living hell. In the course of the First World War, with its widespread destruction of homes, Frenchmen became alarmed at the thought that the citizen, risking his life to save his country, enduring terrible hardships in the freezing, mud-packed trenches, might come home to find his house destroyed or his rent raised above his means to pay. To counteract this danger, rents were frozen. It was a fair wartime measure. But it should never have become a *permanent* law. It should, in any case, have been accompanied by a housing and reconstruction plan that would have made low-price housing available to wage earners while at the same time providing a fair interest return on investment in real estate. This was not done.

Rents were frozen at the 1914 level but prices rose in an inflationary economy in all other sectors. Thus real estate owners, whose costs were rising, found themselves in 1924 collecting rents worth one-tenth of their original value. They therefore refused to spend any more capital in improving or even maintaining their properties, preferring to write them off at a loss. When the postliberation government of 1945 lifted the rent freeze of 1914 on new constructions, it did not help at all. It simply resulted in building for the very rich. For the past ten years luxury apartment buildings have been blooming overnight in Paris and other metropolitan centers, further aggravating the working-class and lower-middle-class sense of grievance. The housing shortage in France is almost unbelievable in a major Western power and a so-called civilized country. Millions of citizens are housed in unheated, crowded and unsanitary conditions. The rural communities are particularly primitive, a percentage as high as one out of three houses having neither electricity, bathrooms, running water, inside toilets or even floors. In Paris itself almost half the lodgings do not have private toilets or hot water. The average age of Paris buildings is a hundred years and whole districts of the capital are older than that. Hardly a week goes by without a story in the papers about a building falling down, just collapsing from old age. The Housing Department of Paris lists some 400,000 people as "inadequately housed," and reports some 35,000 families as "unhoused." What this word means is that thousands of young newly married couples have been unable to find housing of any kind and must live with their parents.

At the liberation in 1944 the rate of obsolescence of French houses, that is, houses officially listed as unfit to live in, was running at about 120,000 a year. The estimated needs of new housing had risen by 1956 to 400,000 a year but the rate of construction was far behind at 250,000 units annually. Thus continued shortages of homes for generations to come is the gloomy prospect of the French, unless the artisanal, inefficient housing trade is converted into a modern industry. At present it takes four months to complete a housing unit in

America, eight months in Germany, one year in Britain and two and a half years in France.

Underpaid, overcharged, heavily taxed and ill-housed, the mass of French workers has turned to Communism. It is not surprising that five million French citizens vote Communist and another two million turn to Fascism. It is only surprising that anybody, let alone the majority of citizens, can still vote for the democratic parties who have borne the heavy responsibility of government in so seemingly hopeless a mess. More than surprising, it is astonishing that the French economy is able to muddle through the mess and has, despite its six grave defects, actually grown stronger in the past decade.

This is very annoying to analysts of French affairs. It is so easy to diagnose the defects of the French, so simple to demonstrate that the system cannot work, that it is doubly irritating to observe that, contrary to all reason and logic, it does. I wish I did not have to admit this. It would be so much more satisfying not to have to deal in paradoxes, never again to write the deadly phrase "but on the other hand." But, on the other hand, the truth is that the French economy is apparently too strong to be wrecked, even by the French.

⤬

In addition to its natural resources the French economy was saved because there were some Frenchmen who were builders, not wreckers, and who knew how to take the best advantage of France's natural strength. The greatest of them was Jean Monnet, a prophet almost without honor in his own country but one of the Frenchmen most admired in the world. Monnet was aware of the shortcomings of the French economic system as he also was sensitive to the limited visions of his compatriots. Born in Cognac in 1888, raised in the vineyards of his family's distillery of brandy, Jean Monnet was a peasant at heart himself. But he outgrew his peasant origins by traveling around the world as a salesman of the famous Monnet brandy, from Paris to Labrador, to China and Russia. He went on to make his own name famous as a financier and economic trouble-shooter for business firms and then for governments.

Back home in France at the liberation Monnet devoted his energies and organizing genius to saving the French economy. The economic heart of France was barely flickering. Monnet prescribed and administered a strong dose of adrenalin, in the form of a five-year plan for rehabilitation and modernization of the basic industries: cement, steel, tractors, fertilizer, transport and energy. He set target dates and goals for each of these sectors and organized special committees, composed of government officials, economists, industrialists and trade union leaders. Monnet gathered around him at his headquarters in the Rue Martignac some of the most brilliant young economists of France. His chief of staff was chemical engineer Etienne Hirsch and his theoretician was Pierre Uri, graduate of the Sorbonne, the London School of Economics and Princeton's Institute of Advanced Studies. Monnet was neither an engineer nor a theorist. He was the high priest of the monks of Martignac Abbey, the most dedicated group of men since the first brain-trust team of the early New Deal in Washington.

Not all of his target dates were met on schedule; he never thought they would be. They were, however, psychological guides to action and in this respect they were a tremendous success. Monnet and his plan gave France the basic platform from which the nation's economic and industrial recovery could be launched. And it was launched with great success. Without the Monnet Plan, the Marshall Plan might have been wasted on France. It would have been difficult, perhaps impossible, to make full use of America's life-saving aid program if the basic industry of France had not been in a position to absorb it. Thanks to Monnet it was. Jean Monnet and George Marshall were the saviors of the French economy and their respective plans enabled the Fourth Republic to break all the industrial and economic records of French history.

The Monnet and Marshall plans provided both rational programs and the capital to finance them. The postliberation nationalization of banks, communications and mines, had taken key levers of the economy out of the hands of the little middlemen of France and provided the broad base of operations for a national reconstruction effort. The nationalization of industry and finances stopped far short of actual Socialism but carried France considerably beyond nineteenth-century capitalism. The Fourth Republic is a halfway house between the theoretical structures of Adam Smith and Karl Marx.

It has been a busy and noisy house. The quarrels of its excitable inhabitants raised such a din in the early days of reconstruction that it drowned out the hum of buzz saws, generators and tractors. Nonetheless these machines were working and things were getting done. Agriculture, despite its fragmentation, boosted farm output by 20 per cent above the average of the prewar years. Industrial production reached new peaks every year from 1946 through 1956, attaining a volume 75 per cent greater than 1938. During that decade the average living standards of Frenchmen rose 40 per cent and the purchasing power of the wage earner increased 25 per cent. In the single year 1953-54 production rose 21 per cent and wages 19 per cent without a rise in prices, the first time in a half-century that expansion was not sabotaged by inflation. French exports increased by the amazing proportion of 89 per cent while total national resources doubled from 1949-55. Oil refining facilities tripled and the tractor pool sextupled.

The most encouraging increase of all was the increased production of babies and a corresponding decrease in the death rate. From 1946 through 1955 the population increased by 1,783,000. On the average there were 835,000 new births a year as compared with a prewar average of 620,000. Deaths fell from 645,000 in 1935 to 520,000 in 1955. France, in the past ten years, has literally been reborn. Despite the muddled state of its affairs, despite imperial conflicts and civil wars, the Fourth Republic, while losing prestige and colonies, has gained citizens and strength in a renaissance as great as any in French history. Frenchmen today are continuing the great traditions of the past, underneath the surface agitations of political crises. In 1956 during the world crisis on the Suez Canal the French were completing a new canal in Alsace that will be longer than the Suez, which the French originally built. The French, in the mid-twentieth century, hold many industrial world records. Among them are:

The fastest locomotive in the world: 199 mph

The fastest electronic calculator, the Gamma, which carries out 5,800 operations a second

The world's most powerful hydroelectric stations, at Pragnères, Cap de Long, Donzère-Madragon and Génissiat

The world's first thermal generator using sea water at Abidjan in the Ivory Coast

The world's highest altitude steel plant at Paz del Rio, in

Colombia (2,600 meters), built by French contractors; also, the longest-spanned viaduct, in Caracas, Venezuela

The world's longest maritime quay at Le Havre: 1,500 meters

The French bathyscape holds the world's record for descent into the sea: 4,050 meters

The French helicopter, Alouette II, holds the world's altitude record for that type of plane: 8,400 meters

This miracle of French recovery has been one of the great unreported stories of our times, or rather one of the great unknown stories, for the facts were reported but were drowned in the torrent of disaster news from France. Statistics on production gains are only published three or four times a year, whereas the crises of France occur three and four times a week, sometimes a day. Good news is, in any case, far less interesting than bad news, so the steady progress, even when reported, generally failed to excite comment. The public, therefore, had a dangerously distorted view on what was happening in France.

The public can hardly be blamed, for the experts themselves could not make up their minds whether France was coming to life or in the last throes of a death agony. The most distinguished and able analysts in Europe were baffled. They wrote, in the 1955 annual report of the OEEC: "France is approaching the point at which there might occur one of those recoveries, of which there have been so many examples in the history of the country.... It seems that little is needed for France either to make a rapid recovery or for the state of economic depression to be dangerously prolonged."

Either rapid recovery or depression! Such is the fragile balance of the French economy, weakened by years of neglect yet alive and vibrant with change and progress. The solution to the mystery of why there is no corpse, despite all the clues pointing to murder, is that France has stubbornly refused to die, although bleeding from every pore and gasping for air. Crimes have been committed daily but France is so strong, its economy so basically sound that it has survived the attacks of the most powerful enemy: its own citizens, the short-sighted, selfish merchants and producers, the mistrustful peasant, the disloyal investors who have no faith in their own nation.

All the ills of the French economy thus derive from social or psychological, not physical causes. There is no defect that the citizens of the Republic cannot correct, no ill they cannot cure. Thus, our examination of the French economy leads to the same conclusion that emerged from a study of politics, parliament and government: all the troubles of France are man-made rather than intrinsic impediments to progress.

The moment has therefore come, in this examination of the Fourth Republic, to consider the central element of French life. Let us, then, turn to the most puzzling yet the most fascinating phenomenon of contemporary society: the Frenchman, the man who holds in his hands the key to the riddle of France.

12 *Manners, Morals and Mores of the French*

The French, they are a funny race,
Parlez-vous?
The French, they are a funny race,
Parlez-vous?
The French, they are a funny race,
They fight with their feet,
And they fall on their face.
Hinky-dinky parlez-vous?

During two world wars hundreds of thousands of American soldiers sang this famous song about the antics of the French. Most of the verses are unprintable. Whatever the color of the words, the sentiment is the same; the French are incomprehensible to the foreigner, particularly to the American who is at first bewildered and then irritated by the contradictions of French behavior.

A Frenchman is rarely seen drunk in public or in private but France has the highest rate of alcoholism in the world. Frenchmen are fervent patriots but they invest their money abroad. A Frenchman is thrifty to the point of miserliness in his private family affairs but will cheerfully raid the public Treasury and laugh at constantly mounting national deficits. A Frenchman prides himself on his logic but turns off the heating system exactly on March 21, the first official day of spring, even though it might be snowing outside. A French deputy delivers fiery speeches in Parliament about the vital importance of putting down the rebellion in Algeria and then votes against the government's bill for increased taxes to pay the cost of putting down the Algerian revolt. The national motto of the United States is "God bless America," of Germany "*Deutschland Über Alles*," but in France it is "*Vive la France*." All the French want is to be allowed to live in peace—yet France has been at war longer than any other country in the world.

This dualism of the French confuses those who do not distinguish between what the French practice and what they preach. If you were to believe what Frenchmen say you would be convinced that they have nothing but contempt for their politicians and are totally disinterested in politics. But if you examine the results of national elections in the past fifty years you will discover that at least eight out of ten registered voters in France go to the polls on election day, one of the best records of responsible political action in the Western world. And, with startling regularity, the voters return to power the same men and the same parties they profess to hold in contempt.

The reason for these contradictions between words and deeds is that the Frenchman has a horror of appearing to be stupid or naïve. He hides his true beliefs behind a defensive cloak of cynicism. He hates to be fooled but even more he hates to have it known that he has been made a fool of. There is nothing worse that can happen to a Frenchman than to be *"cocu,"* to be the victim of infidelity, in private life or in politics. A *"cocu"* is more to be scorned than pitied, for he is a fool. Frenchmen can forgive, even admire, a clever knave but not an honest fool. Therefore a Frenchman plays the cynic, pretends to believe in nothing and in no one. A cynic is foolproof; that is, he only fools himself, which is less painful and embarrassing.

❦

A man's fears, like his hopes, reveal his basic philosophy of life. The fear of looking foolish is the negative expression of a positive force motivating French behavior: the cult of intelligence and of learning. The intellectual is the hero-type of French contemporary society.

Each nation has its hero-type, the model that every man strives to emulate. This image changes with the evolution of a society. In America the hero-type has been successively the frontiersman, the small-town boy who made good in the big city, the self-made man, the tycoon and, in recent years, the executive, the soft-spoken but forceful man of distinction. In France the hero-type has been the aristocrat, the landed gentry, the high official and currently the intellectual. He may be a professor of philosophy or a serious novelist who is a member of the Académie Française. He certainly writes front-page editorials for a Paris daily newspaper, and wears the rosette of the Legion of Honor. He may even be a politician.

In America a politician, even when he is a genuine intellectual, makes a conscious effort to hide his brains. He tries to be just a simple man of the people, uses plain, blunt language, insists upon being called Mike or Jim, rather than Senator or Doctor, even if he has earned those titles. In France the very opposite is true. Intellectuals are proud of their titles and distinctions and would never dream of being folksy, common or inelegant in speech.

French intellectuals participate fully and vigorously in the nation's political life and French politicians, in return, share in the nation's intellectual life. Edouard Herriot was a distinguished writer, while Gaullist Jacques Soustelle is a professor of anthropology. Catholic writer François Mauriac, a Nobel Prize laureat, writes a weekly political diary for the pro-Mendès-France paper, *Express*, and is a vitriolic critic of the orthodox Catholic party. Jean-Paul Sartre and Albert Camus, two of France's most famous novelists and philosophers, were deeply involved in a polemic war for years, after Camus split with the "Stalinists" among the Communist intellectuals. Their debate was given prominent front-page treatment in the press. No press in the world gives as much space and prominence to theoretical and philosophical discussions as the French.

This cult of intelligence is the very best and the very worst quality of the French. It is the force that has created in France the most adult, civilized and literate society in the world. It is also a disease rotting that society. Intellectualism in France has reached a point of intensity and absurdity similar to the scholasticism of the monks in the Middle Ages. The debates in Parliament and the polemics in the press are brilliant and inspiring in language and erudition but have about as much relation to reality as a monkish dissertation on the number of angels that could stand on the head of a pin. The Frenchman, who is the freest, most nonconformist thinker, becomes a slave to his own dogma. A French statesman once said he would rather lose a colony than compromise a principle. By rigid adherence to this inflexible "principlism" the French have succeeded in losing most of their colonies.

The French and British approaches in this respect are diametrically opposed. The British Commonwealth has virtually no formal structure, no constitution, no set of rigid principles. It is opportunistic and realistic, which has permitted it to survive. The French Union, however, has a formal, detailed Constitution, a long, precise set of clauses and principles. It is moralistic and idealistic but it does not work, nor ever will in its present form, for it does not correspond to the human aspirations of the member peoples. The French insistence on abstract analysis and written statutes fails to take into account the human element and thus fails to achieve its ends.

The Frenchman rejects the humanism of the Christian philosopher Blaise Pascal—"The heart has its reasons that reason does not know"—and follows the teachings of the high priest of rationalism, René Descartes: "I doubt, therefore I think; I think, therefore I am." In their passionate Cartesianism the French intellectuals attain a state of sublimation in which they know everything but understand nothing. They become paralyzed, as André Siegfried has commented, by "a skepticism unbefitting them for action." Not every Frenchman is a Cartesian intellectual, nor is every intellectual a skeptic incapable of action. Yet many Frenchmen are either intellectuals or would like to be. The general level of culture, the respect for learning, particularly among the unlearned, is higher than in any other country in which I have traveled, and I have traveled in many.

√ This "intellectualism" of the French is found at every level of society. The café waiter, the taxicab driver, the restaurateur, the so-called "little people" of France are the most stimulating, if frequently exasperating, conversationalists in the world. Of them all, the most anarchistic and voluble is the taxicab driver. I deliberately provoke arguments with them—an easy thing to do—to see what they will say next. Of the hundreds of discussions in cabs one remains in my memory as uniquely, superbly French. It could not have occurred in any other country, except possibly in Brooklyn, where there exists a species of man akin in spirit if not in actual form to the French.

It was midnight in Paris and we were rolling along the Quai d'Orsay toward the Avenue Bosquet, where I live, on the left bank of the river Seine. As we came to the Pont Alexandre III the cab slowed down, for the traffic light was red against us, and then, without stopping, we sailed through the red light in a sudden burst of speed. The same performance was repeated at the Pont de l'Alma before turning left to the Avenue Bosquet.

As I paid the driver I asked him why he had driven through two red lights.

"You ought to be ashamed of yourself, a veteran like you, breaking the law and endangering your life that way," I protested.

He looked at me astonished. "Ashamed of myself? Why, I am proud of myself. I am a law-abiding citizen and have no desire to get killed either." He cut me off before I could protest again.

"No, just listen to me before you complain. What did I do? Went through a red light. Well, did you ever stop to consider what a red light is, what it means?"

"Certainly," I replied. "It's a stop signal and means that traffic is rolling in the opposite direction."

"Half-right," said the driver, "but incomplete. It is only an *automatic* stop signal. And it does not mean that there is cross traffic. Did you see any cross traffic during our trip? Of course not. I slowed down at the light, looked carefully to the right and to the left. Not another car on the streets at this hour. Well, then! What would you have me do? Should I stop like a dumb animal because an automatic, brainless machine turns red every forty seconds? No, Monsieur," he thundered, hitting the door jamb with a huge fist. "I am a man, not a machine. I have eyes and a brain and judgment, given me by God. It would be a sin against nature to surrender them to the dictates of a machine. Ashamed of myself, you say? I would only be ashamed of myself if I let those blinking lamps do my thinking for me. Good night, Monsieur."

Is this bad, is this good? Frankly I no longer am sure. The intellectual originality of the French is a corrupting influence if you are subjected to it for long. There was a time when I thought I knew right from wrong in most cases. I never doubted that it was wrong to drive through a red light. After more than a decade of life in Paris, however, I find my old Anglo-Saxon standards somewhat shaken. I still think it is wrong to drive through a stop signal, except possibly very late at night, after having carefully checked to make sure there is no cross traffic. After all, I am a man not a machine.

ᛒᛒ

Another Frenchman who is not a machine is the famous Paris restaurateur, Roger the Frog.

Roger runs La Grenouille, one of the most popular bohemian restaurants on the left bank in the old Latin Quarter of Paris. His specialty, of course is frogs' legs, hence his sobriquet "the Frog." Physically, however, Roger looks more like a merry, little squirrel. Short, wiry with bright little eyes always twinkling, Roger scurries back and forth among his clients, chattering like a chipmunk, never pausing for breath or punctuation.

His usual greeting to me, in rapid-fire slangy Parisian, goes something like this: "So there you are looking fatter every day probably lapping up Normandy cream in some fancy right-bank brothel that calls itself a restaurant what's the matter with a nice calf's head vinaigrette good for the stomach and something else lower down too how's the family got a letter today from Mike Bessie and Alice C. D. Jackson sent socks for the orphanage there's no table go behind the bar help yourself I'll be back later."

Late at night when the crowd has gone Roger has time to sit and talk with you over a glass of mirabelle or quetsch. It is then that you get to know Roger best, the man underneath the mask of the clown. Roger is a hard-working, moral and gentle man. He supports an orphanage, devotes much of his time and money to the children and is constantly nagging his friends and clients to send clothing and gifts. Roger lives a full, good life, has made many people happy and is a happy man.

His attitude toward his life and his work is typically French. It tells why the suicide rate in France is as low as the rate of industrial production. I heard Roger's personal philosophy one night when I complained that his restaurant was closed on Saturday and Sunday, just when I wanted most to go there. I told him he was losing a lot of business, for those were big dining-out nights.

Roger grinned at me: "Losing business, am I? And what the devil do I want more business for? I'm making enough money now to take care of my family and the orphans. More business? To pay doctor bills perhaps. Don't you think I need a night or two off? You think you're the only old rooster who wants to crow on Saturday night? No, my friend, weekends I don't work. You can go to some other place to eat. It will make you appreciate the old Grenouille more when you come back to us. And it will still be La Grenouille, my home, to receive my friends and not a factory for manufacturing meals and money."

I used to think that Roger was mad but now I know how sane he is. No man can work seven days a week, therefore if Roger were to keep La Grenouille open on weekends he would have to hire a maître d'hôtel to run it for him. But that would be unthinkable. La Grenouille is Roger. Without his lively spirit it would be just another restaurant. This is what distinguishes French restaurants from others, this individual, personal character of the place, the people, the cuisine. It is part of the mores of France, a dynamic element of French folkways and culture. A restaurant in France is not just a place to swill food. Eating is not just a necessary means of keeping the body alive. The restaurant and the café are the true community centers of French life and the process of eating or drinking in France is a social ritual which permits the warmest, pleasantest human contacts in a climate of intellectual freedom that is unique in our world. Other countries—America and Britain for example—have attained political freedom—but none has achieved the complete freedom of the mind, free of all taboos and social frustrations, of the French. Their horizons are unlimited, their curiosity insatiable. Nothing that is human is strange to the French.

Roger and the cab driver are not unique. There are millions of men and women like them in the factories, on the farms and in the civil service of France. The desiccated bourgeois and the despotic bureaucrat are not the only inhabitants of France. It would take several lifetimes to get to know and appreciate the marvelously complex qualities of the remarkable people of France and to understand their refusal to be collectivized or "modernized." Perhaps some day man will achieve the kind of society where the individual's aspirations for life, liberty and the pursuit of happiness will not conflict with the needs of the community. Until then I will always have a soft spot in my heart for men who are not machines.

ᕫᕬ

In my private Pantheon of French individuals there is an old lady who has a niche next to Roger. I met her during the election campaign of 1946. It was in a fishing village in Catholic Brittany the day after elections. The village had voted 90 per cent Communist and I had come to find out why Communism had made such inroads in traditionally anti-Communist, devout Brittany.

As I strolled through town I saw a parade coming down the main street. At the head of the procession was the curé in his ceremonial vestments. Behind him was the Communist mayor, wearing the tricolor sash of office and behind him were the fishermen in striped Breton jerseys and hip-length rubber boots. I followed the procession down the street, then through a narrow lane leading to the beach, where the men climbed into their skiffs and began rowing out to the herring fleet. The priest stood in the prow, holding a huge cross over the water.

I spoke to a group of women, who were standing on the beach watching their men, and one very old lady told me that they were preparing to go through the ancient ceremony of blessing the waters, before putting to sea. I asked her to explain to a foreigner just why men who had voted solidly Communist were still going through this ceremony and why the priest was willing to bless anti-Catholic fishermen. She looked at me in surprise and replied: "Why, our sons are all good Catholics. They vote Communist because the Communists fight hard for our wages and for the price of fish, but still, my son, make no mistake about it, only God can make the west wind blow."

ᕫᕬ

French Catholicism is as nationalistic as it is realistic. When the Vatican threatened to excommunicate Catholics who voted Communist it had little or no effect in France. The French clergy itself warned the Vatican hierarchy of the dangers of a revived "Gallicanism," if too stringent a discipline were applied against the French.

Gallicanism is a kind of national Catholicism. It is an outgrowth of the Gallo-Roman Empire. Just as the Gauls embraced Roman culture politically, but remained Gauls, so did they embrace Christianity without accepting the authority of the Roman Church. The history of France abounds in dramatic examples of this "national Catholicism." Cardinal Richelieu, a Prince of the Church, hired Swedish and German Protestant soldiers to fight against the Catholic Emperor of Austria. Louis XIV attacked and occupied the lands of the Holy See, which was then located at Avignon in southern France.

The most cynical of the "Gallican" kings was Henry of Navarre, first of the Bourbon dynasty. Henri IV was a Protestant, a hard-drinking, hard-riding soldier, famous for his fights and love affairs. It was he who coined the phrase, *"le bâton qui porte paix,"* which we moderns know as "Speak softly but carry a big stick." His political slogan also became popular centuries later in America: "a chicken in the pot of every peasant on Sunday." Of all his realistic aphorisms the most famous was his remark, "Paris is well worth a Mass," spoken on the day he became converted to Catholicism in order to be enthroned as king of France.

This extraordinary character of French Catholicism is a major factor in French society today. It explains such phenomena as the contrast between the spiritual idealism and the material cynicism of the French, and also the existence of left-wing Catholic movements and such organizations as the "worker-priests," which almost caused a split between the French and Roman Church in 1953-54.

A few hundred priests, alarmed at the influence of Communism in their working-class flocks, had accused the Church of being partisan to capital against labor. To win back their lost sheep they became factory workers themselves, shared the toil and hardship of their parishioners and conducted their services only at night, after working hours. Some of them even became Communists. When the Church hierarchy, alarmed by this movement, ordered the worker-priests to abandon their jobs and their blue denims to return to the traditional Church many of them refused. It was one of the most serious crises of conscience ever faced by the French Church and the conflict is not yet completely resolved.

French Catholicism is a unique phenomenon, as individualistic and undisciplined as the French themselves. France is not a "daughter of the Church," as other Catholic countries are, but rather as the French say, "France is the elder sister of the Church," with the accent on the word "elder."

ᕯᕙ

The conflicts of faith in modern France cut across all lines and frequently divide families as well as institutions or political parties. One of the most poignant stories is the story of two sisters, one a dedicated democrat and admirer of America, the other a pro-Communist married to a man who played a major role in the cold war on the Soviet side. Had these sisters been just ordinary women their story would have been only a vignette, of human interest but not of great significance. They were, however, very extraordinary women, of world stature, and the tragedy of their divergent ways was symbolic of the tragic divisions that have split the world. The story of Eve and Irène Curie is thus a story for our times, symbolic of the ideals and passions that can inspire men and women to acts of heroism and nobility but to completely incompatible ends.

I "met" Eve Curie long before I ever saw her, as did millions of other readers of her book, *Madame Curie*. Her sensitive, graceful style, her warm heart and fine mind were all evident in her tribute to her mother. Then I met Eve Curie in person, years later, in a jeep on a road in southern France, the day our troops landed in the invasion of Provence. She was a Free French Army lieutenant, attached to the staff of General Jean de Lattre de Tassigny. World traveler, intimate of the great leaders of the Allied coalition, such as Roosevelt, Churchill and de Gaulle, Eve Curie was a brilliant political analyst.

She was as beautiful as she was brilliant. From the crown of her thick black hair to the tips of her feet she was a perfectly groomed, walking advertisement for Paris chic and charm. She had not inherited her mother's scientific genius—that was the gift of Madame Curie to her first-born, Irène—but Eve had inherited her mother's looks, humanity and quick wit.

Eve Curie is one of the few people in the world ever to have gotten the best of Churchill in a verbal duel. It happened just after the war at a dinner party in the south of France. Churchill had been expounding his postwar policy on the dangers of Russia and the need for a reconciliation between France and Germany. Churchill spoke of his impatience with the policy of General de Gaulle. Finally Eve interrupted Churchill and said: "Mr. Prime Minister, if you can find it in your heart to forgive the Germans can you not also find it in your heart to forgive your ally General de Gaulle?" Churchill roared with laughter and said: "I will try, my dear, I will try."

After the liberation of France Eve Curie founded the paper, *Paris-Presse*, as codirector with another wartime Gaullist, Philippe Barrès. Some years later she sold out her interest and joined the international staff of NATO as staff adviser to Lord Ismay, Secretary General of the North Atlantic Treaty Organization. She served in that capacity until she retired from public life to become the wife of an American lawyer economist, Harry Labouisse. Labouisse had been the chief of the Marshall Plan Mission to France and then the head of the UN Agency for Palestine Refugees.

In twenty-five active years of writing, lecturing, publishing, war correspondence and public service Eve Curie made many friends for France; we Americans have no better friend anywhere than this great Frenchwoman. She has become an American citizen. This is our gain but not France's loss, for Eve Curie is French and wherever she goes she carries the culture and genius of France with her.

Her sister Irène was, like Eve, a brilliant, courageous bearer of the great Curie name, yet in every other respect the two sisters were far apart. Where Eve was a Gaullist, Irène was pro-Communist. Eve was chic and smart; Irène lived in a gray chemist's smock. Eve traveled the world and mingled with the mighty; Irène's world was the laboratory of the Curie Institute and she mingled with molecules and atoms, whose power was less visible if mightier.

I first met Irène Curie on a tennis court at her house outside Paris. I had gone there one weekend, shortly after the liberation, to interview her husband, Frédéric Joliot, then one of the leading atomic chemists of the world. I was startled by her appearance when she came out to the court where Joliot was playing tennis with some of his students. She looked so old, so tired. Her hair was stringy, her teeth crooked and dead. I could hardly believe that this was the sister of Eve Curie.

No one knew it then but Irène Curie was condemned to a slow, painful death. She had given her life for science. An ampule containing radioactive elements had fallen and broken in her laboratory in 1942. Irène Curie, with complete disregard for her own safety, had immediately thrown swabs over the liquid and mopped it up while shouting at her fellow workers to run for their lives. The others escaped, saved by Irène Curie. She paid the ultimate price for her heroism. Radiation penetrated her bones and blood cells. She died in 1956. The genius, the contribution to science and to humanity, of Irène Curie, will remain as a symbol of the best of humanity, long after the world has forgotten the ugly political passions of our times, which caused her and her sister Eve such anguish. Her political convictions, the pro-Soviet activities of her husband, these are temporal. Her work, her faith in science, her example of selflessness, these are as immortal as the name of Curie.

Ꮽᚗ

Why does France produce so infinite a variety of individuals as the Curie sisters, Roger the Frog, Jean Monnet and the little pharmacist who does not want to be big? What makes a Frenchman think the way he does? What makes him different from a German, an Englishman, a Spaniard? It has become a well-worn cliché to say that the French are individualists and that it is their individualism that prevents stable, efficient government, saps the economy, and keeps France divided and weak. This is true and obvious but what is rarely examined is the cause of French individualism.

Surely individualism is not a biological phenomenon. There is no French gene that is passed on in the bloodstream from generation to generation. It is highly unlikely, I would guess, that a French baby sent to America to be raised would grow up to start a new political party at the age of twenty-one. No, what is passed on from generation to generation, in the stream of history rather than the bloodstream of Frenchmen, is a mistrust of all authority, of society itself, and, above all, the conviction that a man must count only upon himself for his own salvation. The French do not believe in the commandment, "Love thy neighbor." They say: "Keep a sharp eye on thy neighbor, for, chances are, he is up to no good."

Frenchmen for centuries have had to fight constantly to defend their homes, their property, their freedom, not only against foreign neighbors but against their fellow Frenchmen. The extension of the domains of the Capetians from the Paris basin to the Atlantic, the Pyrenees, the Mediterranean and the Alps was not a natural expansion but a man-killing conquest of peoples and territories that went on for some eight hundred years, punctuated by raiding parties from Africa, Britain, Scandinavia, Austria and Germany. The most cruel of all wars—religious and civil conflicts—completed the ravages of feudal and imperial wars that set Frenchmen against Frenchmen. Other countries have suffered from war and invasion, of course, but none has the bloody history of the French.

All of the recurrent crises of French history have left their mark on the consciousness of the people. This is what is passed on from generation to generation, in the villages and towns of France. French peasants are all "Minute Men" at heart, always ready to drop the plow and pick up their gun as they have been doing for centuries. The townspeople are perhaps less openly combative but over the centuries they have developed to a fine art the technique of defending their interests and foiling the authorities. I witnessed a pertinent example of this technique during the war scare of 1948, following the Communist coup in Czechoslovakia. In a few days' time it became almost impossible to get gasoline. I soon discovered by checking with French friends that they were buying it up and storing it in jerricans in case they had to make a quick escape. Frenchmen have been making quick escapes through the ages.

The French are ready at all times to resist or circumvent authority. I recall discussing this "uncivic" attitude of most Frenchmen with some prominent citizens at a dinner party one evening, at the home of a good friend, Jean Delcroix, publisher of *La Terre Nouvelle*. Among the guests were a leading art dealer of Paris and one of the biggest real estate operators of France. We were talking about the defense mechanism of Frenchmen, particularly the quality described by the French word "*débrouillard*," which means literally the ability to unscramble or, figuratively, someone who is adept at cutting red tape and getting special privileges.

I said that I did not know a single Frenchman of any standing who was not sufficiently *débrouillard* to have the special "*coupe-file blanc*," a white police pass normally given only to members of Parliament or special officials to facilitate their work. Each one of the Frenchmen present laughed and pulled a *coupe-file blanc* out of his pocket. Not one of them was entitled to have it. Furthermore, each of those men considered himself to be, and was, a solid, law-abiding citizen. They were also, however, expert unscramblers. You have to be to live in France. It is France's equivalent of Britain's "muddling through" and America's "getting along."

This is what is really meant by the term *"incivisme,"* which is more a lack of civic consciousness than bad citizenship. Frenchmen, who always resisted taxes, accepted compulsory military service long before American or British statesmen dared propose conscription for their peoples. The French make a sharp distinction between the nation and its government, and in many ways this is a healthy distinction. A man's ultimate loyalty is to the flag and to the republic for which it stands, and not to any particular incumbent administration. This has always been the traditional American creed, with occasional deviations in times of fear. It is also the traditional French philosophy of loyalty, with less frequent deviations, for no administration is in office long enough in France to test the public's loyalty.

The main difference between the French and American attitudes toward government is that Americans regard their government as a necessary evil, and at times are capable of great affection for their leaders, as in the Roosevelt and Eisenhower administrations, whereas the French regard their governments as a natural enemy to be resisted at all costs and at all times. If we Americans had had the same experience of government as the French we might well react the same way. British historian Phillip Williams put it neatly in his excellent book *Politics in Post-War France*: "The French, like the rest of us, are the prisoners of their past and the outside observer must endeavour to preserve the attitude of Spinoza: 'Do not laugh, do not weep, try to understand.'"

ɕ𝖜ɔ

It is sometimes hard not to weep even when one understands the reasons for French behavior in the public life of the Fourth Republic. One can tell oneself a hundred times that the war and occupation undermined the public morale, that the black market was originally a patriotic device to foil the Germans, that the French are prisoners of their past, but the time comes when you see a man race a woman to a taxicab in the rain and then jump in inches ahead of her, and, with the best will in the world, you cannot excuse him on the grounds that Cardinal Richelieu was a dictator or that France has often been invaded by her neighbors. The fact is that the man is a boor and that many, too many Frenchmen, particularly Parisians, behave badly in public no matter how polite they may be when entertaining friends at home.

Anyone who has ever tried to drive a car in Paris has seen humanity at its depths. Every man for himself and devil take the hindmost is the first precept of the French *"code de la route."* When parking a car in Paris never try to back into the parking space, for you will find a French man or woman in a tiny Renault 4hp sneaking into the space behind your back. If you can find a parking space at all, which is doubtful, go into it fast, headfirst. Regard the streets of Paris as a jungle and be prepared to defend yourself with claw and fang at all times.

A major word of warning to all foreign visitors: do not use an elevator in Paris. If you are a resident then, of course, you will be obliged eventually to do as the French do and play the dangerous elevator game. The game is played with one or two elevators, generally one, for it is rare to find as many as two elevators in any French building. The playing field, that is the elevator cabin, is an average size of one square foot, roughly equivalent to a small closet, but some are very big, large enough to hold as many as four people, if they are all slim.

The field is open, that is the elevator is suspended on thin wire cables in an open shaft. Each floor landing has an iron, openwork grille, so it is possible to put your hand through the grille and push the elevator door open as it comes to your landing. This breaks the electric circuit and stalls the elevator at your level, preventing it from going on up to someone on a higher floor.

My office is on the sixth floor, which puts me at a great disadvantage in the game, for people on intermediate floors are able to "steal" the elevator before it gets to me. My only countermove is to wrench open the grille gate on my floor, which also breaks the circuit. This is known as a deadlock. The elevator remains on the lower floor, suspended between the two broken circuits. Each contestant then stands tensely, one hand on the up button, the other on the circuit breaker. The trick is to be able to close the circuit simultaneously with your opponent but then to break it again as soon as the elevator is exactly on your landing. It is considered bad form for a loser to wrench his gate open when the winner is already in the elevator and moving between floors. However, bad form is part of the game and many are the times that I have been stuck between floors by a poor loser. When that happens you either shout until someone closes the open door or you ring the alarm button to call the janitor. This occurs on the average of about once a month. On other days you get stuck in the elevator by accident rather than by spite, for the elevators in France break down by themselves every tenth trip up or down.

ᔕᖇᑎ

The deterioration of public manners and morals has been in process throughout the twentieth century. It is largely a result of wars and inflation, which sap morale and destroy the traditional virtues of honesty, hard work and thrift. The French are certainly not the only people afflicted with this decline in manners. The roaring twenties, the depressed thirties, the fighting forties and the fissionable fifties have been successive decades of decline in human morality around the world. In France, however, the process seems to have gone on more rapidly and more profoundly than in other countries. This is partly because the French have been the storm center of the Western world, partly because their native individualism and anarchy lends itself more to public bad manners and partly because the legend of *"la politesse française"* leads one to expect something better from the French than the way they behave in public.

Most of my French friends admit that the state of public manners and morals is a disgrace, and "something ought to be done about it," but they resent it when foreigners point this out. I do not blame them, for it is impertinent for foreigners living among the French to criticize their behavior. We Americans do not take kindly to foreigners who sound off about our bad habits. Our usual reply is, "Why don't you go back where you came from if you don't like it here?" Normally I would not be so smug as to set myself up as a judge of French conduct. However, I would be remiss in my duty as a reporter of French affairs if I were to ignore this important aspect of national life. Not all the French are ill-mannered boors, of course, but the decline in public manners has reached a point indicating a serious malaise in contemporary French society.

There are signs, moreover, that the French are beginning to do something about stopping the decline in manners. One day in 1954 the Prefect of Police of Paris, André Dubois, decreed the outlawing of the horn. Until then Paris had been deafened daily by a raucous cacophony of angry klaxons. The horn was used by most motorists as a substitute for the the brake. Many Frenchmen, who normally would never do anything so vulgar as shout, became bellowing fishmongers in traffic. Everyone complained of the noise, but seemed to assume that the other fellow was the guilty one.

Prefect Dubois decided to test the manners and civic pride of his fellow Parisians by making it illegal to blow a horn at any time. To everyone's astonishment Paris became the city of celestial silence overnight. No one blew his horn, not even women drivers. As if by magic every motorist, while still violating all other laws and procedures, suddenly decided to comply with the restriction on the horn. That was almost three years ago and not a horn has blown in Paris since. The experiment was so successful that in 1956 the city of New York followed the example of Paris, with, it must be admitted, a bit less success. You can still hear the occasional moan of a ghostly horn in Gotham but not in old Paname.

ᕱᕓ

The horn-choking experiment indicates perhaps that what the French need is courageous leadership and a sense of self-interest in obeying the law. The clamor of the claxons was so unnerving that every citizen wanted desperately to be freed of it. The combination of an evident need and vigorous leadership by Dubois produced the miracle of compliance. This could mean that much-needed reforms of manners and morals might be effected in other fields of life if a similar combination of stimuli could be found. I would suggest that the place to look for such stimuli, and perhaps to begin the task of creating a sense of community spirit among the individualistic French, is in the schools. Of all the institutions, of all the influences upon French life, the one I believe to be most responsible for the lack of community spirit that divides the French people and weakens their government is the educational system.

A sense of community with others is not, I suspect, a "natural" human instinct. I have spent many a pleasant hour in the Champ de Mars park, just under the Eiffel Tower, watching the children play on the sandpile next to the Carrousel and I would say, after some years of casual research, that the natural tendency of the man-child is to hit his neighbor over the head with a pail or shovel or any handy instrument. Man is gregarious—but he is also aggressive and spends most of his time quarreling with the neighbor whose company he seeks.

A community spirit is thus an acquired characteristic. It can only be acquired at a very early age. Once a man is full-grown it is probably too late to make him public-spirited and civic-minded if the sense of civism has not already been developed in youth. This is precisely the case of Frenchmen. The French educational system does not attempt to develop a sense of civic pride or community spirit in the child. It is keyed to the development of the individual. Its most iniquitous feature, however, is its refusal to allow for individual differences in capacity. Where the American system aims at helping each child attain his own maximum capacity, the French system is based upon individual achievement through competition. The French child is measured not only by his mastery of the subject matter, but above all in relation to all the other children. It is child against child in competitive examinations.

An elaborate honor system grades each child every week, both on subject proficiency and on his relative standing in the class. The examinations are graded on a scale of 0 to 20. A mark of 14/20, or 70 per cent, is a passing grade. Students and parents are more emotionally concerned, however, about the class honors list. A child may have a passing average of 14/20 but only be in the bottom half of a bright class, thus not qualifying for an honors medal. This is a personal humiliation, for the child is publicly branded as inferior.

The medal system is an elaborate one. The most prized medal is the gilt *"Croix de Travail,"* awarded to the top five in the class. The next five students are given the *"Croix d'Application,"* a slightly smaller bronze medallion, thus rounding out an elite circle of the top ten. Those who are very near the top ten are given a consolation ribbon, the "*Ruban d'Encouragement.*" These decorations are awarded weekly. The winners may wear the medals or ribbons until the next honors list is announced. There is no greater tragedy for a bright French boy or girl than to have to hand the precious medal back on a week in which his grades may have slipped a little bit. It is like an officer being cashiered from the army, his insignia of rank publicly torn from his shoulder.

This is a cruel system. The bright children become intellectual snobs, proudly wearing the proof of their superiority. The less bright, the average child, is humiliated and frequently crushed by a feeling of inadequacy. Perhaps I ought to say that my own daughter is generally high on the honors list, so my criticism is not based on a personal grudge but rather on a professional conviction that this is unsound educational psychology. It concentrates on being learned to the exclusion of learning to be a better human being. It is all very well to spur children on to maximum effort, to prod and guide each one to attain his fullest capacity, but this constant competition among them, this harping on distinction or disgrace, can only result in the bitter rivalry, jealousies and discord which I find to be characteristic of French society.

It is in the area of education for citizenship that the French system is most dangerously negligent. It is no surprise to me that French politics are always in crisis and that it is impossible to create a durable coalition of parties in Parliament. Politicians blame it on a faulty constitution. I would put at least part of the blame on the schools. A constitution, as I suggested earlier in this study, can only provide the framework and guiding principles of orderly government. The best constitution is useless when administered by disorderly, unco-operative individuals, which is what most of France's legislators are. They may also be educated, literate men. Their brilliance, however, is lost in the spiritual wasteland of the French community, to a great extent because they never acquired the sense of a community in the jungle of the competitive school system.

There are no organized sports, virtually no group projects, no intramural teams of any kind in French schools. Extracurricular activity offers training in dancing, swimming, acrobatics, arts and crafts, but they almost always train the children for a solo performance.

In 1952 a first, hesitant group-project program was initiated, with the introduction of "new classes" in a few pilot schools. These classes were kept small, a maximum of fifteen students per teacher. Their school day was lengthened to allow for special periods of "supervised group activity." However, only some 25,000 of the 850,000 French children attending secondary schools have been enrolled in these new classes. The shortage of teachers and schoolhouses and the still-rising school population make it highly unlikely that the pilot classes can, in the near future, become standard practice.

Yet a reorientation of method is urgently needed. If it is true that the gene of individualism is passed on through the mainstream of French history, then it is the schools which are the carriers of the gene. It is in the schools that the individualistic, anarchistic Frenchman is molded.

This observer is not alone in thinking so. Authoritative voices are being raised inside France condemning traditional educational methods and preaching the "new" doctrine of education for citizenship. No less a personality than M. Brunold, director of secondary education at the Ministry of National Education, raised this issue in 1954. He sent a directive to all the school principals of France, urging them to develop school projects that would encourage team work and the "communal spirit."

His directive stated:

> In general the French are little inclined toward co-operation. . . . It is deplorable to note our failure to develop a community spirit among our youth, whose activities are excessively motivated by selfish individualism. . . .
> We must declare war on the "System D," put an end to this *"débrouillardise"* that is a degrading deformation of the spirit of enterprise and initiative.[1]

Despite all the pressing reforms so urgently needed in France in all fields, I believe that there is no more fundamentally important project than this basic change in educational psychology recommended by M. Brunold. A thorough reorientation of basic attitudes is needed to provide the nation with workers and leaders who feel themselves to be members of a community. There are new, fertile fields of school children in renascent France today. The teachers who cultivate this

[1] *Le Figaro*, February 8, 1954.

rich human loam can produce the same old crop of self-seeking individualists or develop a new species of public-spirited citizens. Until the seeds of civic consciousness are planted in the schools France is destined to live in continual crisis and disorder. Education for citizenship will not necessarily end crises due to economic or diplomatic conflicts but it can make a big difference in the manner in which these conflicts are resolved.

ᏬᏬ

The French are, of course, aware of the deterioration in public manners and morals and of the strain on the national fabric. They are, at the same time, genuinely mistrustful of collectivism. They regard the free development of man's spirit as their most precious heritage even though it may also be an impediment to their material progress. If they had to choose between spiritual and material progress I believe they would choose the spirit. But do they have to choose? Is there no middle way between soulless collectivism and untrammeled individualism? Is the price of progress necessarily the dominance of the machine over man, the subservience of the individual to the community, the citizen to the State? These are questions that concern all men everywhere who cherish freedom. It is in France that these questions are most insistently asked, for France is the last bastion of the rugged individualist.

The French fortress of individualism has already been invaded, however. France does not live in a vacuum and even if the French resisted change at home they could not stop the world from changing. The revolutions of the colonial peoples, the emergence of Russia as a world power, the decline of Europe and its dependence on another new world power, the United States, all these changes of the past decade have shaken France and are forcing the French to face the realities of a changing world. All of the traditional bases of French imperial and foreign policy have been destroyed. Individualism is now a luxury that the French can no longer afford, at least not the unlimited individualism of the past. Whether they like it or not—and they dislike it intensely—the French of this generation are faced with the greatest challenge to their civilization and way of life in the long history of their country. Their success or failure in meeting this challenge remains in doubt. Whatever happens, however, one outcome is already certain: the traditional individualism of France will die in the process.

The France of the pharmacist who did not want to be big, the France of the Gnips, of the bakers and the thousands of little candlestick makers, this France is dying out, or, if this France is not dying, then France herself may be. The France of tomorrow, to survive as a strong, healthy nation, must be the France of Eve and Irène Curie, of Jean Monnet and Etienne Hirsch, of atomic scientist Francis Perrin and Productivity Commissioner Gabriel Ardant. It would, however, be a tragedy for all the world, as well as for France, if there were no room in the new France for men like Roger the Frog or the taxicab driver who trusted his God-given brains more than the signals of an automatic lamp. A world without these men would not be a pleasant world.

The France of the future need not exclude such men. Individualism is not a negative force only. Indeed a community is no stronger than the strength of its individual members, providing that their individualism is not exclusively self-seeking. If ever there were a time in French history when the nation needed selfless patriotism, courage and ingenuity it is certainly in these troubled times.

☙

Our study thus far has been, in effect, a report on the private life of a person named France. It is now time to follow the adventures of this extraordinary person through one of the most exciting and perilous chapters of French history: a trip around the world, from Dien Bien Phu to the mountains of the Rif, through the djebels of the Atlas and deep into the interior of Africa. There is no more action-packed and tragic story in the long history of France than the record of the Fourth Republic's global adventures in the past decade. It is the story of France's attempt to convert the old Empire into a new Union of overseas peoples, and to find France's new place in the postwar world. The crisis of the French Union, more than any single issue, has influenced and shaped the life of the Fourth Republic. The decline or recovery of France depends upon the outcome of that crisis.

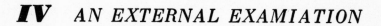

IV *AN EXTERNAL EXAMIATION*

13   *The Dream of l'Union*

Française

A martial roll of the drums announced the arrival of the President
at the gates of the Palace of Versailles. The President entered the
hallowed halls with a slow step and a solemn mien. He had come
to say farewell to the delegates of the French Union, the new
"commonwealth" of Overseas France that had replaced the prewar
Empire.

Seven years had passed since Vincent Auriol had been elected
first magistrate of the world's second largest commonwealth. His term
of office had come to an end. It was January 1, 1954 and the drums
were rolling for the last time at Versailles to honor the "Father of
the French Union." Auriol seemed hardly conscious of what was
happening. He walked like a man in a dream.

"Yes, I have been dreaming," President Auriol told the delegates.
"The dream came to me in London when I went there for the
coronation of Elizabeth. What a magnificent sight that was! People
and sovereigns from every corner of the globe had come to pay their
respects to the Queen. There I saw the British Commonwealth in all
its glory. I came home thinking about that spectacle. Then I had a
dream, a dream that the same glory, the same grandeur had come to
Paris."

It was the Fourteenth of July in Auriol's dream and the traditional
Bastille Day military parade was forming up for the march down
the Champs Elysées and through the capitol. All Paris was dancing
in the streets. Celebrating with the Parisians were their brothers
from Overseas France. Tall, strong Berbers from the Atlas Mountains of Morocco waltzed across the cobblestones with petites
Parisiennes. Burnoosed Tunisians sipped mint tea with blue-denimed
Paris workers. Vietnamese and Sudanese, Malagasy and Martiniquais,

213

men from every corner of the old Empire, men of every color, race and creed had come to fete France's Independence Day, for they were free and equal partners in l'Union Française, a world-wide brotherhood of one hundred million Frenchmen.

His voice heavy with emotion, President Auriol concluded: "This dream was not realized in my term of office. I leave it, however, as a legacy for my successor, President René Coty. I hope that someday soon you will all see this dream become a reality."

Rarely has a dream been so wild a fantasy as this dream of Auriol's. The day he put his dream into words a bitter war was being fought in the rice fields of Tonkin. In Morocco, Arabs and Frenchmen were not celebrating the New Year; they were shooting each other down from speeding cars, with machine guns spitting hate and death. Burnoosed Tunisians were not sipping mint tea at French cafés. They were hiding on rooftops and tossing over grenades on the French below.

Before 1954 was out, Auriol's successor, President Coty, had been forced to accept the loss of some thirteen million "brothers" in the partition of Vietnam at the Geneva Conference. And a month before Christmas, 1954, a new revolt erupted in the Aurès Mountains of Algeria. Auriol's dream was not only a fantasy. It had become a nightmare.

What had turned the dream into a nightmare? Would the nightmare ever end? If not, what would become of France, shorn of her overseas territories, reduced to the status of a small European state?

❧

The story begins with the fall of France.

The tall, stiff-backed General stalked into the studios of the BBC, grim-faced but exalted with confidence and courage. It was June 18, 1940 and France had fallen. Charles de Gaulle never doubted for a moment that France would rise again, providing that Frenchmen did not lose heart. His first thoughts in those dark moments were for the Empire, whose resources, he sensed, could help keep France free and fighting. De Gaulle's deep, solemn voice rang out with self-assurance: "Believe what I tell you, for I know of what I speak, and I say that nothing is lost for France."

Then like a priest chanting a litany, he intoned these words: "For France is not alone. She is not alone. She is not alone. She has a vast Empire behind her."

The Empire was indeed vast, the second largest in the world. The tricolor of France flew over four and a half million square miles of lands, rich in minerals and men for the liberation armies de Gaulle was calling to his banner. The island of Madagascar alone was bigger than the motherland of France. The colonies of Equatorial and West Africa together were as large as the United States of America.

One of the world's biggest sources of aluminum had been found in Conakry, French Guinea, in West Africa. In Mauritania the French could draw upon one hundred million tons of iron ore and geologists had located deep veins of copper, a metal missing from the motherland. Across the Atlantic in South America the French had not even started to mine a deposit of forty million tons of bauxite. Halfway around the world, in Indochina, the French controlled extensive rubber plantations and rice fields. The Empire abounded in tungsten, antimony, coal, iron, cobalt, molybdenum, zinc and manganese. There was also great promise of oil in the Sahara.

Most of these treasures were virtually untapped at the time that de Gaulle reminded his compatriots that France had a vast Empire. French colonists had not been industrial-minded, nor had French industry developed a mass-production system requiring a full exploitation of the Empire's resources. They had only scratched the surface of the fertile imperial soil. Instead of mining the bauxite deposits in Guiana they had built a penal colony there, the dread Devil's Island of Cayenne. The "vast Empire" evoked by de Gaulle was largely a mass of uncharted jungle and savanna. Yet the image of a vast Empire was reassuring and brought an immediate, positive response.

The first response to de Gaulle's appeal of June 18 came on June 20, from the Pacific, when New Hebrides joined "La France Libre." A month later de Gaulle knew that his crusade was well launched when the Cross of Lorraine was hoisted over the Chad, in Equatorial Africa, by its Paris-educated Negro Governor, Félix Eboué. This was stirring news, for Africa had to be the base of operations for the campaign

of liberation and the greatest reassurance, or so it seemed then, was
to learn that Africa had been rallied to the colors by a Negro
leader.

The French Army of Liberation formed its ranks in the Chad, for
the march north to the Mediterranean, under the command of a
general named Jean de Hautecloque. The General soon changed
his name to protect his family, which was still living under the
German occupation. He called himself Leclerc.

General Leclerc mobilized the first Free French units and blooded
them in combat against the Italian Fascist troops in Libya. Men
from those first Chad legions marched with Leclerc to make junction
with the Allied forces that landed in North Africa in 1942. Many
Chad veterans were still with him when his Second Armored Division
won the greatest honor of the war for Frenchmen. They spearheaded
the liberation of Paris.

France, demonstrably, was not alone.

∽

A great change had taken place however. The very fact that the
Empire had saved France meant the end of the Empire. You cannot
refuse freedom to a people who fought to help you regain your own.
De Gaulle knew that, although he never accepted the full consequences of the changed relationship between France and the
colonies. In 1944 he granted French citizenship to sixty thousand
Algerians who had fought in the French armed forces. But that was
only a half-measure, understood as such by the Algerians, and the
other colonial peoples. They sat and watched sullenly, then with
open anger, as the same old colonial system was put back in place
by the liberated French.

Frenchmen still owned the best lands in 1945. Frenchmen still
had the best jobs. And when an African was given the same job as a
Frenchman he was paid only half as much. Colonial students, trained
in the great schools of France, came home to find a color line they
had never seen in Paris. A Moroccan engineer was offered a job as
a bus conductor. A Tunisian lawyer could become only an office
boy or a clerk in a French office. French officials came back to
organize a Central Exchange and the currency became French. Black

market operators made fortunes trading piasters in Saigon. Vietnamese doctors could not get foreign exchange to buy drugs.

Resentment broke out into open revolt in the Constantine Department of Algeria on May 8, 1945, V-E Day. Bloody rioting there marred the celebration of victory in Europe. France, indeed, was not alone. France had a tiger by the tail.

In the summer of 1945, to meet the new challenge, de Gaulle proposed that all the overseas territories elect deputies to the Constituent Assembly that was to draft the charter of a new French Republic. Perhaps the strongest impulse for a new deal in the colonies came from the Resistance parties of France, the Communists, Socialists and Catholics, who were imbued with idealism and rededicated to the principle of liberty for all peoples. It was this ferment of forces, some negative, some positive, that produced the dream of l'Union Française, the dream of converting the old Empire. The magic word was "Union."

The term, Union Française, coined by de Gaulle's Minister of Colonies Paul Giacobbi, became a patriotic slogan. It was simple, clear and inspiring. Everyone understood what union meant and no reasonable man could decry it. The fact that no one, including Giacobbi himself, had any concrete plans for the nature, form and functions of such a French Union, was, to Paris politicians, the greatest virtue of the concept, for it permitted many interpretations, satisfying all factions. For the Left the key word was "Union." For the Right it was "Française." This was, of course, its greatest failing, for if everyone understood what union meant, it also meant different things to different people and had to result in conflict.

To colonial leaders, l'Union Française meant an association of free and independent states, equal in rights and bound together in a federal union, whose strongest, but not ruling, member was France. To most Frenchmen, Union Française meant an association of unequal states, since only the wildest-eyed visionary could argue that Togoland was the equivalent of France. The French Communists opposed any ties between France and the colonies. The Catholics, on the other hand, were dedicated to a new crusade, and their leaders, such as former history teacher Georges Bidault, regarded the Union as a means of assuring the grandeur of imperial France.

In months of debates these conflicting views produced a constitutional monstrosity of face-saving compromises and self-canceling clauses. Rights and liberties granted by one clause of the French Constitution were taken away by another. Article 80, for example, asserts that all overseas nationals enjoy French citizenship but it goes on to state that "special laws" shall determine the conditions under which they may exercise their citizenship rights. In American terms this is a poll-tax escape clause. The French, who pride themselves on their racial tolerance and are always critical of the American disenfranchisement of the Southern Negro, practice the same policy in their colonies, and, even worse, have written discrimination into their Constitution.

Similar discriminatory provisions are found in Article 75 which says that countries in the category of "Overseas Territories," which are, in principle, a part of the French Republic, are "liable to evolve" to full departmental status one day. However, no specific timetable for such an evolution is provided. On the contrary, Article 75 explicitly states that any change of status "can only be brought about by a law voted by Parliament." Dress it up as one may, it still remains that the territories are colonies and will remain so until the *French* deputies decide *unilaterally* that the colonials are ready for full and equal citizenship.

The most flagrant violation of the principle of union is seen in the contrast between the preamble of the Constitution and Article 62, the most controversial of all the union clauses. The preamble states that the "French Union" is composed of nations and people who "pool *or co-ordinate* their resources" for mutual security and prosperity. Article 62, however, obliges the "members of the French Union to pool all the means at their disposal to guarantee the protection of the whole of the Union." Article 62 deliberately omits the two key words of the preamble: "*or co-ordinate.*" There is an enormous difference between a voluntary choice of pooling or *co-ordinating* resources and an automatic obligation to "pool all the means" a nation possesses. Article 62 in effect gives the president of the French Republic a constitutional right to raise troops, levy taxes, requisition crops, in fact simply take over any member country at will.

Paul Mus, one of France's leading historians, has written that

Article 62 was put in at "the insistence of Alexandre Varenne," a former French governor general of Indochina.[1] He quoted a Vietnamese official as telling him, after reading the Constitution, "This isn't a link, it's a noose."

෧ඐ

Political practice was as far removed from equality as was constitutional law. The overseas territories sent representatives both to the Union Assembly and the French National Assembly, but in neither case in proportion to population. Out of a total of 627 deputies in the National Assembly 544 are representatives from metropolitan France, leaving only 83 seats for the overseas representatives. Yet 60 per cent of the population of the French Union is overseas. The overseas area sends one deputy to Paris for every 800,000 inhabitants whereas the metropolitan average is one for 75,000.

These injustices and inequalities are largely a result of the French trying to reconcile the irreconcilable. France could not possibly allot parliamentary seats on a proportional basis, for the differences of civilization and culture among the territories of the Union and between the overseas and Continental peoples are too great, too varied to be resolved equitably in one formal structure. But if this is true then it is nonsense to talk of a "Union of one hundred million Frenchmen." The French with their usual passion for abstract idealism and for statute law denied themselves the easy flexibility of the British practical common-law approach. The British, in addition to being imperialist, are also empirical, which is a method highly compatible with co-ordinating the ill-assorted territories of a global commonwealth. Anyone present in London in June, 1953 saw, as President Auriol did, the triumph of British empiricism in the parade of colonial peoples from all over the world who came to pay homage to Queen Elizabeth.

I watched that symbolic pageant from the reporters' booth high on the scaffolding opposite Westminster Abbey. The highlight was the appearance in the parade of Jawaharlal Nehru, Prime Minister of a country that had remained in the Commonwealth only on condition that it did not have to recognize the sovereignty of the British Queen.

[1] Paul Mus, *Vietnam: Sociologie d'une Guerre.*

Nehru, paying his respects to a Queen he did not recognize as his sovereign, proved by that act the unifying force in the principle of "free consent." He came because he did not have to come. It was evidence that a commonwealth could exist without a rigid, formal constitution, whereas a union was not automatically created with one.

Auriol's dream of a similar pageant in Paris was unreal because it contained only the externals and not the inner wisdom of the British Commonwealth. What Auriol failed to point out in his Versailles farewell address was that Nehru was the Premier of a free and independent India, who had come to London voluntarily, whereas men like Ho Chi Minh, Nehru's neighbor in Indochina, were not celebrating in Paris because they were fighting a war of independence against a France that was trying to perpetuate the past.

It took the French a long time to admit that the French Union, as originally conceived, was dead. By 1956, however, it could no longer be denied that radical revision of the Constitution was needed to take account of a new situation. Vietnam, partitioned at the Sixteenth Parallel, had broken all ties with France. Newly independent Morocco and Tunisia, no longer "protectorates," were negotiating a new status, based on the principle of "independence in interdependence," without a reference to Title VIII of the French Constitution. Everywhere throughout the socalled "Union Française" rapid, dynamic change was in progress, the same change that had shaken the British and Dutch empires. The French were the last of the imperial powers to recognize the end of an era.

It was a bitter end for France because of the very great contribution that France had made to the welfare of the colonial peoples. French aid to the colonies was a relatively greater philanthropic project than American Marshall Plan aid to Europe, for it represented a higher proportion of the French national income and a greater drain on the resources of a war-devastated country, than did the cost of the Marshall Aid to rich America. In 1954 alone the French gave some two hundred million dollars to North Africa at a time when North Africans were assassinating Frenchmen. One French economist told me that five hundred Frenchmen had been killed during the period of the two-hundred-million-dollar grant. In other words, he said bitterly, "We are paying them a reward of four hundred thousand dollars a head for every Frenchman murdered."

The first two modernization plans, for the decade 1947-57, provided more than five billion dollars of economic aid and investment capital for the territories of the French Union. This was one of the most daring gambles that France had ever undertaken, this pouring out of funds for territories that were either in open or potential revolt against France. It was, in its way, a new dream, a much different dream from Auriol's fantasy of one hundred million Frenchmen, for it was based on mutual self-interest, the reality that makes dreams come true.

The newly independent states of Morocco and Tunisia need investment funds. Their own resources in money and technicians are not adequate. Moreover, their leaders are French-educated, French-speaking, and willing to accept help from France. Many are anxious to maintain ties with modern, democratic France rather than backward, feudal Islam or the Communist world.

It is difficult, however, if not impossible, for the overseas peoples to look toward France as their mentor and guide through the early days of independent growth. The passions of past conflicts are not soon forgotten. Many powerful, rich French colonists still live among them and behave as though nothing had changed. The French Army is still based in "independent" Morocco and Tunisia and there are constant clashes between French troops and new native units. In October, 1956, France's Secretary of Defense for Algeria, Max Lejeune, declared that French troops would "protect the lives and property of French citizens resident in Morocco," a declaration resented by Moroccans, who compared it with Hitler's "protection" of the Sudeten Germans in Czechoslovakia. French anxieties about their nationals' security in North Africa are certainly understandable but unilateral declarations such as Lejeune's are incompatible with national independence. The Anglo-French invasion of Egypt on November 6, 1956, then widened the breach between the French and the Arab peoples of North Africa.

Whether or not these conflicts can be resolved, whether a new, real union can be created out of the dream fantasies of the old charter is a highly hypothetical question at this moment. The future looks bleak for the concept of a global French Union in this age of renascent nationalism in the former colonial territories. The future of any nation or community of nations is a product of the past and present, and the history of French colonial relations has not been conducive to the trust and friendship on which union must be built. The ability of the French to salvage something from the liquidation of the old Empire is, therefore, highly dubious. Even if they were to succeed in crushing the Algerian rebellion the hatreds that would be engendered in that bloody repression would not soon be dissipated.

In the past twelve years I have traveled extensively through the French Union, and have seen this hatred in its most destructive fury. I am, thus, not sanguine about the future. I was in Hanoi when Dien Bien Phu fell and I saw the exultation of the people of Vietnam, even of the most staunch anti-Communists, who could not help but cheer the defeat of the colonialist forces. I have ridden in convoys through the Aurès Mountains and watched French Légionnaires "rake out" a native douar with brutality. The faces of their victims still come back to haunt me on sleepless nights. In Morocco, in Tunisia and in Black Africa I have seen the arrogance of the colonial master race and felt myself humiliated by the humiliation of the subject peoples. A hundred Albert Schweitzers could not heal the wounds of those whose souls were lacerated.

The record of the past decade in French Union history is thus not a pleasant story to tell but it is a gripping one and one that must be told, for it illumines the present and foreshadows the future. If the eventual outcome were only the concern of France it would be of little interest except to specialized students of French affairs. Unfortunately, for the rest of the world, anything that happens to France and to the overseas territories is of the greatest concern to all. The war in Indochina became a war of global interest and at the very end almost precipitated the entire world into an atomic war. North Africa is of even greater strategic importance and big-power concern. It is doubtful that France would have invaded Egypt, in defiance of both the United States and the United Nations, if Nasser had not been sending arms to the rebels in Algeria. No nation today can afford to be indifferent to or uninformed on the crisis of the French Union.

It is to those areas of the world, therefore, that we turn now in an examination of the Fourth Republic and the moribund Union Française.

14 End of a Dream
in Indochina

The dream of French Union ended in the tragedy of Indochina. This tragedy was played on a world stage, whose range extended beyond the rice fields of Indochina to Chungking and Moscow and around the globe to the banks of the Seine, the Thames and the Potomac. Much of the tragedy was acted out in the wings of world power politics, hidden from the eyes and ears of the audience. It took ten years for the full tragedy to unfold. Many times during those ten years a happy ending was in sight. That is what makes the story of Indochina a tragedy, for the true tragic element of any story is that it need not have happened.

I was a spectator, and at times a participant, in every major scene of that tragedy, from the fall of 1946, when Ho Chi Minh told me that war was imminent, to the spring of 1954 when I flew over Dien Bien Phu and saw the flames of revolution engulf the last bastion of French power. I cannot, therefore, pretend that this report will be detached or fully objective. It is difficult to achieve complete objectivity about a human tragedy through which the writer has himself lived and in which his own country's security was seriously threatened. Indeed, for one terrible moment the entire world teetered on the brink of atomic war on the rim of the hills of Dien Bien Phu. Such a story cannot be told with detachment. It will, I hope, be told without conscious prejudice or passion.

ᴄᴛᴐ

Prologue: The stage is set.
The Time: August 16, 1945, to September 16, 1946.

No one day, no one event can be said to be the exact time and cause of a great war. Yet there is in every war one critical moment, when peace is hanging in the balance, when the clouds of war are gathering, one day, or week, or month whose events symbolize and heighten all the elements of the drama.

Such a day was August 16, 1945, the day after the Japanese surrender to the Allied powers.

The events of that day took place in widely separated places: in the delta of the Red River in Tonkin; in Paris, Ceylon and in Chungking; finally, in the ancient, imperial capital of Hué, in central Annam. In those places, on that one day, events took place and forces were set in motion that were to decide the fate of Indochina and almost plunge the entire world into atomic war.

In *Tonkin*, on August 16, 1945, Communist underground leader Ho Chi Minh emerged in the open to declare himself President of a "free Vietnam." It was a day of anarchy in the land. The day before, the Japanese had surrendered to the Allies, so their occupation troops in Indochina had no authority. The Allies had not yet been able to send their own occupation forces. The Vichy French administration had been smashed by the Japanese on March 9, so there was a momentary vacuum of authority in Indochina. It was into that vacuum that Ho Chi Minh moved on the sixteenth of August.

His Vietminh "party" emerged from the underground at a carefully staged public meeting of the "People's National Liberation Committee." The Committee acclaimed Ho Chi Minh as "President" and exhorted him to lead the people to "independence and freedom."

In *Paris* on August 16, 1945, another principal actor was cast for his future role in the tragedy, when Admiral Georges Thierry d'Argenlieu was appointed by General de Gaulle as "High Commissioner for Indochina," with instructions to re-establish French sovereignty there. D'Argenlieu had been one of de Gaulle's earliest "*compagnons*" in the Free French days. He had come out of a monastery, to which he had retired after the First World War. A Carmelite monk, whose name in the order was Père Louis de la Trinité, d'Argenlieu was a warrior-priest, a throwback to the medieval crusaders of Cluny. The reconquest of Indochina was a crusade for d'Argenlieu and he was to fight it with religious fervor.

In *Ceylon* on August 16, one of France's most illustrious soldiers, General Leclerc, straining to get to Indochina before Ho Chi Minh could consolidate the revolution, pleaded with Allied Supreme Commander Vice-Admiral Lord Mountbatten to send occupation troops in all haste to "preserve law and order." Mountbatten understood the urgency and sympathized with Leclerc's argument but he did not have the troops, shipping or planes available.

In *Kunming*, on August 16, 1945, Jean Sainteny, who had been named France's Commissioner for North Indochina, pleaded with Chinese and American officials to provide transport for himself and for the five thousand French troops, under the command of General Alessandri who had been in China since escaping from Tonkin after the Japanese coup in March. The Chinese refused to provide troop transport. They had plans of their own for Indochina.

In *Chungking*, on August 16, 1945, French diplomats tried to buy Chinese support by concluding a treaty that returned to China the prewar leased territory of Kwangchowan, along with other important economic concessions. The Chinese accepted the bribe willingly enough and Chiang Kai-shek publicly disavowed any Chinese ambitions to claims to Indochina, but he said nothing and did nothing about supporting French claims there.

In *the imperial palace of Hué*, on August 16, 1945, Emperor Bao Dai took a decision that greatly strengthened the claims of Ho Chi Minh. Bao Dai had been watching events anxiously all day, getting hourly messages from his agents, who reported wild public acclaim for the "Independence Army." He promptly sent an imperial delegate to Hanoi to invite Ho Chi Minh to form a new imperial cabinet. As proof of his nationalist ardor the Emperor also sent a telegram to Premier de Gaulle in Paris, warning him: "Even if you come to re-establish a French administration, it will no longer be obeyed. Each village will be a nest of resistance. Your officials, your colonists, will themselves ask to leave an atmosphere in which they will be unable to breathe."

If each of the separate moves made on August 16, 1945 were to be pursued without change, the result could only be catastrophe, for the forces they set in motion were irreconcilable.

On August 26, Ho Chi Minh won an important victory. Emperor Bao Dai recognized the Revolution and abdicated his throne, renouncing his dynastic name and assuming the role of plain citizen Vinh Thuy, his birth name. President Ho promptly appointed Citizen Vinh Thuy "Supreme Adviser" to the Liberation Committee and announced that on September 2 he would proclaim the independence of the Democratic Republic of Vietnam. He was moving swiftly to win popular support and international recognition.

On September 2, Ho Chi Minh appeared before a mass meeting at Hanoi and read to the people the Declaration of Independence. It began with these words: "We hold these truths to be self-evident. That all men are created equal, that they are endowed by their Creator with certain inalienable rights, and that among these are Life, Liberty and the Pursuit of Happiness."

He concluded: "Vietnam has the right to be free and independent and, in fact, has become free and independent. The people of Vietnam have decided to mobilize all their spiritual and material forces and to sacrifice their lives and property in order to safeguard their right to liberty and independence."

As Ho spoke, two American planes flew low over the city and over the crowd, their stars clearly visible. The people cheered and cheered the planes of their "American allies." Watching the demonstration from a window overlooking the scene, frustrated and helpless to stop the march of events, was Jean Sainteny, Commissioner of France, who had succeeded in making his way from China, only to end up under virtual house arrest in the palace of the Governor General from which France had once ruled Indochina.[1]

Sainteny was furious at the appearance of the American planes and at Ho's clear bid for American support. He felt that Ho's opening words were a cynical travesty of the American Declaration of Independence, chosen for propaganda purposes, but he also sensed the determination and realism of the closing words. The threat to fight to the death was not propaganda. It was only a matter of time before French troops would arrive and the threat would be put to the test.

[1] See Sainteny's book, *Histoire d'une Paix Manquée*. (Paris, 1954) for his full report on these crucial early moves.

The test was not long in coming, for the prologue to the tragedy was now complete. The scene was set, the principal actors in place, or in the wings, waiting for their cues. The curtain was ready to rise on Act I, the Colonial War of Reconquest.

ͼ੪ͽ

Act I: The Colonial War.
The Time: October, 1945.
Scene 1: South of the Sixteenth Parallel.

On October 5, 1945, General Leclerc, hero of the march from the Chad, marched into Saigon.

His troops had finally arrived by sea from Marseilles. The British Occupation Commander, General Douglas Gracey, was happy to have French reinforcements for his lone Anglo-Indian Division. He allowed Leclerc to move into a command position at once, although he was not authorized to do so by Supreme Headquarters. Four days later, however, both Gracey and Leclerc had Allied diplomatic sanction for their actions, when the British Government signed an agreement with the French, recognizing their jurisdiction south of the Sixteenth Parallel and promising to help France transport more troops to Saigon. Encouraged by the news from London, the French immediately launched their offensive to reconquer Indochina.

On October 10, French and Anglo-Indian troops marched into Pnom-Penh, capital of Cambodia. General Leclerc promptly arrested the Cambodian Premier, who had declared independence for his country a month before, and shipped him off to France to be tried as a "collaborator of the enemy."

Leclerc kept the operation going under the guise of a minor series of "mop-ups" of bandits and outlaws. It was, in fact, not a mopping-up nor a police operation. It was a full-scale offensive of reconquest of all the territory below the Sixteenth Parallel and the brutal repression of all native opposition. By the end of 1945 all south Indochina was solidly in the hands of France again. France had advanced halfway down the road to disaster.

ͼ੪ͽ

Scene 2: North of the Sixteenth Parallel.

A very different course of events had been under way north of
the Sixteenth Parallel, in Tonkin.

The Chinese had arrived there on September 15, just three days
after Gracey and the British had arrived in the south. However,
unlike Gracey, the Chinese commander did not welcome French
military assistance. The first thing he did on arrival was to set his
troops to dismantling all French fortifications in the north, particularly the outposts at Lao Kay and Mon Cay on the Chinese frontier.
The Chinese were going to see to it that the French did not return
to power on their border.

They were, in addition, determined to prevent Ho Chi Minh from
consolidating his power. It did not suit Chiang Kai-shek to have an
independent, above all a Communist, regime to his rear. Thus the
first threads of international power politics were being woven into
the plot early in the first act. The Chinese began immediately to stir
up local opposition to Ho, by financing anti-Communist groups and
fomenting unrest and disorders to weaken Ho and diminish his
prestige.

Ho Chi Minh countered by seeking popular support and moral
sanction by the Allies. On November 11 he dissolved the Communist
party, decreed a ban on opium, alcohol, prostitution and gambling.
He abolished the hated salt tax and head tax. He won the support of
the two million Catholics of the north and, that accomplished, he
set the last, crucial stage of his plan for power into motion. He
proclaimed national elections for Vietnam.

On January 6, 1946, for the first time in Vietnamese history men
and women over the age of eighteen went to the polls to select their
"national" representatives. As expected they voted overwhelmingly for
Vietminh candidates. The election certainly was not "free" or democratic, but it could not be disputed that Ho had won, no matter what
the circumstances.

Ho Chi Minh immediately claimed authority over the entire
country. No Vietnamese leader, Vietminh or otherwise, could tolerate the continued existence of a French colony in the south.

The French colonists and soldiers were equally determined not to
deliver their rich colony to the "rebel gang" in the north. High

Commissioner Thierry d'Argenlieu, the Carmelite monk, saw it as his "sacred duty" to re-establish order, to "liberate" the Vietnamese from their "native tyrants" and to restore the "precious gift" of French culture and civilization.

There was still a chance to prevent tragedy but time was running out rapidly. Soon France would have to decide to fight or to negotiate. If they waited too long after the elections, the whole world would recognize Ho's regime.

ↀ

Scene 3: The Uneasy Truce.

Both sides were weak and knew it. Both wanted to get rid of the Chinese occupant. Both knew they had to come to terms, at least temporarily.

When compromise is to the advantage of both sides, particularly when they have mental reservations about the concessions they would make, then agreement is not hard to achieve.

On March 6, 1946, France and Vietnam signed a "Treaty of Association." France agreed to recognize the Democratic Republic of Vietnam "as a free State, with its own Government, Parliament, Army and Finances." In return Vietnam agreed to become a permanent part of "the Indochinese Federation and the French Union."

Nine days later the French concluded an economic treaty with China, and the Chinese began pulling out of the country. French troops began disembarking at Haiphong, while Ho ordered his chief military lieutenant, Vo Nguyen Giap, to rush the training of his own army.

The two sides were speeding toward a head-on collision like locomotives out of control.

ↀ

Scene 4: Betrayal in Laos.

On March 20, 1946, General Alessandri, who had finally been able to take his troops out of China, marched into Laos to relieve the Chinese occupation forces, which were pulling out as a result of the Chungking agreement.

Laotian nationalists who tried to block the occupation by Alessandri were promptly shot. Village after village was occupied by force as Alessandri pushed his offensive through Laos, through the same villages where, in March, 1945, he had himself fled from the Japanese Army and had been helped by Laotians to escape into China. Alessandri rewarded them by destroying any village that resisted the return of French rule. By August all resistance had collapsed. France was again master of Laos. Soon the French would be so deeply dug in that there would be no easy way out.

ഗ✦ഗ

Scene 5: Stabbed in the Back.

While General Alessandri was marching through neighboring Laos, the Vietnamese, seeing the trap closing, pressed for immediate negotiations to implement the March 6 treaty. A conference was convened in Dalat, on April 18, to consider the issue of Vietnamese diplomatic representation in foreign countries and other treaty clauses.

It was another opportunity for the French to show good faith and offer peace and friendship. It was another failure, for High Commissioner d'Argenlieu had a very personal interpretation of the treaty clauses. For him the word "federation" simply meant French sovereignty over the federated territories. Furthermore, he flatly refused to set a date for holding a promised referendum on territorial unity, arguing that guerrilla fighting made it impossible to hold a valid referendum.

The Vietnamese decided that there was only one hope left, one chance to establish their national sovereignty, and that was to go to Paris to appeal for justice and respect for treaty pledges. They still had faith in France and counted, above all, on the Communist and Socialist deputies in the National Assembly to defend the cause of independence for the colonial peoples.

It was a serious miscalculation.

The French Socialist party had just suffered a serious setback in the national elections in June, whereas the Communists, who were then in the government, were trying to show the people how patriotic they were. Neither party was in a mood or position to support Vietnamese nationalism. Thus, instead of going over d'Argenlieu's head, the Vietnamese gave him an opportunity to stab them in the back.

On June 1, just a few days after Ho Chi Minh had set sail for Paris, Commissioner d'Argenlieu engineered an audacious coup.

D'Argenlieu hastily set up a "free Republic of Cochinchina," putting at the head two local politicians, who were also French citizens, Dr. Nguyen Van Thinh and Nguyen Van Xuan. Xuan was, at the time, a colonel in the French Army. The scheme was to present both Ho Chi Minh and the French Government in Paris with a *fait accompli*, for if there were a free Republic of Cochinchina there could be no question of holding a referendum on territorial unity. D'Argenlieu, of course, had absolutely no authority to recognize a Cochinchese Republic even if it had been legitimate, let alone a puppet fashioned by him. He used as his pretext the argument that the Cochinchinese people feared "Vietnamese imperialism." It was the duty of France, reporters were told, to protect the people of the south from the aggressive designs of the north.

This pretext also served d'Argenlieu for a second coup. While French and Vietnamese delegates were deep in negotiations at Fontainebleau, outside Paris, Admiral d'Argenlieu arbitrarily convoked another conference of his own, back in Indochina, at Dalat, August 1. Not only did he summon delegates from the phony Republic of Cochinchina, but this time he went further than anyone would have dreamed. He invited delegates from "Southern Annam." That was really a stroke of genius, for, in point of fact, there was no such place as "Southern Annam," in the political sense of the term. D'Argenlieu had simply carved another chunk out of the body of Indochina.

D' Argenlieu's coup broke up the Fontainebleau Conference. Disillusioned and bitter men, the Vietnamese delegates left Paris. They felt that the French Government was either unwilling or unable to control its proconsuls.

Only one man stayed behind to salvage something from the wreckage of Fontainebleau: Ho Chi Minh. He went to see Jean Sainteny, who had come to Paris with him, and pleaded with him to urge his government to some face-saving gesture. Sainteny, in his memoirs on Indochina, quoted Ho as saying to him and to the Minister for Overseas France, Marius Moutet: "Do not leave me like this. Give me some weapon against the extremists. You will not regret it."

Nothing was offered to Ho but vague promises.

Ho Chi Minh left Paris never to return again, for he knew then that he would shortly be leading his people in war against the French. That is what he told me on September 11, 1946, shortly before he departed. It was the most extraordinary interview I have ever had in my career as a foreign correspondent. It lasted four hours, as he analyzed in geat detail all the issues of the conflict, and then, to my astonishment, forecast the future, predicting the early outbreak of war, describing how it would be fought and how it would end.

ᲮᏯᎧ

Scene 6: The Tiger and the Elephant.

Ho came into the room dressed in the plain, high-collared tunic popularized at the time by Stalin and Chiang Kai-shek. He wore no decorations, no insignia of any kind. A small, thin Oriental, Ho had large, burning eyes, under a high brow that dominated a narrow face, made even narrower by a long, wispy beard that descended from the point of his chin.

The interview began pleasantly but not very promisingly. He parried my questions with a smile and a quip at the start. When I asked him to tell me why he thought he had won so great a majority in the elections, he laughed and stroked his chin whisker: "My people like me because I have a long beard. It is very rare for an Annamite and is a sign of venerable age and wisdom."

When I asked him about his background, where he had come from in his youth, Ho said, "Who knows who a man is? Does a man himself really know? His mother and father give him his name and tell him where he came from. This is of no importance. What is more important is to know where he is going."

I took the cue to ask Ho where he and his government were going, whether he would create a Communist state in Vietnam. Ho smiled again, waved his hand and said: "Communism takes different forms in different countries, as does capitalism. Our circumstances are very special in Vietnam. For example, if I wanted to create a Communist state, I would certainly nationalize the banks. Well, we hardly have any banks at all in Vietnam. We must first create wealth in our country before we can share it." I pressed the point, asking him to confirm the fact that he himself was a Communist and a graduate of the Moscow school of revolution. He laughed at the question: "I learned about revolution not in Moscow but right here in Paris, capital of Liberty, Equality and Fraternity."

It was only after several rounds of small talk that Ho finally stopped sparring and came to the point, and I learned why he had taken the trouble to spend an evening with an American correspondent. Here, from the notes I wrote that night, is a transcript of the interview:

"Your country," said Ho, "can play a vital role for peace in southeast Asia. America is loved by our people. The memory of Roosevelt is still strong. You never had an empire, never exploited the Asian peoples. The example you set in the Philippines was an inspiration to all of us. Your ties with France are strong and durable and you have great influence in this country. I urge you to report to your people the need there is now to swing the balance toward peace and independence before it is too late for all of us. Do not be blinded by this issue of Communism."

I protested that the Communist issue was an important one in America, that our people did not think Communism was compatible with freedom and would hesitate before straining our relations with France, with whom we shared common ideals, by giving support to a revolutionary government about which we knew so little.

Ho Chi Minh nodded understanding of this attitude but went on to say: "My people hunger for independence and will have it. If men you call Communists are the only men who lead the fight for independence, then Vietnam will be Communist. Independence is the motivating force, not Communism. The Communists are a small minority in our country. The strongest political element is nationalist. On the issue of independence and the unity of North and South we are all in agreement, Communists, Catholics, Republicans, peasants, workers. If we must, we will fight together for those aims."

I promptly picked up his lead and asked whether he thought he would have to fight.

This was his astonishing reply:

"Yes, we will have to fight. The French have signed a treaty and they wave flags for me, but it is a masquerade. We do not have the true attributes of independence: our own customs control, our own diplomatic representatives abroad, our own currency. Our country is truncated. They have set up puppet, separatist regimes in the south. Yes, I fear that in the end we will be forced to fight!"

I expressed my surprise: "But, President Ho, that is extraordinary. How can you hope to be able to wage war against the French? You have no army, you have no modern weapons. Why, such a war would seem hopeless for you!"

"No, it would not be hopeless. It would be hard, desperate, but we could win. We have a weapon every bit as powerful as the most modern cannon: nationalism! Do not underestimate its power. You Americans above all ought to remember that a ragged band of bare-footed farmers defeated the pride of Europe's best-armed professionals."

"But that was in 1776!" I countered. "The weapons of war and the organization for a modern war have advanced so that I would seriously doubt that a ragged band of farmers could do the same again. There were no planes then, no napalm bombs, no radio communications. . . ."

"They can be procured if they must be," said he, waving my argument aside. "And are you forgetting some recent examples of what ragged bands can do against modern troops? Have you already forgotten the heroism of the Yugoslav partisans against the Germans? The spirit of man is more powerful than his own machines. And we have other weapons that are most effective against machines. We have swamps that are better than antitank guns. We have thick jungles that planes cannot fly through and where the trees are a shield against fire bombs. We have mountains and caves where one man can hold off a hundred, and we have millions of straw huts that are ready-made Trojan horses in the rear of any invading army."

"Then it will be a guerrilla war?" I asked. "A war of harassment and attrition?"

"It will be a war between an elephant and a tiger," Ho replied. "If the tiger ever stands still the elephant will crush him with his mighty tusks. But the tiger does not stand still. He lurks in the jungle by day and emerges by night. He will leap upon the back of the elephant, tearing huge chunks from his hide, and then he will leap

back into the dark jungle. And slowly the elephant will bleed to
death. That will be the war of Indochina."

Those were the words of Ho Chi Minh on September 11, 1946.
On December 19 the tiger struck.

ᕳᕲ

Scene 7: War!

In French history books it is now written that the war in Indochina broke out on December 19, 1946, when the Vietnamese Army
deliberately attacked the French in Hanoi. The facts are correct as
far as they go. The Vietnamese did attack on that day and knew it
was an overt act of war. December 19, however, was not in reality
the beginning of the war in Indochina. The first shots had been fired
a month earlier in the "Haiphong incident." The trouble began on
September 10, while Ho Chi Minh was still in Paris. On that day
French General Morlière moved his troops into the customs shed
at Haiphong harbor in violation of the March 6 treaty. There had
been sporadic trouble in Haiphong harbor for some days. Vietnamese
guards on shore had fired at a French patrol boat, which was inter-
cepting a Chinese contraband junk. French soldiers from a near-by
garrison came running to the harbor and a fight broke out between
the two groups. Fighting continued in Haiphong for two days between
French and Vietnamese armed forces, while government and military
officials tried to restore order.

Admiral d'Argenlieu, in Paris at that time, was getting daily reports
of the fighting. When he heard of the Haiphong incident he went
promptly to see Premier Georges Bidault and urged him to authorize
strong action "to teach the Vietnamese a lesson." Bidault agreed that
a lesson was called for and when d'Argenlieu specifically asked,
"Even going so far as using cannons?" Bidault replied, "Even that."[2]
That was all d'Argenlieu had to hear. He immediately wired to
General Valluy at his headquarters in Saigon and Valluy relayed
the order to Morlière. General Morlière messaged back that the
fighting was already over and that order had been re-established in
Haiphong. Valluy ignored Morlière's reply and telegraphed directly
to the commander of French troops in Haiphong itself, Colonel

[2] Ellen J. Hammer, *The Struggle for Indochina*, pages 183-85.

Debès, ordering him to take firm action against those who "had treacherously attacked you." The order instructed Debès to "make yourself complete master of Haiphong."

The Colonel immediately sent an ultimatum to the Vietnamese to evacuate the port and the French section of the city in two hours' time. When the Vietnamese did not reply, Colonel Debès ordered all the batteries of the army and the big guns of the navy cruiser *Suffren* to shell the Vietnamese positions. The shells tore into Haiphong without warning and with terrible force. In a few minutes the Vietnamese quarter of town was completely destroyed. Under the wreckage were thousands of corpses torn to bits. The streets were littered with dead and flames rose over the city. More than six thousand Vietnamese were killed, thousands more injured and homeless.[3] If ever there was a criminal act of war the French bombardment of Haiphong was one.

Morlière later followed up this "lesson" by ordering the Vietnamese to evacuate Haiphong city in addition to the port. The Viet Minh thereupon issued a proclamation to the people to stay calm and united and to be ready for action. The French promptly landed two companies of troops at the naval base in Tourane.

Ho Chi Minh, back in Hanoi by then, sent despatches to Paris warning the government that colonial extremists were violating agreements and dishonoring the name of France. Ho was hopeful of help from Paris, for the Bidault Cabinet had fallen and the new premier was the Socialist statesman Léon Blum who, twenty years before, had befriended Ho Chi Minh, and who all his life had been a champion of democratic freedoms and people's rights. Ho's messages to Blum, however, were held up by French censorship in Hanoi for more than a week and were only delivered to the French Premier after war had broken out.

Tensions mounted in Hanoi as Ho awaited an answer from Blum, not knowing that his message had not even been delivered. Vietnamese extremists in the Vietminh pressed him to declare war and began to take matters in their own hands. Frenchmen were shot down on the streets of Hanoi. Giap's soldiers began building barricades,

---

[3] Some estimates run as high as ten thousand casualties. I have used the figure of six thousand, admitted by Admiral Battet, as reported by Paul Mus in the paper, *Témoignage Chrétien*, February 10, 1950.

piling sandbags in front of public buildings, putting roadblocks on all important arteries into town. French parachutists moved into Hanoi to take up positions around French installations and they were attacked by snipers and grenade-throwers up on roofs. The French moved in greater forces to occupy all high buildings and wipe out the snipers.

On the morning of December 19 General Morlière sent another demand to Giap that he disband immediately the Vietminh militia of some fifty thousand armed men. This time Giap did not wait for Morlière to turn his demand into an ultimatum.

On the night of the nineteenth, the Vietnamese attacked in force, infantry troops advancing under the cover of an artillery barrage, supported by machine guns and mortars. Sappers blew up French installations, cut power and water lines, drove the French troops out of the Vietnamese Government buildings they had occupied.

General Morlière ordered an immediate counterattack. His forces were much stronger than Giap's, his artillery heavier, and he had planes. There could be no question about who would win the Battle of Hanoi. Ho Chi Minh must have been told by Giap that he would be beaten in a head-on battle. He certainly never intended to fight a pitched battle that early. The situation, however, had gotten out of hand, and extremist elements on both sides were straining at the leash. On the night of December 19 the Vietnamese tiger snapped the leash and clawed the elephant. It was the beginning of a war that was to last almost eight years, the longest war of our times.

The curtain had come down on the first act of the tragedy, the colonial war. The second act, the civil war, was about to begin, after an intermission.

ⵞ

The intermission lasted the full year of 1948, a year of transition.

General Leclerc had undergone a complete reversal of his thinking about Indochina. He had come to the conclusion that France had to come to terms with nationalism in Vietnam, that French sovereignty could not be imposed upon the Vietnamese.[4] Paris politi-

---

[4] In a secret report to the government in the summer of 1947, Leclerc stated that there would be no solution by force in Indochina: "The capital problem from now on is political. It is a question of coming to terms with an awakening xenophobic nationalism." This secret report was revealed by Mendès-France

cians also realized that times had changed and that France could
not fight a frankly colonial war of reconquest in Asia in the year
1947. Some disguise had to be found for colonialism, some answer
to Vietnamese nationalism.

They found the disguise and the answer, they hoped, in the person
of Ex-Emperor Bao Dai.

Bao Dai had not stayed on as Supreme Adviser to Ho Chi Minh
for very long. Early in March, 1946, Ho had asked him to go to
Chungking to try to speed up negotiations for a Chinese withdrawal.
Bao Dai, who had long been awaiting an opportunity to abandon
his role as Citizen Vinh Thuy, jumped at the opportunity and
left immediately.

Bao Dai did not stay in Chungking however. He had no desire to
be a diplomatic agent of Ho Chi Minh. He left very soon for
Hong Kong where he established himself quietly in exile, waiting to
see who could come out on top in his homeland.

During the spring of 1947 both sides began to send emissaries to
see Bao Dai in Hong Kong. Ho sent a well-known nationalist figure,
Ho Dac Lien, to try to persuade Bao Dai to mediate the conflict
with the French and bring peace back to his country. The French
sent, among others, Paul Mus, political adviser to General Leclerc
and a former close friend of Ho Chi Minh.

Admiral d'Argenlieu and his friends were also interested in Bao
Dai and his possible usefulness as a rallying point for anti-Vietminh
nationalists. D'Argenlieu and his advisers had been thinking of using
Bao Dai as a puppet emperor early in 1947. Within only two weeks
of the outbreak of war in Hanoi, d'Argenlieu's political adviser,
Léon Pignon, wrote a policy paper that stated, "Our objective is
clear: to transpose to the field of Vietnamese domestic politics the
quarrel that we have with the Vietminh. . . ."[5]

When the French suggested that he return from exile in Hong
Kong to rally his country's nationalists, Bao Dai agreed that this was
a splendid idea but, he pointed out, in order to rally his nationalists
he would have to champion the cause of nationalism. "What concessions were the French prepared to make for that cause?" Bao Dai

in a speech to the National Assembly on November 22, 1950. It can be found
in the *Journal Officiel* of that date, on page 2044.

[5] Devillers, *Histoire du Vietnam*, Paris, 1952, page 364.

wanted to know. Although a puppet, Bao Dai was not stupid and could drive a hard bargain if he had any cards to play.

The French were prepared to make many concessions to get Bao Dai back. He was their only "front," their only hope to split the nationalists. They were not worried about concessions to him, for after defeating Ho they could take care of Bao Dai. He would not be hard to handle. As they say in French: *"Il y a toujours moyen de s'arranger."* A means of arrangement, moreover, would not be hard to find: Bao Dai needed money and the French were prepared to pay a considerable price for his co-operation.

All through 1948 the bargaining continued. Bao Dai refused to settle for anything less than "unity of the three Kys," the same demand that Ho had made to d'Argenlieu and that had led to the war. He would return as Emperor of all Vietnam—Tonkin, Annam *and* Cochinchina—or he would not return at all. From this position Bao Dai refused to budge.

With the Vietminh getting stronger every month and the colonial war getting more and more unpopular at home and abroad, the French were forced to yield. They gave in to Bao Dai's demands, recognized the reintegration of d'Argenlieu's phony "Republic of Cochinchina" to Vietnam, in a formal treaty signed on March 8, 1949.

The agreement with Bao Dai was hailed as an example of France's generosity and a proof that the war was not a colonial war. It had become, they claimed, a civil war between Vietnamese "democrats" and Vietnamese "Communists." France, as the motherland of the French Union, was said to be merely doing her duty under the terms of the Constitution by coming to the aid of a free Vietnam torn by subversion and rebellion.

The intermission had ended. The curtain was rising on the second act: Civil War.

 measure

Act II: The Civil War.
Time: The year 1949.

Never in history has there been such a "civil war." If the results of the travesty had not been so tragic, the second act would have been a farce.

The new "State of Vietnam" never got into the act at all, in the so-called civil war against the Vietminh. It had neither a constitution, which Bao Dai kept promising but never promulgated, nor an army, which the French kept training but never formed.

Bao Dai's soldiers were recruited by the French and incorporated into the French Expeditionary Corps, commanded by French officers. They wore French uniforms and had the status of "French Union forces." By the end of the war there were some Vietnamese units actually fighting as complete units, but never many of them. The Commander-in-Chief of the "State of Vietnam," General Nguyen Van Hinh, complained to me bitterly in Saigon in April, 1954, at the height of the battle of Dien Bien Phu, that *he had never once been invited to sit in on a general staff meeting*, even as an observer. The majority of the troops in the Expeditionary Corps—by that time some one hundred thousand of them—were Vietnamese, but their General was not consulted on how they were to be used.

However, in the early stages of the civil war there seemed to be no urgent need for a Vietnamese Army. The military situation was relatively stable throughout 1949. The French Expeditionary Corps commanded the main centers of population, its outposts were well dug in throughout the delta and along the Chinese border. The French felt that they could sit tight and let time take its course. The Vietminh, they thought, would eventually tire or be squeezed back to unimportant hill country in the northwest and nationalists would slowly be attracted back by the sight of a free, united Vietnam prospering under French guidance. That was the rosy scenario of the "Bao Dai solution," as the French saw it.

It was never played that way. The nationalists in the Vietminh movement did not rally to Bao Dai. Those outside the Vietminh remained suspicious and neutral. Catholic leader Ngo Dinh Diem refused a Bao Dai offer to be prime minister and said: "The national aspirations of the Vietnamese people will be satisfied only on the day when our nation obtains the same political status which India and Pakistan enjoy."

Independence was still the rallying cry of the nationalists. They recognized the fact that the French had granted unity in theory but they did not trust that unity so long as the French kept the real control of the unified country. At the end of 1949, nine months after the creation of his State of Vietnam, Bao Dai had made little or no headway in the "civil war."

It was at that point, in December, 1949, that an event occurred which was to shake all Asia, and above all Vietnam since it happened on its borders: Red China burst upon the scene with a decisive defeat of Chiang Kai-shek's forces. When Chiang's troops fled the mainland, the Chinese Communist troops raced south to plant their flag on the frontier of Indochina. On the third anniversary of the December 19 attack in Hanoi, Vietnamese and Chinese Communist soldiers met on the international bridge at Mon Cay.

The third war was about to superimpose itself on the other conflicts in Indochina: the Cold War.

ᏻᏯ

Act III: The Cold War.
Time: 1950-1954.
Place: Everywhere.

Nineteen-fifty was the year of the cold war in Indochina, freezing any last hope of a peaceful settlement, if any still existed.

In January the Vietminh announced its recognition of the Communist regime in China and was promptly rewarded by China's return recognition of the "Democratic Republic of Vietnam." The Soviet Union immediately followed suit and even anti-Stalinist but still Communist Marshal Tito of Yugoslavia accorded recognition to Ho Chi Minh.

Until then the United States press and many American public figures had been sympathetic to the Vietminh and supported the "anticolonial war of independence." The State Department, however, supported France and its puppet Bao Dai. Dean Acheson was deeply involved in the policy of building a strong military alliance in Europe to contain Soviet aggression. France was the linchpin of the Western defensive chain. The State Department felt that it had to support France for that reason, despite the anticolonial tradition of the United States.

The perfect justification was found in the Sino-Soviet recognition of Ho Chi Minh. In an official declaration on February 10, 1950, Dean Acheson stated that it shattered "any illusions as to the nationalist nature of Ho Chi Minh's aims and reveals Ho in his true colors as the mortal enemy of native independence in Indochina." That same month the United States formally accorded its own recognition to the so-called "State of Vietnam," that is, the formless regime of Bao Dai. Some thirty other countries followed the United States lead, while a dozen or so followed the Sino-Soviet lead.

The deep freeze of the cold war closed in on Indochina.

United States military aid to France under the North Atlantic Treaty and Mutual Security agreements was then building up rapidly in Europe. At the outset it permitted the French to send more equipment to Indochina, although no direct aid for Indochina had yet been authorized. A mere trickle in 1950, United States aid became a mighty torrent by 1955, growing in volume from $96 million the first year to $800 million in the final year. In all, America poured $3,730 million into French Indochina in financial, military and end-item aid.

The Vietminh watched that torrent grow with dismay and fury. They saw victory being snatched away in the very last moment. They turned in desperation to China for military aid and speeded up the process of eliminating all non-Communist elements from the movement. The most extreme Communist elements had been pressuring Ho Chi Minh for months to tighten up the Nationalist movement. After their 1950 offensive was stopped by French General Jean de Lattre de Tassigny, and American aid increased, the Communists took over the Vietminh completely.

Acheson was proved right in the end. Vietnamese nationalism had become completely perverted by Communism. Ho Chi Minh had been proved right too, for he had predicted to me that if the fight lasted long enough, the whole resistance movement would eventually become Communist. That may have been his objective anyway. I believe it was. Ho was a veteran Communist and Soviet-trained revolutionary, there is no doubt about that. I also believe, however, that he was flexible enough to have tried to create an independent Communist state. Like most Vietnamese, Ho Chi Minh feared the Chinese, even the Communist Chinese, just as Communist Tito feared Soviet Russia. I believe Ho Chi Minh might have become an Asian Tito up to 1950. After 1950 all hope was lost. The curtain ending Act III was an iron one.

From then on all three wars of Indochina, the colonial, civil and cold wars, were fought simultaneously, until they reached a triple climax in the final act of tragedy, at Dien Bien Phu.

ono

Act IV: Climax at Dien Bien Phu.
The Time: May, 1954.

Hardly anyone had ever heard of Dien Bien Phu when the French set up a fortress there in November, 1953. It was an obscure jungle clearing in the Thai country, on the invasion route to Laos. General Henri Navarre, French Commander-in-Chief, set up a roadblock there against a Vietminh push in that direction.

From a tactical point of view it was a very dangerous position to hold, unless you also commanded the heights surrounding it. Dien Bien Phu was at the bottom of a bowl of land, ringed by hills on all sides. For anyone with artillery on the heights it would be like shooting fish in a barrel.

When I asked Navarre in Hanoi, in April, 1954, how he had allowed himself to be caught in this trap, he replied: "When we went into Dien Bien Phu the Viets did not have any artillery and there was no danger from the heights. It was only because the diplomats agreed at the Berlin Conference in February to convene a peace conference later at Geneva, that the Chinese began to send big cannon to Giap. They wanted to go to Geneva in a strong bargaining position. By then it was too late for us to get out."

What an extraordinary admission of lack of foresight by a commander-in-chief! The French had known for months that a big power conference was impending—they had been demanding one themselves—and Navarre had certainly known that the Chinese Communists were supplying the Vietminh. Apparently he simply gambled that the Chinese would not supply heavy artillery.

Dien Bien Phu was the perfect place for General Giap to fight a pitched battle against the French. After seven years of hit-and-run tactics the tiger at last had trapped the elephant in a deep pit and could claw him at will. The gallant defenders of Dien Bien Phu never had a chance. They fought with supreme courage, a do-or-die

defense that will live on in the annals of military history, but all
for nothing. It was a stupid, criminal slaughter of brave men.

An even greater crime was almost committed at the height of
the battle, one that would undoubtedly have plunged the entire
world into a suicidal war. Foreign Minister Bidault called in United
States Ambassador in Paris, Douglas Dillon, on April 3 to request
an American air strike at Dien Bien Phu. Goaded by mounting
criticism at home, alarmed at the prospect of going to Geneva as
the representative of a defeated side, Bidault threw all caution to
the winds in asking for an American air intervention that might well
provoke a mass Chinese invasion of Indochina, and even world war.

Dillon relayed his request and promptly received a negative reply
from Washington on the air strike. Dulles, however, agreed to give
France bombers and also supply transport for a French strike. Dulles
indicated, moreover, that an American air strike might eventually
become possible but only if there were "united action." By that he
meant the creation of a Southeast Asia Treaty Organization—SEATO
—with the British participating.

That seemed to be in the making when Dulles flew to London
and Paris on October 13 and joint communiqués announced that
agreement had been reached on "collective defense" in Asia. An
American intervention seemed imminent on April 16 when Vice-
President Nixon told the American Society of Newspaper Editors,
". . . if, to avoid further Communist expansion in Asia and Indochina, we must take the risk now by putting our boys in, I think the
executive has to take the politically unpopular position and do it."

Dulles was then supposed to meet with the British and French
Ambassadors in Washington on April 20 to start the work of creating
the "united front" that he thought he had created in London. However, just before the meeting was supposed to start, the British
Ambassador telephoned Dulles to inform him that "My government has instructed me not to attend the meeting. The British
Government does not desire such a meeting before the Geneva Conference has had a chance to study most carefully the chances for peace
in Indochina."

Dulles was very angry. He felt betrayed by his closest friend and
ally. There was nothing he could do, however, but put the best face
on it. The order of business of the meeting was immediately changed

from a conference on Indochina to a conference on Korea, and the British Ambassador attended.

British officials told me at the time that Churchill and Eden were also very angry. They had been shocked by Nixon's revelation of American intentions. They claimed that they had not agreed with Dulles to do more than create a SEATO *defense* pact, but not an endorsement of an *offensive* action in Indochina.

Later, Dulles, in a session with Congressional leaders began to backtrack. He said the administration had not intended an intervention in Indochina. He summarized events of the preceding weeks and briefed the Congressmen on the British refusal to proceed with united action before Geneva. Then he flew to Paris for a NATO meeting on the eve of the Geneva Conference.

On his arrival in Paris Dulles was taken aside by Bidault who asked him urgently to reconsider his refusal to order an American air strike at Dien Bien Phu. Dulles called an emergency meeting of his top advisers and sent an urgent signal back to Washington to inform the President. American officials met for four hours. Dulles finally informed Bidault that the United States would still consider only "joint action."[6]

Bidault understood that this was tantamount to an American refusal. He knew the British had already turned down such joint action a week before. He knew the Americans well enough to understand that if they had thought an air strike on Dien Bien Phu feasible or important enough they would have agreed, with or without British approval. Truman had not waited for British approval before intervening in Korea. However, Bidault had no choice left but to go to his British allies and seek their consent. He promptly went to see Eden, who was in Paris for the NATO meeting, and officially requested British intervention at Dien Bien Phu, in the framework of "collective defense." It was April 24 and Giap had already pierced the outer defenses of General de Castries and was closing in on the heart of the encampment.

The next morning, Sunday, the British Cabinet met in extraordinary session. The majority of the cabinet members told Sir Winston that it would be folly to permit an American air strike at Dien

---

[6] I gathered and verified this detailed account in personal talks with Bidault, Dillon, Navarre, and many other informed and responsible officials.

Bien Phu. British military experts thought it could not in any case save the garrison that late in the battle, while it might provoke a Chinese counterattack with the risk of a general war in Asia. Why, they asked, after seven years of war in Indochina, on the very eve of an armistice, should we risk an even worse explosion that might lead to world atomic war? The British reply to Bidault was thus a sharp "No."

The next day, Monday, April 26, the Geneva Conference began. The same day the full details of the rejection by America and Britain of Bidault's request were in the press and on the world's radios. Giap must have heard the news by radio monitor immediately. He certainly stepped up the rate of attack. Assault waves of suicide troops battered down the last defenses of the garrison. On May 7, 1954, exactly nine years to the day that the victorious Allied generals received the unconditional surrender of the Nazis, Dien Bien Phu fell. The final curtain had fallen on the tragedy of Indochina.

৵৵

Epilogue: Geneva and After.

Everything that happened after May 8, 1954 was an anticlimax. Dien Bien Phu had been the end of the trail for France. There was nothing left to be done but to withdraw.

In Paris events moved swiftly to bring about the disengagement.

The Laniel Government was defeated in a vote of confidence and the Assembly turned to the one man who had denounced the Indo-chinese War from the start, Pierre Mendès-France.

Mendès electrified the Assembly and the world with a startling proposal: a thirty-day contract to end the war in Indochina or resign as premier. It was an audacious proposal, designed to impress the Chinese and the Vietminh as much as the French Assembly. He counted on Chinese and Russian fears that America might change its mind and send its atom bombers to Indochina after all.

Mendès won his gamble on the very last day, at the very last minute, of his thirty-day deadline.

The Peace of Geneva was not a brilliant affair for the French or for the Allies but it was much better than anyone had dared hope after the fall of Dien Bien Phu. The Communists got half the

country at the peace table but they had already won it on the battle-
field and were in an excellent position to win more if the war had
continued.

The greatest fear of diplomats at that time was that Mendès
had conceded too much by agreeing to hold elections to unify North
and South Vietnam by July, 1956. It was believed then, with good
reason, that Ho Chi Minh would sweep those elections and get the
whole country.

It did not work out that way.

The July, 1956 deadline passed without the elections being held.
The new Premier of South Vietnam, Ngo Dinh Diem, who had
finally returned home after the fall of the Bao Dai regime, had refused to allow elections to be held, arguing that he had not been a
party to the Geneva Treaty. The Communists did not seem anxious
to push the issue. A new regime was in power in Russia too and a
new phase of world politics was under way. All sides agreed to let
sleeping tigers lie for the moment.

Thus Indochina at the moment of this writing is dormant. Nothing, however, has been solved and trouble may break out at any
time. If it does, it will be the Americans who will be faced with a
new challenge. Indochina is no longer a French responsibility, nor
ever again will be.

ᐇ

The greatest writer of tragedy said that the evil men do lives after
them, while the good is interred with their bones. In the lives of
nations the opposite is often true. The good that France has done
in Indochina will endure. It is only the evil that was interred at
Dien Bien Phu.

The century and a half of French life in Indochina was not a
senseless waste. Only the seven and a half years of a senseless war were
wasted. It will take a long time for the wounds to heal but it would
be a denial of history to assume they never will. Other nations have
fought bitter, cruel wars in the past and then found new ties in new
times. Who would have predicted in 1776 that Britain would become the most trusted ally of the United States? Who would have
believed in 1944 that within ten years France and Germany would
sign a military alliance for the first time in their history? If the

French and the Germans can become brothers-in-arms, anything can happen in history. France will never again be master of Indochina, but there is no irreparable hatred that will separate forever those two peoples who lived together for so long.

That is the key to the future of French-Vietnamese relations and, above all, to the future of those territories of the dream Union over which the French flag still flies. That dream may have been shattered in Indochina but other, more real unions can be constructed. Yes, anything can happen, or almost anything. The one thing that cannot happen is the imposition of French rule by force of arms. The words of General Leclerc written in 1947 are still valid today, a decade later:

"The capital problem from now on is political. It is a question of coming to terms with an awakening xenophobic nationalism, of channeling it in order to safeguard, at least in part, the rights of France."

Every word in that report, save one, is a fundamental truth of contemporary history. The one false note today, as then, was struck by the word "rights." France had no "rights" in Indochina. France had only interests to safeguard. This is the heart of the matter, the original sin that destroyed the many virtues of the colonial era. The French thought that their civilizing mission gave them certain vested rights. They had forgotten the lesson of the great Revolution of the eighteenth century. The only inalienable rights are the Rights of Man, to life, liberty and the pursuit of happiness.

The "rights" of a colonial power are as temporary as the rights of a parent. They end the day the child or ward has reached his majority. The whole purpose of parenthood is to prepare the child one day to leave the home and establish one of his own. That is the day of the successful parent's greatest reward, of the unsuccessful parent's cruelest punishment.

A refusal to accept this fact of life in Indochina shattered the French dream of Union and led directly to the rude awakening in North Africa, where another, and perhaps the greatest tragedy of modern French history, is at this moment approaching its climax.

15 *Nightmares in North Africa*

France is smaller than Texas but larger than the United States.

That is to say, metropolitan France, on the Continent of Europe, is smaller than Texas, a country of only two hundred thousand square miles, whereas Overseas France, in Africa, is a vast land of some four million square miles, extending from the Mediterranean deep into the interior. The French distinguish between two different regions in that huge territory. The Mediterranean lands are called French North Africa; the interior region is called Black Africa.

Frenchmen are lost in the wide spaces of Black Africa, where only seventy-five thousand Frenchmen rule over some thirty million black Africans. In North Africa, however, the French are a large, powerful minority. More than two million Frenchmen live among the twenty-two million Moslem peoples of the three North African countries: Morocco, Algeria and Tunisia.

Algeria, which lies between the other two countries, is the giant of North Africa, sprawling across 850,000 square miles of territory, four times bigger than the motherland. Morocco, on the west, contains some 150,000 square miles for approximately the same population as Algeria, nine and a half to ten millions. Tunisia, on the east, is a tiny country of only 48,000 square miles and less than four million inhabitants.

In the year 1956 Tunisia and Morocco won their independence from France, reducing French North Africa to the single territory of Algeria. And Algeria, in 1956, was in rebellion against French rule, demanding its own independence, with the support and encouragement of its newly liberated neighbors.

The future of North Africa and of Black Africa depends upon the outcome of the struggle for Algeria. Many Frenchmen believe that

249

the fate of the Republic is itself at stake, that France could not survive "an Indochina in Algeria." This is an appropriate analogy, for, although the particular circumstances may be different, the crisis of North Africa had its origins in the tragedy of Indochina.

The war of Indochina was an electric charge that set off the dynamite which had long been stored by the French in North Africa. As in Indochina, the explosion could have been prevented at any time. The French, however, set the fuses themselves. In Indochina the explosion of revolution ended the dream of French Union. In North Africa it plunged the French into a nightmare in which they are still tossing today.

∾

The first fuse: Tunisia

The first fuse was lighted when General, later Marshal, Alphonse Juin, who was to play a major role in the explosion of Africa, arrested the Bey of Tunisia and deposed him from his throne.

Juin had been incensed by the Bey's refusal to grant passage through Tunisia to the French Army of Liberation, after the Allied landings in North Africa late in 1942. No doubt the provocation was great, for the Allies had to move their armies freely, to cut off the Nazi forces, but Juin acted hastily and brutally, with no consideration for the reaction of the Tunisian people.

Until then the Tunisian masses had been largely indifferent to a national independence movement which had been confined to a few intellectuals. After the deposition of the Bey, however, the people became ready recruits. There were two principal nationalist groups active at the time: the Neo-Destour (New Constitution) party and the trade-union UGTT, the General Union of Tunisian Workers. The respective leaders were both highly intelligent, French-educated men, Habib Bourguiba and Ferhat Hashed.

Bourguiba fled Tunis when he learned that a warrant for his arrest was being prepared. He went to Cairo, where a North African Defense Front had been established. Later he made his way to the United States, and did not return to his homeland until 1949. By then Juin had left Tunisia and tensions had eased somewhat under a moderate, civilian resident general. France was deeply involved in the Indochinese War and needed peace and order in North Africa. It was one of the many opportunities to save French North Africa, to regain the friendship of the people there.

French Foreign Minister Robert Schuman, discussing the Tunisian question, told the Senate in Paris, on July 19, 1950: "We cannot maintain indefinitely direct administration by the French. That is precisely the purpose of the reforms we have in mind."

The reforms he referred to were based on demands put forward by Bourguiba in April, calling for home rule in Tunisia. Schuman did not accept all of Bourguiba's demands but he did agree to negotiate with a new Tunisian Government "institutional modifications which would lead Tunisia by stages to internal autonomy."

A new Tunisian Government was formed under Premier Chenik and included members of the Neo-Destour. Hopes were high for peace and friendship. Thereupon the colonial clique, which had wrecked similar hopes in Vietnam, promptly set about sabotaging Schuman's reform program for Tunisia.

Senator Antoine Colonna, one of the multimillionaire landowners of North Africa, sent a memorandum to the French Government in October, 1950, claiming that the Tunisians were incapable of self-government and warning that "once Tunisia is free, she will, whatever her promises, join the other camp—maybe the Arab League, or the U.S.A. or the U.S.S.R."[1] The colonialists always raised the specter of rival powers lusting after French territories, particularly the United States, whose influence they feared the most, because they knew perfectly well that America was not an imperial power and was more likely to support native nationalism.

Despite Schuman's promises, the officials of the Foreign Office, yielding to Colonna's threats, drafted a letter rejecting the idea of home rule by an all-Tunisian Government. The Quai d'Orsay instead favored a new principle, put forward at that time by the colonialists, the principle of "cosovereignty," which meant a joint Franco-Tunisian Government. The letter told Tunisians that France had earned the right to participate in their government because of France's "great share in the economic life of the Tunisian state and its contributions to its budget."

This cynical claim was a clear violation of the terms of the Protectorate, which granted France only the right to administer military

[1] See Jean Rous, *Tunisie, Attention!*, Paris, 1952.

security and foreign affairs, but it was finally endorsed by Robert Schuman, under pressure from his own party, the MRP, and from the colonial lobby. The most dangerous concession that he made, however, was his agreement to replace the incumbent, moderate Resident General by a diehard reactionary, who turned out to be a kind of Tunisian d'Argenlieu.

The new Resident, Ambassador de Hautecloque, set the tone of his administration when he arrived in Tunisia early in 1951 aboard a warship. On land he put on a parade, a military show of force, to impress the natives with his determination to brook no nonsense. One of his first official acts was to order the Bey to dismiss the nationalist ministers in his government.

The Bey, no more amenable to threats than his deposed predecessor, ignored the order. Instead of dismissing his ministers, he sent the Neo-Destour leader, Salah ben Youseff, to Paris, where the United Nations was in session, to protest against France's conduct in the Protectorate.

Nationalist demonstrations broke out throughout Tunisia. There were riots in Bizerte in January and at Cape Bon in February. De Hautecloque ordered out the Foreign Legion to put down the demonstrations. The Legion began one of its infamous "*ratissages*," literally a raking-out operation, a house-by-house search, conducted in a most brutal manner. Légionnaires looted, raped and killed in an orgy of lust.

Resident General de Hautecloque once again ordered the Bey to dismiss his nationalist ministers, blaming them for fomenting the riots. At the same time he arrested Habib Bourguiba, as a warning to the Bey. The Bey still refused to dismiss the Chenik Cabinet.

Then news came through from Paris that the Afro-Asian bloc would present the complaint of Tunisia to the Security Council at a meeting scheduled for April 1. De Hautecloque, in a towering rage, marched into the palace on March 25 and ordered the Bey, for the third and, he warned, the last time, to dismiss Salah ben Youseff and all the ministers of the Chenik Government.

The Bey's answer was to send a telegram to Paris, to President Vincent Auriol, protesting de Hautecloque's "high-handed behavior."

Auriol, the dreamer of union, was apparently unable to act, for the

Bey was still waiting for an answer when de Hautecloque carried out his threat. The Resident General arrested the Premier and deported both Chenik and Bourguiba by plane, although he had absolutely no authority to take such action against a regime he was supposed to be "protecting."

De Hautecloque followed up his coup by arresting thousands of Tunisians suspected of nationalist sentiments. The true figure will probably never be known. Tunisians claim that as many as 25,000 people were thrown into jail in the spring of 1951. The French insisted that arrests did not exceed two thousand and that most of those rounded up were merely taken into "temporary protective custody" and released in a few weeks. The truth in such cases, however, is less important than what people believe to be true and the Tunisians believed that tens of thousands of their compatriots had been arrested and tortured by the French.

Their worst suspicions of the French were confirmed and the most violent hatreds set loose at the end of 1952, when French colonials took matters into their own hands to dispose of the one nationalist leader still at large, the one man even de Hautecloque did not dare arrest, union leader Ferhat Hashed.

On the morning of December 4, as he was on his way into Tunis, Ferhat Hashed was shot down by assassins from a speeding black Citroën car, the trade-mark of French gangsters. The assassins were not mere gangsters, however. They were French colonials, members of the secret terror organization, a kind of Tunisian Ku-Klux Klan, called the Red Hand.

Many of the French colonists in Tunisia were of Sicilian and Corsican descent. Some were Spaniards and Maltese who had settled there and acquired French citizenship. They represented only 4 per cent of the total population of Tunisia. Yet it was these little Frenchmen of Tunisia, this legion of post office clerks, bank tellers and bus conductors who were used as a pretext by the handful of great landowners, like Senator Colonna, to invoke the "presence of France" and the need for police and troops to protect "the lives of Frenchmen."

The plot succeeded because of the weakness of the governments in Paris, the vain dreams of glory and grandeur of men like Bidault and General Juin, and the power and influence of the colonial lobby, allied with some of France's biggest newspapers. They invented the myth of a peaceful, happy North Africa being sabotaged by Moslem fanatics, Communist agitators and American secret agents.

The North African lobby spent huge sums to hold rallies in Paris and distribute pamphlets throughout France, warning that France would be finished as a world power, and that French factories would have to shut down three days a week if France lost its military bases and its markets in North Africa.

Finally there was Indochina to point to as a horrible example of what would happen if a firm hand was not used in North Africa. Two arguments were current in 1952: (1) if we are soft in North Africa, then it will go down the drain like Indochina; (2) if we lose Indochina, then all we have left is North Africa. "North Africa is France's last stand!"

৵৩

The myth became reality when Dien Bien Phu was lost. The defeat of France in the jungles of Indochina reverberated through the mountains of North Africa. It was an eye-opener for the nationalists, as revealing as the Japanese defeat of the British in Singapore had been to the Asian peoples.

Dien Bien Phu did more than open the eyes of the colonial peoples to their own strength. It opened the eyes of the French to the bankruptcy of past policy. It brought to power Mendès-France, the first genuinely anticolonialist premier of the Fourth Republic, with the single, brief and ineffectual exception of Léon Blum in December, 1946. It was the climactic turning point of imperial policy in Tunisia. The advent of Mendès set forces in motion that could never again be halted.

Just as he had startled France and the world with his dramatic thirty-day gamble for peace in Indochina, so did Mendès break with tradition in North Africa, by announcing that he would personally fly to Tunisia to see the Bey at his palace in Carthage and begin in earnest to carry out France's old pledge of home rule in the Protectorate. A mountain of strength and self-confidence, Mendès did not fear to go to Mohammed.

His master stroke was his persuasion of Marshal Juin to endorse his Tunisian policy and to accompany him on his mission to Carthage. When Juin stepped into the plane with Mendès, on the morning of July 31, 1954, the jig was up for the die-hard colonials in Tunisia.

Juin, at the time, was Commander of the Central European Front of the NATO forces and he knew that a war of reconquest in Tunisia was not feasible and would not be tolerated by the Allies or by world opinion. He knew, too, that Mendès could not be stopped from his decisive mission. Juin, born and raised in Bône, Algeria, also must have been thinking ahead to the climactic struggle for that key territory, which would require France's undivided efforts.

If Mendès put the colonials to rout with "*le coup de Juin,*" he also spread dismay and confusion among his friends both in Paris and in North Africa. Many of them warned Mendès that "to sup with the devil one must have a very long spoon." The Tunisians were suspicious of any policy, of any man, endorsed by Marshal Juin. The fears and suspicions mounted as weeks and months went by while negotiations with the Mendès Cabinet dragged on in endless haggling over details, just as they had under the Bidault-Schuman regimes.

And then, just as the Tunisians were successfully concluding their treaty with Mendès, and hope for a new deal was at last in sight, Mendès-France was thrown out of office by the National Assembly in Paris, in a debate on his Tunisian policy.

The confidence debate of February 5, 1955, was one of the most cynical and vicious of the many debates I had witnessed at the Palais Bourbon since the liberation. It also was one of the rare occasions when part of the truth about what the French had been up to in North Africa was publicly and incontestably revealed.

The revelation came when the Catholic party deputy, Alfred Coste-Floret, was imprudent enough to attack Mendès. He accused him, of all things, of keeping nationalist leaders in prison, an astonishing charge from a man whose own party had been in office when the arrests had taken place.

Mendès snapped back, with scathing sarcasm: "The prisons full, my dear colleague? Let me tell you that the prisons of Tunisia *once* had as many as five thousand prisoners. Today there are only a few hundred left, and they are serving time for civil, not political, crimes. The prisons *full*, my dear colleague? Why, it seems to me that your reproach must be addressed to previous governments." (Coste-Floret's brother had been Minister for the Colonies for almost two years, in earlier governments of the Fourth Republic.)

Mendès continued: "I can say the same for Morocco. When this government took over, it found the prisons of Morocco bursting with prisoners. We found men in prison who had not been sentenced, who had not even been brought to trial, but who had been kept in prison for three and four years, and even longer."

Mendès paused dramatically, leaned forward across the lectern and said: "Listen to this: we found in the prisons of Morocco a child of eight years who had been locked up for more than a year."

Then, his face white with anger, he pounded his fist on the lectern and shouted at Coste-Floret: "And it is to this government, which emptied out the prisons, which gave hope back to despairing families, it is to this government that you dare speak of prisons and of repressions!"

There was a painful silence in the Chamber. The deputies sat and stared straight ahead, looking neither at Mendès nor at Coste-Floret. Coste-Floret lowered his head and remained mute in his seat. Mendès, his anger exorcised, tried to put the debate in its true light: "The problem today, I insist upon saying, as clearly as possible, so that each one of you is free to decide his vote and personal conduct, is not to change a prime minister. This debate, whether you like it or not, is to make a choice on North Africa."

The deputies did not like it. They made their choice: 319 votes against Mendès-France and only 273 for him. That was the end of the Mendès-France Government. The colonial lobby had triumphed. Or so it thought.

Parliament might throw a Mendès-France out of office but it could not extinguish the flames of hope that he had lighted in Tunisia. In fact a majority of the deputies who voted against Mendès was reconciled to granting home rule to the Tunisians, even if the minority of the colonial clique still plotted to hold back the clock of history.

Mendès-France was defeated on February 5 not because of Tunisia but because a few days earlier he had announced that he would be ready to put his economic new-deal program into operation just as soon as he had concluded the Tunisian treaty. The economic royalists in Parliament, the delegates of the powerful wine, beet, alcohol, trucking and other lobbies joined forces with the colonial lobby to throw Mendès out of office.

Proof that Tunisia was only a pretext for the vote of "no confidence" in Mendès-France was not long in coming, and with it the turning point of French policy in North Africa.

Mendès was succeeded in office by his own closest friend and cabinet associate, Edgar Faure. The circumstances under which Faure succeeded Mendès broke their friendship, but there was no split of any kind between the Edgar Faure policy and the Mendès-France policy on Tunisia.

Faure simply took up the treaty at exactly the point where it had been when Mendès was overthrown, and, by June, 1955, concluded the negotiations for home rule in Tunisia. Announcing the advent of a new era in North Africa, Faure presented the Tunisian Conventions to Parliament, almost the same document that Mendès had drafted, and won a rousing vote of approval from the same deputies who had denounced this program only a few months before.

Having granted home rule to Tunisia, it was obvious that France would have to follow through with the same grant of home rule, sooner or later, to the sister Protectorate of Morocco. At the very least, France was obliged to set a date immediately for negotiations with the Moroccans. Premier Faure told party leaders that this would be his next step.

It was easier said than done, however, for by the summer of 1955, France had become almost hopelessly entangled in Moroccan affairs.

All during the long years of struggle in Tunisia sinister forces had been at work in Morocco. The same General Juin, who had lighted the first fuse in Tunisia when he deposed Moncef Bey, was later appointed French Resident General in Morocco, and, like a confirmed pyromaniac, had promptly begun playing with matches around the Sultan's palace. The resultant explosion blew the lid off France's North African policy and propelled both North Africa and France into an uncertain future, for which neither was prepared and whose outcome is still uncertain.

The story of how that happened, and how the conflagration spread to Algeria, rivals the tragedy of Indochina as a record of violence, treachery and governmental irresponsibility.

༄

THE SECOND FUSE: MOROCCO

A Roman captain once sent back a report from Morocco, in which he wrote: "The people here can be conquered but cannot be subjugated." He called the people "Berbers," from the Greek-Latin word for "barbarian." The same people had been called "Moors" by the Greeks, meaning "people of the west." By whatever name they were called, the Berbers demonstrated to every would-be conqueror the wisdom of the Roman soldier's commentary.

The French, however, were fortunate to have a Berber warrior for an ally rather than an adversary. Si Hadj Thami El Glaoui, Pasha of Marrakech, offered his services to Marshal Lyautey to help him "pacify the country," when the French arrived in 1912 to establish their "Protectorate" over Morocco.

El Glaoui was a feudal warlord, who saw the French as his natural allies against the Sultan and the Arab rulers of Morocco. A descendant of the original Berber warriors, El Glaoui had never reconciled himself to Arab rule. There were more than one hundred thousand Berber tribesmen in the Atlas Mountains around Marrakech and El Glaoui had visions of making himself the "Sultan of the South." He commanded twenty thousand loyal Berber horsemen, the fiercest fighters in Africa.

The French accepted El Glaoui's help eagerly. He was the ideal instrument of an imperial, divide-and-conquer policy. For forty years the French were to use El Glaoui as their trump card against the Sultan and Arab nationalism.

Moroccan nationalism, like Tunisian, was the dream of a few intellectuals. As in Tunisia, too, it received its first important stimulus from events that took place following the Allied landings of 1942.

The greatest spur to Moroccan nationalism was President Roosevelt's decision to see the Sultan of Morocco at the time of the Casablanca Conference. The fact that the President saw the Sultan without any French official present during the talks convinced Moroccans that Roosevelt was on their side against the French. The word soon spread that Roosevelt had promised the Sultan to help him win independence. With powerful America as an ally, and with France still occupied by the Germans, the nationalists felt the time had come to strike.

The nationalists made their first move on January 11, 1944, when they presented a Declaration of Independence to the French Resident General. His answer was to order mass arrests of nationalist leaders. This only inspired more Moroccans to become nationalists. Repression never has been the answer to nationalism.

The next great boost for nationalism came in April, 1947, when Sultan Sidi Mohammed ben Youseff visited the International Zone at Tangier and delivered an address in which he spoke, for the first time publicly, of statehood for his country. The Sultan shocked the French when he expressed his admiration for the Arab League. It was the first reminder to the West that Morocco was a Moslem nation and was looking over its shoulder of mountains at Cairo.

There were many other forces generating change in Morocco during the early postwar years. Morocco had become the California of North Africa, an American-style boomland, prospering from a kind of reverse gold rush. French capital, alarmed at the socialistic reforms and Communist infiltration of the liberation government in Paris, had fled the motherland and sought refuge in Morocco, a Paradise of rich minerals, cheap labor, low taxes and few Communists.

Casablanca, which had been a fishing village before the French arrived, mushroomed into a giant metropolis of 750,000 people. Skyscrapers shot up almost overnight and the port became the most active in Africa.

French merchants and traders flocked to Morocco like hungry crows to a cornpatch. Stories of fortunes being made in a new land of Cockaigne brought an invasion of get-rich-quick speculators, who descended upon Casablanca with the hoarded gold that they had never been ready to invest in their own motherland.

Given the caliber of the Casablanca carpetbaggers, it was inevitable that social strife would follow in their wake.

Arabs from the rural regions were recruited as cheap labor in the new factories before adequate housing had been built for them in the cities. The slums of Casablanca mushroomed more rapidly than the skyscrapers. Homeless workers huddled together in miserable shacks built of discarded gasoline cans, the familiar "*bidon*" of the military forces. These *"bidonvilles"* covered vast areas of polluted land, stinking of refuse and excrement, a breeding ground not only of disease and crime but of nationalism. The slum dwellers looked out of their tin-can shanties at the skyscrapers of wealth and lusted to have their country back.

In the areas where there were no slums, where the French had built schools and hospitals, nationalism was growing even more rapidly. Misery alone is not the cause of revolt. It is only the dry rot that kindles the fires. Revolt is sparked by hope and fanned by education. No matter what the French did—whether they cleared the slums or let them fester—nationalism grew stronger every day.

I ventured to express this opinion one day in Rabat to Resident General Léon-Augustin Guillaume, an able soldier, who had spent most of his career in North Africa. He listened to me patiently and courteously, but insisted that this was a typically naïve American theory. Americans, he said, always judge North Africa by American standards, which do not apply there. "You Americans always confuse the nationalists here with your own American forefathers, seeing them as fighters for independence against a colonial tyrant. You are quite wrong. The Moroccans are not the historic equivalents of the American colonists. If you must seek historical parallels, then the truth is that the Moroccans are the Indians, the indigenous peoples."

Guillaume concluded with an apologetic smile:

"Your American colonists never had to cope with a native nationalism, because they drove the Indians off the land, killed most of them, and cooped up the survivors on reservations. We French, however, did not drive our 'Indians' off the land. Instead we showed them how to care for it, with modern farming methods. We explored the subsoil and found great mineral treasures. We did not steal those treasures from them by offering them glass beads in exchange. We nationalized the phosphate fields of Morocco, for the Moroccan State, so that all of the profits would go to the Moroccan people. And you Americans call us colonial exploiters! Really, my friend, it is most exasperating."

Guillaume was right, in the context of his basic premise. It was the basic premise, however, that was wrong and therefore everything he said, and later did, was wrong. The premise, the same one that was operative in Tunisia and had operated in Indochina, was that France enjoyed special rights in those countries to which France was making so great a contribution.

If it is true that France had not killed her Indians, or driven them off the land, it is also true that France refused to accept the logical consequences of that humanitarian policy. France helped the natives grow in numbers and in health but would not admit that they were also growing in age and maturity and were rapidly reaching the time when they would want to stand on their own.

The time did come, however, in the mid-twentieth century, when France was still living in a nineteenth-century dream world.

∾

The trouble began in February, 1951. The Sultan, who had been to Paris on a state visit the year before, had renewed his Tangier demand for statehood, and had been told to negotiate the issue with the Resident General in Rabat. The Resident General was Alphonse Juin. When the Sultan pressed his demands, General Juin turned him down flatly and lectured him sternly on his "troublesome and dangerous behavior." When the nationalist party, Istiqlal, took up the demands and began to make them a public issue, Juin played the cards the French had ready for just such an emergency: the Berbers.

El Glaoui beat the drums, mustered his horsemen and sent them on the warpath, down from the Atlas Mountains. The Berber horsemen surrounded the old capital city of Fez and then began to ride to Rabat, where the Sultan's court was installed. When the French made no effort to contain the Berbers, the Sultan capitulated. He had his Grand Vizier denounce the Istiqlal, dismiss its members from his cabinet, while the Sultan himself issued a proclamation of loyal friendship with France.

General Juin did not have to depose the Sultan, as he had once deposed the Bey of Tunisia. The threat alone had been enough. From February, 1951 on, the Sultan was virtually a prisoner in his palace.

The Sultan had not, however, abandoned his hopes for independence. He was merely waiting for an opportunity to restate them publicly. To my surprise, I became that opportunity.

I had tried, on each of my reporting tours of Morocco, to see the Sultan, but without success. However, when I arrived in Rabat, about a year and a half after the 1951 coup, the situation had considerably eased. General Juin had been replaced by General Guillaume, who had lifted many of Juin's restrictions.

I was received at the palace in Rabat on November 9, 1952, just a few days after the American national elections. Thus, the first question I asked the Sultan was a request for his comment on General Eisenhower's victory. The Sultan replied: "General Eisenhower first came to my country exactly ten years ago this week, at the head of the invading armies of liberation. The Moroccan people thus rejoice at the results of an election which is surely a new victory for peace and the liberation of peoples." From the very outset, therefore, the Sultan stressed emancipation as the heart of his aspirations.

The Sultan went very far in his interview with me. It was, I believe, the first interview he had granted to an American correspondent since the Allied landings in North Africa. The Sultan knew that it would be widely published throughout the world. In that interview, for the first time since his Tangier speech of 1947, the Sultan publicly called for revision of the French Protectorate.

The Sultan answered some twenty questions in all. The highlights, which are still pertinent today, were:

1. Morocco is linked to the nations of the Arab League by cultural, spiritual and ethnic ties. It is, however, also linked to the West by geography. "It is our hope, therefore, that our country can become the bridge between West and East."

2. "Communism is in flagrant contradiction with the principles of Islam and our national traditions."

3. Morocco was one of the first foreign nations to recognize the young Republic of the United States. "It is our hope that relations between our countries will be guided by this spirit and adapted to new circumstances."

Of all the questions that I asked the Sultan, only one of them went unanswered. It was: will an independent Morocco extend the leases of the American Air Force bases in that country?

The Sultan's interpreter said to me: "His Majesty cannot answer that question. You see, the French granted the bases to you Americans without consulting the Sultan. Officially the Sultan does not know that there are foreign military bases on his territory." Later a palace official asked me to make it clear in my broadcasts that the Sultan, once independent, would be happy to negotiate new leases for American bases in Morocco.

On November 11 the French papers in Morocco and inside France carried the full text of the interview. The colonial press was wild with anger, denouncing not only the Sultan but this reporter, too, accusing me of being an American *"agent provocateur."* Strict censorship was imposed upon the palace following my interview and the Sultan's every move, every audience, was regarded with mistrust.

Within a few weeks' time the situation worsened very rapidly because of developments in Tunisia. The news of the murder of Ferhat Hashed led to protest strikes throughout Morocco on December 7 and 8. The strikes gave the colonialists an opportunity for a new wave of repressions.

The Prefect of the Casablanca region, Boniface, a tough and ruthless man, ordered his riot squads to break up the protest demonstrations. Hundreds of Moroccans were beaten up and many died in the fighting. Hundreds more were arrested in a *ratissage* similar to the Cape Bon operation, in Tunisia.

Not content with a police operation, the colonialists moved to play the Berber card again, but this time a final trump card that would dispose of the troublesome Sultan once and for all. It was the fatal decision that irrevocably wrecked all hopes for a peaceful settlement of the Moroccan problem.

∽

The plot was prepared during the winter and spring of 1952. The plan was to press new demands upon the Sultan. The scenario of the plot was the same as in 1951 when El Glaoui sent his horsemen down from the hills of the Atlas Mountains to Fez and Rabat. However this time El Glaoui was not merely threatening the Sultan. He was determined to dispose of him once and for all, divesting him of all authority, until he finally was moved to protest or to refuse to sign away his remaining rights. At that point El Glaoui would ride again.

The plot worked with only a slight change in the scenario. When El Glaoui sent his horsemen down from the hills the Sultan capitulated and signed the decree depriving him of his last legislative authority. There was no pretext left to use against him. El Glaoui, however, did not even bother to seek a pretext. He simply denounced the Sultan publicly and convened a meeting of vassal pashas and caids to select a new sultan. His choice was a cousin of the Sultan's, Sidi Mohammed ben Arafa, a weak and submissive old man.

While all this was going on, French Resident General Guillaume was, coincidentally, on vacation in France. Guillaume was ordered by the government to fly back immediately to call off El Glaoui and stop the dangerous *coup d'état*. Foreign Minister Georges Bidault told him to "avoid bloodshed at all costs."

Guillaume, after his return, telephoned back to Bidault to report that El Glaoui refused to call off his coup, and that it could not be stopped without sending troops into action to drive off the Berbers. Bidault yielded and told Guillaume to let the coup take its course, but to protect the lives of the Sultan and his family.

On the afternoon of August 20, 1953, Sultan Mohammed ben Youseff left his palace under tank escort and was taken to the airport, where he was flown to Corsica as a "guest" of the French Government. The next morning El Glaoui's hand-picked "Council of Notables" carried out instructions and "elected" Moulay ben Arafa as the new Sultan of Morocco.

In Rabat General Guillaume delivered himself of one of the greatest understatements in history, when he commented: "We did not wish for this."

ও৲৹

The *coup d'état* was at first a great success. The Moroccan nationalist movement was weak, unarmed and caught off guard. The depressed French might have been able to turn the coup to their advantage by winning over the Moroccan people through a liberal social and economic policy, as well as a political grant of home rule to a passive, puppet sultan.

Nothing of the kind was done, for the very good reason that the colonialists, who had engineered the coup with El Glaoui, had no intention of instituting liberal reforms once they were the masters of the country. All their talk of reforms was merely a cover to justify their use of force.

The California-style boomland of Morocco became a Chicago gangland of terrorism within six months. The nationalists rallied their forces after the initial surprise and began guerrilla warfare. Hardly a day went by without a bomb exploding in a public place, a strip of rail being torn up on a main line, or a "collaborator" of ben Arafa falling in the street, a knife in his back.

The Sultan himself was a target for terrorism. Twice he was attacked by assassins. The terrorists invaded El Glaoui's own fortress and threw grenades at him inside the Koutoubia Mosque of Marrakech, in February, 1954. El Glaoui miraculously escaped death but three of his guards were killed and twenty-four injured by those grenades. When terrorists were able to invade the stronghold of El Glaoui, it became obvious that the very foundations of French rule in Morocco were shaking.

The colonialists thereupon organized vigilante committees and secret "counterterror" bands like the Red Hand in Tunisia. The terror and fear knew no bounds. Not only did they murder Moroccans; they also killed one of the most distinguished Frenchmen in Morocco, Jacques Lemaigre-Dubreuil.

Lemaigre-Dubreuil had been one of the organizers of the resistance to the Nazis in Algeria, after the fall of France. He had played an important role in the underground intelligence network helping organize the American landings. His was the other face of France in the colonies. He was, like the other French leaders of Morocco, a wealthy businessman, but he had an enlightened view of the role of Big Business interests and French-Moroccan co-operation. He was therefore hated by the colonials, who considered him not only an adversary but a traitor to his class.

Lemaigre-Dubreuil was shot down in his home in June, 1955. Just before his murder, he had personally given Premier Faure a list of names of men marked for murder by the maffia of Morocco. His name was on the list and he demanded action to break up the gang. Lemaigre had obtained the list from an undercover police agent, Forestier, who had died in a mysterious accident shortly after having turned over the murder list to the paper *Maroc-Presse*. Premier Faure, who had just concluded negotiations for the transfer of home rule to the Tunisians, was shocked by the revelations of the crisis in Morocco and speeded up his plans to deal urgently with that problem.

Edgar Faure, one of the most cunning and subtle minds in France, conceived a plan to solve the Moroccan crisis. The plan was to "suggest" to puppet Sultan ben Arafa that he abdicate voluntarily and transfer his sovereignty to some sort of Regency Council. At the same time the French would bring Ex-Sultan ben Youseff back from the island of Madagascar, to which he had been transferred after a brief stay in Corsica following the August, 1953 coup. Ben Youseff would be comfortably installed in France, with all honors and personal liberty, on his promise that he would not return to Morocco or interfere with the evolution of events in his country.

Faure hoped that ben Youseff, who had fallen ill in the Madagascar climate, would consent to the plan, and then the nationalists could be won over by giving them representation in a Regency Council. The idea was to push the dynastic dispute into the background by eliminating both claimants to the throne, but voluntarily, rather than by another *coup d'état*. It was a brilliantly conceived plan. There was only one thing wrong with it. Faure never carried it out.

The sabotage of the Faure Plan, and the concessions made by Faure himself to the demands of the opposition, have been recorded for history in the memoirs of Gilbert Grandval, the man whom Faure appointed to carry out the plan. Grandval was Resident General in Morocco from July 7 to August 22, 1955, a period of six decisive weeks that shook Morocco and broke France's grip on North Africa.

ᲦᲦ

On July 7, 1955 Gilbert Grandval flew into Rabat, full of optimism and courage for the mission ahead. Within a week Grandval's optimism was severely jolted when nationalist terrorists threw a bomb at a crowded café terrace in the village of Mers-Sultan. Several Frenchmen were killed, many wounded. It was the signal for a wave of counterterrorism by the colonialists. In three days of violence the toll of dead was 55 Moroccans and 11 Frenchmen. The police had arrested 150 "terrorists." Resident General Grandval noted in his memoirs that all 150 were Moroccan. He began to see what he was up against and how difficult it would be to convince Moroccans that he was an impartial and just administrator.

On July 19 Grandval sent Paris a report on the three-day campaign of terror and warned the Minister for Moroccan and Tunisian Affairs,

Pierre July, that the "Plan" must be put into operation swiftly. "It is absolutely indispensable that important decisions be taken before the August 20 anniversary of ben Youseff's deposition." For the next week, July 20 through 27, Grandval devoted all his efforts to laying the groundwork for the plan.

On July 29 Faure sent an emissary from Paris to instruct Grandval to slow down. Faure said he needed more time to win over opposition members of Parliament. Grandval sent a message back reasserting the absolute necessity of completing the plan before August 20.

On August 2 Grandval received a report from one of his staff, informing him that El Glaoui's son, Si Brahim, had gone to Paris, carrying a letter to Faure from his father. El Glaoui warned Faure that ben Arafa would never abdicate voluntarily. That same day the paper *Paris-Presse* published the contents of El Glaoui's "confidential" letter.

Since the opposition force had begun its offensive, Grandval felt the time had come to take action himself, despite Faure's injunction to slow down. Therefore Grandval went to the palace, on the morning of August 5, and told ben Arafa of the plan, suggesting that he abdicate the throne. The old man did not protest, nor seem surprised. He said he would consider it and asked Grandval to put the request in writing, which Grandval refused to do. The next day, August 6, exactly two weeks before the feared target date, Minister Pierre July called Grandval to tell him that the cabinet had met for nine hours, in a stormy session, with powerful opposition to Grandval's "tight timetable."

Uneasy and suspicious, Grandval decided a few days later to fly to Paris. He took off at midnight, August 9. The next morning he saw Faure, who received him warmly, congratulated him on his fine work and assured the Resident that everything was proceeding according to plan, without any change in the original concept, except possibly "the slightest delay in the timetable." It was necessary, Faure said, to submit the plan to the Comité de Co-ordination pour l'Afrique du Nord, which would meet the next morning.

Grandval wearily reiterated his warnings against any delays, even the slightest. Once again he said, "There will be a catastrophe on August 20." Faure told him to stop worrying.

The next morning, August 11, the North African Co-ordination

Committee began its deliberations. The meeting lasted two days and then, on the morning of the thirteenth, Faure issued a communiqué, saying, "The Committee has worked out a plan, a calendar and a method" for solving the Moroccan crisis. He told reporters that Grandval would proceed immediately to Rabat to begin operations and that the Resident would return to Paris on August 18, at the conclusion of the first phase of the plan. By September 12, said Faure, all phases of the plan would have been decided.

The new "plan" called for creation of a "Council of Five," all French ministers, who would be authorized to follow the development of Moroccan affairs and more particularly to approve the nomination of a new Moroccan Government. In reply to Sultan ben Arafa's letter, it was left up to him to constitute a government. Whether this government was constituted or not, it was decided in any case that on August 25 negotiations would start for a new juridical relationship between Morocco and France. Should the Sultan fail to constitute a new government—which was considered a certainty by all French ministers—the negotiations would be held with the representatives of the different political parties and trends of opinion in Morocco.[2]

On the following day Grandval came and expounded to Edgar Faure that this plan was unacceptable, and that he could not accept it. It simply underlined the fact that ben Arafa was a puppet, picking names out of a French hat. The Moroccans so designated would have no authority, no dignity. The only possible result would be to strengthen demands for ben Youseff's return to the throne.

Grandval told Faure he would have nothing to do with the execution of such instructions. Faure told him to keep calm and think it over. After much soul-searching, and a quarrel with Faure that led to an abortive resignation, Grandval returned to Rabat for one last try.

But his efforts were all in vain, for he could not get a decision from Paris. Ben Arafa, prodded by El Glaoui, did not abdicate. No one went to Madagascar to see ben Youseff. Instead of proceeding with the plan, Faure announced that a "Franco-Moroccan Conference"

[2] The contents of this paragraph, as they appeared in the first edition, were amended following a communication from Mr. Edgar Faure.

would be held at Aix-les-Bains, an elegant watering place for the tired
and overfed rich of Europe.

The fatal day of August 20 arrived and, as Grandval had predicted, nationalist riots broke out as the partisans of Sultan ben
Youseff demonstrated their anger on the second anniversary of his
deposition. A bloodthirsty tribe descended from the hills and
destroyed the village of Oued Zem, massacring forty Frenchmen,
women and children. The French engineers and personnel at the
phosphate mines of Khouirbga were attacked by another armed
band. Before the day was over, all hope of peace and compromise
was shattered.

Grandval was not only furious with the government for having
failed to take action; he suspected even worse. In his book he
hints at high treason and says that he turned over a secret report
to the government for investigation. Grandval asserted that he had
not been informed by the military of the attack on Oued Zem
until hours after it had started, and he said that he could not
understand why a village, so near to military and air bases, had been
left defenseless, as Oued Zem had.

Grandval returned to Paris, resigned and began to write his
memoirs, for he felt that his countrymen had to know the truth
before all Africa was lost by the same tragic errors and sabotage.
His memoirs, *Ma Mission au Maroc*, published in Paris in 1956,
are a companion piece to the memoirs of Jean Sainteny, the French
Commissioner for North Vietnam. The two books, by dedicated
French public servants, document the death agonies of the French
Union.

⁓

From August 20 on, France's position in Morocco disintegrated
rapidly. Puppet ben Arafa folded his tent and stole silently away
in the night. General Catroux flew to Madagascar to arrange Sultan
ben Youseff's transfer to France, but it was no longer a transfer,
no longer an *"amende honorable"*; it was a triumphal march back to
the throne.

The Sultan flew first to Beauvallon, on the Riviera, then to Paris,
where he was escorted with all the honors of a sovereign to a
requisitioned hotel at Saint Germain-en-Laye. The hotel became
immediately a mecca for Moroccan notables who came as pilgrims

to worship at the feet of the Sultan. The most extraordinary pilgrim of them all was El Glaoui, the mighty warrior, whose horsemen had once circled the palace and driven the Sultan from his throne.

The game was up when El Glaoui threw himself at the feet of the Sultan and begged forgiveness, calling on God "to punish those who have done you harm." I watched that abject scene in the salon of the Pavillon Henri IV, and saw its effect upon the hundreds of Moroccans present that day. Sultan Mohammed ben Youseff became in an instant the undisputed master of Morocco. El Glaoui was finished. In fact he did not last long on earth. His old body was rotted with cancer and he died soon after his final humiliation.

On November 6, only one month after Edgar Faure had again stated that the Sultan would not return to his throne, France signed a Declaration, at the Celle-St. Cloud, implying the principle of the independence of Morocco, and providing for ben Youseff's speedy return. In fact, the French begged him to return at once, for the situation in Morocco was getting out of hand, as the Sultan's partisans began to riot and clamor for their king.

On November 10, 1955, Sidi Mohammed ben Youseff, now recognized as Mohammed V of free Morocco, flew back to Rabat in triumph.

I saw the Sultan there at his palace, where I had first interviewed him exactly three years before. He seemed tired and worn but he showed no bitterness to the French. On the contrary he seemed far more anxious about the lawlessness and hatreds that had been set loose in Morocco. He spoke to me at length about the need for peace, order and friendship.

In his traditional Speech from the Throne of November 18 the Sultan praised God for the deliverance of his country, but went out of his way to praise the French too, for their contribution "to the evolution and particularly the economic prosperity" of Morocco. He promised to safeguard the interests and rights of the French and said, "Our wish is to see Moroccans and French co-operate for the prosperity of Morocco and, for the good of all, to consolidate their relations and safeguard the friendship of our two countries."

The Sultan recognized that the end of the French chapter of his country's history did not mean the end of the history of Moroccan relations with France. However, before a new, more profitable era could begin it was necessary to write finis to the old. This was done by the spring of 1956 when a formal Treaty of Independence was signed, annulling the Treaty of Fez, thus bringing to an end the Protectorate. A similar end was written to the Tunisian story when the Treaty of Bardo became a dead letter on Tunisian Independence Day, in March, 1956.

Neither one of these episodes of history ended with the grim finality of the Indochinese tragedy. Indeed, insofar as Tunisia and Morocco themselves were concerned, there was *theoretically* a chance that the end of the old history was only the beginning of a new and more fruitful history.

Unfortunately for France, neither Morocco nor Tunisia could be considered by themselves, in isolation from the third and largest territory of North Africa, Algeria. And in Algeria the French began fighting a full-scale war against nationalist rebels late in the fall of 1955, just as they came to the crossroads of a new future in Morocco and Tunisia.

The link between the territories of North Africa and the future of France was described dramatically by Mendès-France, in June of 1956, when he told the Radical party, "There is one point on which we must not nurse any illusions: the situation in Morocco and in Tunisia will not improve so long as the Algerian drama is prolonged. The truth is that in Algeria is being decided the fate of all North Africa and indeed the fate of the French Union itself."

16 Awakening in Algeria

November 1, 1954 was a gray, grim day, as it almost always is in France. Even the weather seems to go into mourning as Catholic France prepares its annual pilgrimage to the cemeteries to honor the dead during the All Saints' Day and All Souls' Day ceremonies. On November 1 death cast its shadow over Algeria, in the form of a communiqué from the Government of Algiers.

"In the course of the night thirty acts of violence . . . were committed in different parts of the Algerian territory." With these words the communiqué announced an uprising that was to become, within two short years, a civil war whose flames threatened to spread throughout North Africa. Yet at the time no one in France seemed alert to the full implications of the revolt in the Aurès Mountains.

The Prime Minister, Pierre Mendès-France, dismissed it as an "act of terrorism" of a few fanatics. He told the National Assembly, in a special report on November 12, that "the criminal designs of a few men will be broken by a repression without weakness." The House cheered when Mendès declared: "The departments of Algeria are part of the French Republic; they have been French for a very long time; their population, which enjoys French citizenship, and is represented in Parliament, has given enough proof of its attachment to France so that France cannot allow its unity to be brought into question. Never will France, never will any Parliament, never will any Government yield on this fundamental principle!"

In that one, brief, concise and utterly erroneous declaration Mendès-France echoed the line that had been the leitmotif of every French Government for ten years and was to remain the policy of succeeding governments through 1956, by which time this disastrous self-deception had resulted in the spread of the rebellion

272

from the remote mountain passes of the Aurès throughout all of Algeria and had obliged the French to send, futilely, a half-million soldiers to carry out Mendès' vain pledge of a "repression without weakness." By that time Mendès had recognized his errors and was in opposition to the policy he had himself laid down. In a speech to a Radical party meeting in the spring of 1956 Mendès conceded that the priority problem in Algeria was "political, not economic or military." As for "repression without weakness," Mendès-France reversed himself completely by saying, "There is not a single example in history of a regular army defeating a national rebellion. Remember Spain, Mexico, Indochina!" It is a pity that Mendès himself had not remembered history earlier. He might have changed the course of current history in France if a man of his stature had awakened to reality sooner.

Although Mendès recanted on the issue of repression he did not renounce the main principles he originally expressed and which, he said, every French Government would have to embrace. Every government to date has indeed hewed close to the line he traced in November, 1954. In March, 1955, Edgar Faure told the Assembly, "There is no such thing as an Algerian State," and his Foreign Minister, Antoine Pinay, stalked out of the United Nations in protest against the General Assembly decision to put the Algerian question on its agenda. Pinay, like Mendès, insisted that the Algerian departments were part of the French Republic and thus an internal problem which did not come within the competence of the UN. This was also the position taken by Socialist Premier Guy Mollet in 1956. Thus Socialist Mollet, liberals Faure and Mendès, conservative Pinay—Left, Right and Center—all seem to agree on certain fundamental principles: that Algeria is an integral part of the French Republic; that its population enjoys French citizenship, that it has been French a very long time and has given proof of its attachment to France; that there is no historical precedent or justification for an independent Algeria; and that no French Government, therefore, will ever yield on this fundamental principle.

I have stated that in my opinion the policy speech of Mendès, containing these principles, was utterly erroneous. I do not mean to suggest in any way that Mendès was consciously, deliberately making a false statement. I am certain he believed what he said when he said it. I am equally convinced that he would not make the same statement today. In fact he has already retracted part of his November, 1954 statements. It is, however, worth going over these statements point by point for, by and large, the great majority of the French deputies and the people are still blinded by these erroneous principles and by their own propaganda. They have been told so many falsehoods and have repeated them so loudly and constantly that they can no longer distinguish the reality from the myths about Algeria.

ᕙᕗ

1. *"The departments of Algeria are part of the French Republic."*

This statement of Mendès-France is a legal fiction that he, as a skilled lawyer, could not have swallowed if he had not been carried away by his own mystical nationalism.

Algeria, or rather the coastal strip from Oran to Constantine, was declared to be a part of the French Republic by the postliberation drafters of the Constitution. They carved out three "departments": Oran, Algiers and Constantine. Later they added a fourth, the department of Bône. However, nine-tenths of the vast territory of the interior and the Sahara were not included in this "departmental" structure. Moreover, the whole of Algeria was administered by a "governor general," which is a colonial office. No department of the motherland has a governor general. Departments are supposed to be administered by a prefect. The departmental structure of Algeria is a thin cloak for the old imperial administration and anyone who opens his eyes can see through it.

2. *"They have been French for a long time."*

France invaded Algeria in 1830 when Charles X, last of the Bourbons, sent his fleet to fight the Barbary pirates and his army to avenge his honor. His honor had been injured, he felt, because the Dey of Algiers had slapped his envoy in the face with a fly swatter in an argument over an unpaid French debt to the "Regency of Algiers." The French are hardly in a position to discuss historical precedent, for the history of the conquest of Algiers is anything but glorious. It began as a farce and has ended in tragedy.

France, America and Britain all recognized the sovereignty of the

dey and all had signed commercial treaties and treaties of friendship
with him between 1793 and 1830. The thesis that there was no
Algerian State is thus highly contentious. It is based solely upon
the argument that the dey's authority did not extend very far inland
and that most of Algeria was a barren land of nomads. The same
might be said of Algeria under the French, for until very recently
the French never wandered far beyond the fertile coastal strip. It
is only in the last five years, out of more than a century of rule, that
the French have suddenly become interested in the vast Sahara territories and the possibility of finding oil there.

Even if the French contention that there never was an Algerian
State were true, that does not by itself mean that there never should
be an independent State in Algeria. It is, indeed, historically shaky
theorizing and morally absurd to say that a nation cannot be created
because it had never before existed. There was no American nation
before 1776. There was absolutely no historical precedent or justification for a French Republic before 1793. The forefathers of Mendès-
France and Guy Mollet revolted against the tyranny of the king and
proclaimed a French Republic. Do they now deny the same right to
the Algerian people?

Is this, indeed, a matter of right and wrong at all? Or is it rather
a matter of fact and fiction? It is a fact that a great number of
Algerians have taken up arms. It is a fiction that they have given
enough proof of their attachment to France to deny their desire for
independence. Too many Algerians are giving daily proof of their
desire to be detached from France to maintain this fiction. One might
argue about whether they are wise or foolish to revolt, or even
whether France should or should not come to terms with the
revolution, but surely one cannot argue the right or wrong of the
question. Any group of men has the right to aspire to and fight for
national independence and for freedom, no matter how long they
have lived under foreign domination or colonial rule. Men revolt
against their own national governments if they are discontented. How
can France, the country of revolution, deny its very meaning?

3. *"The population enjoys French citizenship."*

The verb *"réjouir"* in French has two connotations: it means to
possess and also to enjoy. Only a small proportion of the Algerian

population actually possesses full French citizenship and very few, indeed, enjoy the full benefits of this possession.

General de Gaulle granted citizenship to sixty thousand Algerians at the liberation. The Constitution then proclaimed all Algerians to be French citizens but the Algerian Statute of 1947 set up special conditions restricting the enfranchisement of Algerians. Only seventy-five thousand out of almost nine million Algerians have ever become full citizens for voting purposes. To say, therefore, that the population enjoys French citizenship is an enormous exaggeration at least quantitatively speaking. It is, moreover, just as exaggerated qualitatively, for those who do have citizenship do not enjoy equal rights and privileges. Algerian citizens are second-class citizens. My source for this assertion, among others, is Pierre Mendès-France. In a speech to the Radical party in 1956, Mendès, talking of the future of Black Africa, said:

"Nothing would be more dangerous than to apply in Black Africa the same methods which did such harm in North Africa, where the Moslem peoples of Algeria welcomed the inauguration of universal suffrage as an immense progress but soon perceived that in practice it was only a façade and a deceit."

Mendès was referring to the phony elections of April, 1948 in Algeria, as great a travesty of free elections as any Soviet puppet show. The candidates were hand-picked by the French Administration and the ballot boxes were stuffed so efficiently that in one district a candidate won more votes than there were registered voters. The distribution of seats was also rigged by law. The legislature was divided into two "colleges," or houses, of sixty members each; one represented French citizens, the other "local statute" citizens. On a population basis this was manifestly undemocratic. The sixty French representatives spoke for 1.2 million constituents, whereas the sixty non-French deputies represented 8.5 million constituents. Thus the French were given one congressman for every 20,000 inhabitants whereas the "locals" were given one representative for every 141,000 voters. Mendès was right, in 1956, to call this a façade and a deceit." He was wrong to claim, in 1954, that the population "enjoyed" French citizenship.

The only policy statement on Algeria that any of the premiers has made which has so far proved correct is the declaration that no government will ever yield on the principle that Algeria is inseparably tied to France. Someday, however, that principle too will have to be yielded. Algeria is not French. The population does not enjoy French citizenship. The French could not even afford to give full citizenship to the large, rapidly increasing Algerian population even if the Algerians desired it. If all Algerians were enfranchised there would be 100-150 Algerian deputies in Parliament. France, as her leaders once feared, would become "a colony of her colonies." France also could not afford to give the Algerians the full benefit of French social security laws and family allocations. The cost would bankrupt France. The French are quite right when they say that the differences in education and civilization between the primitive Algerian masses and the French are too great for complete equality. But, if this is true, they cannot also assert that Algeria is France and Algerians French.

◊

The government of Socialist Premier Guy Mollet took the fateful decision to implement the Mendès-France pledge of "repression without weakness." Ironically Mendès-France thereupon resigned as Minister of State in that cabinet in protest against the policy of force. Mollet denied that force was his only resort. He kept insisting that he wanted a "political solution" for Algeria. But his party colleague, Robert Lacoste, Minister Resident in Algeria, was the real policymaker of the government and his was a policy of brute force to put down the rebellion. By the summer of 1956 the Mollet Government had sent 500,000 soldiers to Algeria, more than triple the force that had been sent to Indochina.

Lacoste and Mollet stated that "order must first be restored" before any fundamental reforms could be effected. This was the same disastrous position that Socialists Léon Blum and Paul Ramadier had taken in 1946 and 1947 on Indochina. It flies in the face of all the lessons of history. "Order" presupposes victory of one side over the other. Victors are seldom generous in their concessions to those they have conquered. Above all, the Mollet Government has refused direct negotiations with the rebels, just as the Ramadier and succeeding governments refused to deal with Ho Chi Minh. If they will not negotiate, then it means a fight to the finish rather than reforms and a new deal. This indeed, is what Lacoste has sought: a fight to the finish.

This policy has led the French into the most desperate and dangerous adventures. Two events, in the fall of 1956, changed the course of North African history and shook the entire world. The first was a dramatic air-kidnaping of Algerian rebel leaders; the second the French-British invasion of Egypt.

The air-kidnaping was an extraordinary cops-and-robbers stunt that virtually wrecked French relations with Morocco and Tunisia. It occurred just when chances were brightest that the Moroccans and Tunisians might help bring peace to Algeria. Bourguiba had invited the Sultan of Morocco to visit Tunis, for the first official conference between the two newly independent leaders of North Africa. He had announced that they would consider means of mediating the French-Algerian conflict. In a euphoria of excitement he had printed delegate and press badges of white silk with a green dove of peace carrying an olive branch.

The Sultan of Morocco then announced that he had invited Algerian rebel leaders to Rabat and would take them to the conference with him. He had previously informed the French of this plan. They had not objected but had warned him not to "receive the rebels with official honors," for that would be an offense to the French. The Sultan at first took this warning seriously. The five rebel leaders, led by Ben Bella and Mohammed Khider, the military and political "brains" of the rebel organization in Cairo, were discreetly received at the palace at night, with no public ceremony. However the next day press dispatches from Rabat reported that the Sultan had declared the rebels to be his friends and had invited them "to consider yourselves at home in my country." He put his private plane at their disposal to fly them from Rabat to Tunis. Moroccan crowds cheered the Algerian revolutionists as heroes.

The French were furious. The Sultan had never invited the French "to consider yourselves at home" in Morocco. On the contrary he had made it quite clear that the French were foreigners in free Morocco. Moroccan terrorists were still burning French farms and giving moral encouragement if not actual material aid to the Algerian rebels. The French press broke out into a rash of angry denunciations of both the Sultan and Bourguiba.

Then the incredible happened. The crew of the Sultan's private plane received radio instructions from Algiers, to land there instead of proceeding to Tunis. It was a French crew working on contract for the Sultan. The pilot decided that his first duty was to his country and not to his employer. Thus, instead of flying to Tunis, he flew to Algiers, circled around in the clouds for an hour and a half, so that his revolutionist and armed passengers would think they were flying on schedule, and then landed at the Maison Blanche Airport of Algiers. The rebel leaders, unsuspecting, walked out of the plane into the arms of the French police and were promptly thrown into jail.

At that very moment, in Tunis, government officials were scanning the skies in search of the plane of their guests. When they learned what had happened there was an explosion of rage. The Sultan was wild with anger and shame at the trap into which he had unwittingly led his personal guests. He accused the French of piracy and treachery. They had no right to seize his plane, flying his flag. Unquestionably it was a violation of international law and behavior. The French hardly bothered to justify it. Instead they boasted blatantly about their bravery and daring. "At last a return to virility" was the headline in the paper, *Paris-Presse*, above a blood-and-thunder editorial that sounded more Wagnerian than French.

The Moroccans and Tunisians immediately canceled plans for further negotiations with the French on interdependence. Millions of people throughout the Arab world staged protest strikes and demonstrations. French embassies and schools were attacked by angry mobs from Damascus to Annam. The French Undersecretary of State, Alain Savary, a Socialist colleague of Guy Mollet, resigned from the government in protest. Mollet accepted his resignation and announced his complete support of Lacoste's coup. For it was, again, an administrative coup by a proconsul. Mollet admitted in Parliament that he had not known about this kidnaping plan until the last moment. He told the deputies, "I do not admit this in order to shirk the responsibility for the action but rather because I do not want to take credit for it." The House, particularly the Center and Right, lustily cheered the new "strong-man Socialist." Mollet had suddenly become the hero of the most reactionary forces in France.

He had, however, blasted the hopes of many Moroccans and Tunisians who had not expected Socialists Lacoste and Mollet to play the swashbuckling role of a Juin or a d'Argenlieu.

Mollet played his new role to the hilt. He never faltered, never hesitated once his mind was made up. He had the rebels transferred to a military prison outside Paris, refused the Sultan's demands to release them and, in effect, told the Sultan and Bourguiba that they had better understand France's determination not to show any weakness in North Africa. France, said Mollet, still proffered the hand of friendship to the North African people but would not tolerate any support or sympathy for the enemies of the Republic. The once mild-mannered, soft-spoken Socialist teacher of English grammar had become the little Napoleon of the Fourth Republic.

Nothing could have been more Napoleonic than Mollet's next and most startling move: the invasion of Egypt. Of all the remarkable episodes of French history the joint Anglo-French invasion of Egypt on November 5, 1956 was one of the most astonishing and disastrous. It came very close to sparking off World War III and it gave the Soviets an opportunity that Russians had been seeking for two centuries and more: a chance to get a foothold in the Middle East.

At the moment of this writing, toward the close of 1956, the consequences of this dramatic act are still incalculable. That it was a defeat for the West is undeniable. How bad a defeat, how recoverable a setback cannot yet be seen. Some of the immediate consequences are, however, already clear. The prestige of France and of Britain has been irremediably damaged. They both revealed that they are no longer great powers of world stature. Having decided upon an invasion of Egypt, to occupy the Suez Canal, they were forced to quit under Soviet threats and American pressure before they had attained their objective. Anglo-French troops had only captured Port Said when they were halted by a governmental order to cease-fire. The cease-fire order was sent out only a few hours after Russia had announced it would send "volunteers" to aid Nasser and had sent truculent notes to Paris and London warning them that they might be bombed.

Mollet did not want to quit under pressure. He, and most of the French, were fighting mad, ready for anything. Their courage was both inspiring and irresponsible, for it was out of all proportion to the limited objectives of the operation. But despite their courage and spirit the French had to call off the operation when Eden informed Mollet that Britain was going to call a cease-fire. Eden had been under heavy attack from the Labor opposition and had also suffered defections from his own ranks. His personal protégé, Anthony Nutting, had resigned from his government, as did his personal spokesman, William Clark. Public opinion in Britain was sharply divided. Eden could not go on in the face of so many pressures. And Mollet could not "go it alone." Thus Britain and France, in different moods and for different reasons, both found themselves in the same boat: friendless, alone, defeated, no longer the mighty powers who once ruled the world, unable to carry out an independent foreign policy against the combined opposition of the U.S.A. the U.S.S.R. and the UN.

The repercussions of this revelation on the Arab world in general and on North Africa in particular were enormous. The Algerian rebels, who had been stunned by the capture of five of their leaders, took on new heart. The Moroccans and Tunisians, still angry, became even more violent in their denunciations of the French. Even the most pro-Western leaders, like Bourguiba, were forced to take sides with their Moslem coreligionists against the invaders of Egypt. It was at that very moment that Tunisia was accepted as a member of the United Nations and Bourguiba announced that his first vote would be against France.

In an open letter addressed to "My French Friends" published in the Paris paper, *Express*, Bourguiba wrote of his cruel dilemma:

The vote of free Tunisia will be against France but it would be a mistake to believe that we are happy about this conflict. I had hoped sincerely that Tunisia would be a bridge between the Occident and the Orient and that our first independent vote would have been in favor of France. Although that has proved to be impossible I still cannot bring myself to despair, for the first time in my life, of the wisdom of the French people and their government. The day may yet perhaps come, if the Government of the Republic acts swiftly enough, when French civilization will be truly defended in world councils by the leaders of a French North African Confederation.[1]

[1] *Express*, November 16, 1956, supplement No. 282.

This is the dream, fading rapidly but still cherished, of Bourguiba, the Sultan and many other new leaders of Morocco and Tunisia: a coalition of the three North African countries, freely associated with the French Republic, in a confederation of political, economic, military and diplomatic interests. It is a North African version of the dream of a French Union, based upon a voluntary association of free and independent states who have many reasons to act in concert. There would be no fundamental conflict of interests between the North African countries and France if they were all independent nations.

Those who pretend that the Moslem religion would separate the two entities and draw North Africa into the orbit of the Arab League—and this is a principal argument of the nationalistic, colonial Right—do not seem to realize the full significance of their argument. If they are correct then they are saying that there is no hope of peace ever in North Africa. If Algerians, Moroccans and Tunisians are enemies of France by their religion then how can one also argue that Algeria is French and North Africa a part of the French Union? Either Bourguiba is right and there is still hope, no matter how slim, or Senator Colonna and his ilk are right and there is no hope for the future. France must either gamble on the friendship of a free North Africa or get out of North Africa completely. It should be evident after the Egyptian fiasco that France cannot impose her will upon some twenty-two million North Africans indefinitely. Sooner or later the French will have to recognize the existence of an Algerian state. The sooner, the cheaper in terms of men, money and a chance to salvage something from the wreckage of the French Union.

∽

How to get out of Algeria is as important as, and for the moment more important than, whether to pull out. The majority of French political leaders, and the great majority of the people, now know that Algeria is not French and must one day become an independent nation. Few will admit this publicly yet but many Frenchmen are beginning to confess in private conversations that some new relationship between France and Algeria must be devised. The basic questions being studied are: what kind of status for Algeria and how can it be achieved politically?

Premier Guy Mollet launched the idea, in March, 1956, of a "Franco-Algerian State," in which a balance of power would be created to protect both ethnic groups—the Europeans and the Moslems—from domination by either one: "no economic domination by the rich European minority; no political domination by the majority Moslem population." Just how this could be accomplished Mollet did not say. Nor did he say clearly whether he would or would not agree to direct peace negotiations to this end with rebel leaders. This is a vital factor in finding a solution to the Algerian problem. Peace and a new status can only be negotiated between direct adversaries or imposed by a victor. Few Frenchmen still believe in a full military victory that would enable the French to dictate terms but they have not yet quite reached the point of negotiating with the rebels. Indeed they argue that there are no rebel leaders with whom they could negotiate.

There is no doubt that the Algerian revolutionists are anything but a cohesive group. They are fighting for power among themselves. There is no Algerian Ho Chi Minh, no Bourguiba to speak as a responsible leader capable of negotiating a treaty and carrying out its terms. Yet there is an evident lack of desire for peace in this argument, which, valid as it is, is not the real reason for refusing to negotiate. The French could find an "interlocutor" if they really wanted one. Indeed throughout 1954 they were secretly negotiating with rebel representatives in Cairo, Rome and Zurich. Premier Guy Mollet admitted to Parliament that he had sent his party colleague, Pierre Commin, to confer secretly with the rebels.

Bourguiba in his open letter to the French said he was "fed up" with this argument that the Algerian National Liberation Front was divided and politically immature. He said he had wanted to put that argument to the test by inviting the rebel leaders to the Tunis Conference. However, instead of risking a fair test, he said, the French kidnaped the rebel leaders.

By that act the French proved that they were not really trying to prepare public opinion for talks with sincere partners; they were not seeking a solution, they were trying to keep Algeria French. Well, in the first place that is not possible and even if it were we would not accept it. There is no true Franco-Tunisian interdependence if they try to revive the old slogans of French Algeria. The Algerians will continue to fight and the Tunisians cannot help but give them their fullest support.

There could be no clearer warning to France than that, particularly from a Bourguiba, who is the best, and just about the last, important friend France still has in North Africa.

ᏉᎳᎤ

The gradual awakening of the French to the fact that some new status must be formed for Algeria has been necessarily slow and painful. They have regarded Algeria as French for more than a century. It is not some distant Oriental colony; it is in their own backyard. More than a million French men and women live in Algeria and they cannot be abandoned. These French Algerians were born there, for generations past, and many of them regard Algeria as their true homeland. They are more Algerian than French and have no desire to return to a "motherland" they hardly know. The French in Algeria are the Boers of North Africa. Thus Algeria is a much more complex and emotion-packed problem than Indochina ever was. Algeria indeed is not a colony. It is a settlement. The French created Algeria out of the desert and irrigated the land with their sweat and their blood. They do have some rights in Algeria that cannot be summarily dismissed.

This is an anguishing problem for France's allies as well. The traditional anticolonialism of Americans is to a great degree misplaced in Algeria, for it is not a classic colonial case. The Algerian rebels are not the equivalents of Washington, Jefferson and Franklin. There are many primitive, fanatic men among them. A free Algeria would not necessarily be a democratic Algeria, either internally or in its foreign alliances. American and British statesmen are aware of the uniqueness of the Algerian question. They have, despite American public opinion, reaffirmed their solidarity with the French on this issue. Sir Gladwyn Jebb, the British Ambassador to France, expressed his government's solidarity early in March, 1956. The British declaration was followed by an even stronger one from the American Ambassador, Douglas Dillon. On March 21, Dillon told the Diplomatic Press Association of Paris: "The United States firmly supports France in its search for liberal, equitable solutions for Algeria." At the end of the speech Dillon drew cheers from the French when he said that France can count on "the total support of the United States."

In fact this "total support" was somewhat less than total, for the sympathies of the American people were still not with France, and American trade unions actively and openly supported the Algerian cause. Dillon was completely sincere in his assurance of total support but only within the limits of diplomatic solidarity. There was nothing comparable to American support of France in Indochina, nothing like a giant aid program or joint strategy meetings. The French themselves did not want it in Algeria.

France and Britain drew closer together during the Suez crisis. The United States drew a little further away, alarmed by the hysteria and war-mongering of its principal allies, who had once criticized America for losing its head during the Korean and Formosan crises. The Suez crisis was closely linked to the Algerian crisis. Both were results of the wave of nationalism that rolled across the former colonial countries in the wake of World War II.

The Western powers, formerly dominant in the world, have had great difficulty readjusting to this historic, global revolution. The emancipated nations are having the same trouble adjusting to their new national responsibilities. These adjustments, made in an emotional climate, in the midst of another even greater readjustment between the democratic and Communist powers, inevitably have generated more heat than light.

❧

For France, more than for any other world power, the colonial revolution has been an agonizing problem.

The loss of Algeria can only lead to the very early loss of the huge territories of Black Africa, France's last frontiers. L'Afrique Noire has been outwardly quiescent but inwardly rumbling all through the years of fighting in North Africa. Neighboring countries have won their independence, and the accession of black men to independent government has been a great inspiration to others still ruled by whites. Kwame Nkrumah, who administers Britain's neighboring territory, the Gold Coast, is the hero and inspiration of French West Africans.

The West African native leader who sees the Gold Coast as the model for his own land is a French-educated Negro tribal chieftain, Félix Houphouet-Boigny. Houphouet became chief of the Akwe tribe at the age of five when his father died. Although a chief, he was "requisitioned" by a minor French colonial functionary to be his houseboy. Later, after he had completed his education, and gone to medical school in Dakar, Houphouet had to work as a laboratory assistant because only white men were permitted to practice medicine. The proud French boast that they are not racists was untrue in the colonies. It was one of the many ugly facets of French colonialism that were carefully concealed from the people of metropolitan France.

Houphouet-Boigny rose rapidly among his own people and at the liberation of France was sent to Paris as a deputy from West Africa to the Constituent Assembly. Like Algeria's Ferhat Abbas and other colonial deputies, he walked out in disgust at the betrayal of pre-liberation promises to the colonial peoples. He went back to Africa, back to the tribes in the jungle, and organized a powerful political force, the Rassemblement Démocratique Africain. Although he had earlier become a convert to Catholicism, Houphouet concluded an alliance with the Communists, which shocked the French colonial administrators more than his reversion to tribal life.

In 1950 Houphouet had a change of heart. He broke with the Communists, announcing that the alliance had been only tactical. He denounced the Communist program of independence, telling his people that their society was still too primitive to be independent. Houphouet told the French that he would return to Paris to try to revive the dream of French Union.

In February, 1956, Félix Houphouet-Boigny celebrated his fiftieth birthday as the first Negro cabinet minister in French history. Socialist Premier Guy Mollet had appointed him Minister of State, charged with the mission of drafting a new version of the French Union clauses of the Constitution. Thanking the Premier for his confidence in him, Houphouet-Boigny replied: "Act quickly. My people trust me and will follow. But they will not stand still. The war drums will again beat in the jungle if our aspirations are held in check."

Mollet did move quickly. In July his government promulgated a new decree-law for Black Africa, abolishing the Jim Crow, double-college, electoral system of Algeria. The *"loi-cadre"* instituted single-college, universal suffrage and granted a large measure of decentralization and internal autonomy to the overseas territories. Whether Mollet had moved quickly enough only the future will tell, and the future of French Africa will not be determined by the French alone.

France is only one of many powers interested in the future of Africa, and France is in the weakest position to meet the competition of rivals. Not only is the colonial past a barrier to future friendship but France needs almost all her energy to develop her own resources, her own long-neglected industry.

Even more hostile to France's African policies than the great powers, are the small, newly independent nations of what once was called the Dark Continent. No longer living in the darkness of the primeval jungle, all Africa, like all Asia, has ended its sleep-walking through history. France cannot keep its African colonies dormant when its neighbors are alive with hope.

All that France can expect for the future is a chance to maintain contacts, not colonies, in Africa. France indeed can only hold its contacts and friendships by giving up its colonies. There is still a slim but rapidly fading chance to stake out developmental areas in the Algerian Sahara and in Mauritania, where there are vast almost un-populated areas rich in copper, iron and oil. The Algerian rebels and the Moroccans are already looking covetously at these potential treasures and trying to claim sovereignty over desert regions where they never exercised control and never colonized themselves. France's moral and legal claims to the Sahara are stronger than those of rival claimants but they will be lost too if the war in Algeria continues much longer. By trying to hold too much too long France may lose every-thing and Africa may become the graveyard of the Republic as well as of the dream Union of France.

17 *Lost in a Strange,*
New World

The dream of a French Union was not the only dream that dazzled Frenchmen in the first decade of the Fourth Republic. Nor were Frenchmen the only men to dream of a brave, new world in the aftermath of the most destructive war that men had ever fought.

The dream of a World Union sustained men even when the forces of evil were tearing the world apart. In Algiers, in 1943, the Allied Radio was called "The Radio of the United Nations." The Atlantic Charter was a rainbow of a future dedicated to democracy for all freedom-loving peoples. Inside Europe, in slave labor factories and concentration camps, men dreamed of a new community of peoples that Europeans had not known since the decline and fall of Rome.

These were not idle dreams. All of them saw the light of day, within a few years of the liberation. The United Nations, the World Bank, the World Health Organization, European Economic Co-operation, this was the stuff that the dreams were made of, dreams translated into reality.

Reality, alas, rarely measures up to the dream. None of these organizations, despite their many and often remarkable accomplishments, realized to the full the aspirations of the dreamers. Many men were to share the bitter disillusions and confusion of the French in a postwar world that was new but not brave, a world divided, alternately burning and shivering in the fevers of hot and cold wars.

❧

The French were lost in the strange, new world of liberated Europe. All of the familiar landmarks of the past had been destroyed. The "Liberator," Charles de Gaulle, hardly recognized the country he had fought to restore to freedom and its place in the world. From the strongest power in Europe, France had fallen to the rank of the weakest, among the larger nations. From one of the smallest parties in prewar France, the Communists had become the largest party. For liberated France the struggle for survival did not end with the war; it began. It had to be fought on two fronts, inside and outside of France.

De Gaulle flew to Moscow in the winter of 1944, while war still raged, to seek a way out of his double dilemma. There were two men in Moscow who could help France on both fronts: Stalin and Maurice Thorez. It was de Gaulle's illusion that he could play a balance-of-power game between East and West, and at the same time, tame and control the French Communists.

In Moscow he negotiated a Treaty of Friendship with the Russians. De Gaulle also amnestied French Communist party leader Maurice Thorez, who had been living in exile in Russia ever since he had fled France during the war and had been sentenced in absentia for desertion.

De Gaulle's policy was a failure from the start and could not be otherwise. A powerless France was incapable of playing a balance-of-power game and neither West nor East looked to France as a bridge or a link. Roosevelt, although sympathetic to France's difficulties, discounted France as a world power and laughed at the idea of France becoming one of the Big Four of the postwar world. Stalin had nothing but contempt for the "decadent French." France was not invited either to Yalta or to Potsdam. Churchill, alone, befriended the French although he was constantly at odds with de Gaulle.[1]

Thorez returned to Paris and, for a while, kept his part of the bargain with de Gaulle by calling on the Communist party to "roll up your sleeves and rebuild France." This co-operation lasted only one year, however. By the fall of 1945 Thorez had split with de Gaulle and by the fall of 1947 the "Party of Renaissance" had again become the party of revolution.

[1] For official documentation of the Roosevelt-Stalin policies on France, see Chester Willmott's *Struggle for Europe*, Robert Sherwood's *White House Papers*, and Winston Churchill's memoirs.

The first two postwar years were years of painful awakening from wartime dreams, for the French and for all the once-allied peoples.

❧

The first sign that the Allied coalition would not last long beyond the final victory came at the San Francisco Conference in June, 1945. Russia and the Western powers failed to agree on a United Nations seat for Poland because the Russians backed the claims of Poles who had been in Moscow during the war, while the Western powers insisted upon the legitimacy of the London-based Polish Government-in-Exile.

Three months later, at the London Conference of Foreign Ministers, Molotov rejected a British proposal for an inquiry into conditions in Soviet-occupied Rumania and Bulgaria. The French, with historic interests and friendships in the Balkans, listened with dismay to Molotov's arguments, for he made it starkly clear that in the future Eastern Europe was a Soviet sphere of influence, off-bounds to the Western nations.

The former allies drew further and further apart during 1946. The Soviet threat to Iran opened the eyes of the UN to the reality of the postwar world. The Communist rebellion in Greece then opened the eyes of America to the power vacuum in Europe. It led to the Truman Doctrine, the first realization that United States security extended beyond the limits of the Americas in time of peace.

The Truman Doctrine, in March, 1947, coincided with the Big Four Conference in Moscow, on the future peace treaties for Germany and Austria. At that conference any illusion still left about Soviet intentions vanished, for Stalin opposed every French demand, particularly French plans for control of the Ruhr and the Saar.

Within a month of the Moscow Conference the French Communist party broke its alliance with the democratic parties inside France and Premier Ramadier fired the Communists from his cabinet, just a few days before the second anniversary of V-E Day.

The Allied coalition, outside France, also burst apart, a month later. The final split came just before the second anniversary of the UN Charter. It had in fact already occurred in Moscow, but appearances were still being preserved in March. In June, however, the final break came when General George C. Marshall delivered his historic address at Harvard University, a speech that inspired Europe and shook Russia as much as the power of the American invasion forces had thrilled Europeans and shaken Hitler three years before.

∽

Europeans were quick to sense the meaning of Marshall's address and to seize the opportunity for collective security in the West.

On June 7, only two days after the Harvard speech, France's quick-witted Foreign Minister, Georges Bidault, instructed his Ambassador in Washington to inform Mr. Marshall of France's "greatest interest" in his suggestions. The next day, at a news conference in London, Britain's tough, little Socialist Foreign Secretary, Ernest Bevin, a veteran organizer of the London docks, made his move to organize European economic co-operation. He publicly thanked Marshall for his "generous offer" and promised speedy action by the British Government.

On June 14, Bevin called Bidault to suggest a conference in Paris. Bidault agreed to meet Bevin immediately and also sent a cable to Moscow, inviting Molotov to meet them later. On June 22, Molotov replied, accepting the invitation and suggesting that the conference be held in Paris on the twenty-seventh.

Molotov arrived in the French capital that day with a delegation of some fifty political and economic experts, a sign that he took the Marshall proposals seriously. However, despite the appearances of Soviet interest, the result was negative. Molotov objected to every French and British proposal for the creation of a joint European economic organization.

The conference ended on July 2, when Molotov walked out, stating as his reason that the French-British plan for a central authority would lead to interference in the internal affairs of the member states and endanger their independence—an impertinent charge from a man who was snapping the whip over the Soviet satellites of Eastern Europe.

The Kremlin had made a great mistake, perhaps the greatest diplomatic blunder in modern history.

Bevin and Bidault both admitted later to friends and associates that they had been very worried when they saw Molotov arrive in Paris with so huge a delegation. They feared he might agree to join a

European organization and that his "Yes" might be more deadly than his "No." At an informal cocktail party at his hotel Bevin told some of us reporters, "I was afraid of the Soviet kiss of death. If Molotov had agreed, I doubt that Congress would be willing to appropriate money for an economic aid program."

෬౦

The European Recovery Program was only the start of the search for security in postwar Europe. Before 1947 had ended Europeans discovered that military security was as important as eonomic security, for the Soviets had grown more menacing ever since Molotov had walked out of the Paris Conference.

In the fall of 1947 Russia had organized the Cominform, as its answer to the Marshall Plan. French Communist Jacques Duclos was present at that Communist underground meeting in Poland and had returned to France with instructions to wreck the Marshall Plan. A wave of Communist-led strikes rolled over France in the critical winter of 1947-48.

In Britain Ernest Bevin watched events on the Continent with increasing alarm. When the London Foreign Ministers' Conference on Germany broke up in November, with East and West further apart than ever, Bevin decided the time had come to talk about military security.

He invited George Marshall to a private dinner at his flat in Carlton Terrace, on the night of December 16, 1947, and there proposed a military counterpart to the Marshall Plan.

Marshall liked the idea but told Bevin to proceed with caution while he sounded out opinion back in Washington in the course of getting a Congressional appropriation for the economic aid program.[2]

Bevin's new plan received an unexpected boost from the Soviets. At the very moment that Marshall was conferring with Congressional leaders back in Washington, the Communists pulled a *coup d'état* in Prague. It was the most convincing proof of Bevin's argument for collective security against Soviet expansionism.

"*Le coup de Prague*" also brought about an immediate change in French attitudes. Although a willing member of the economic alliance,

[2] Theodore H. White, *Fire in the Ashes*, New York, Sloane, 1953, pages 287-88.

France was still reluctant to accept a definitive split between East and West. After Prague, however, Bevin found willing ears in Paris for his plan of a Western military alliance.

In the spring of 1948 the British and French moved rapidly together, building the military foundation for a future alliance with America. They signed a Treaty of Western Union at a conference in Brussels. This pact created a military alliance of Britain, France, Belgium, Holland and Luxembourg. However, it was a framework rather than a power alliance, for none of its members had any real power. It would mean nothing if the United States did not send its men over to fill in the frame.

Nineteen forty-eight was a year of anxiety in Europe but it was also, unfortunately, an election year in the United States, the traditional moment for Americans to withdraw from the world and fight among themselves. It was certainly no year for anyone to hope to put through Congress such precedent-breaking proposals as a peacetime foreign alliance, with an American commitment to fight if an ally were attacked.

Europe had to wait. American leaders were not idle, however. They issued directives to the State Department and the Pentagon to tackle the problems involved and be ready with constitutionally and politically acceptable formulae when the time came to act.

The Americans were ready soon after Truman's inauguration. They had found a way to satisfy Europe's demands for collective security without violating the Constitution. It was the formula contained in Article 5 of the North Atlantic Treaty, which committed all members to go to the aid of each but left the nature of the aid to each country's own decision. It was clearly a moral commitment to go to war in defense of an Atlantic ally.

On April 3, 1949, the representatives of twelve nations assembled in Washington and signed the document instituting the North Atlantic Treaty Organization, thereafter to be known as NATO. It was, and is, the most powerful voluntary association of nations, for the purpose of self-defense, that the world has ever known. The original twelve nations became fourteen when Greece and Turkey joined NATO in February, 1952, and then fifteen when the Federal Republic of Germany became a member in 1955.

The territories of the member nations stretch from the Arctic to the Equator, from the Dardanelles to the Panama Canal, a total land area of almost eight million square miles, covering half of the northern part of the globe. Its peoples are more than four hundred million strong. Their factories produce four-fifths of the world's goods. Three out of every four oceangoing freighters fly the flag of a NATO member and use a NATO port for their trade.

However, despite their manpower and material resources, the only real "protection" that the member peoples of NATO enjoyed when the treaty was signed was the possession by the United States of atomic bombs and the means to deliver them. This was not the kind of unique protection that could give them comfort. The world dreaded and hated the terror weapon, even those peoples who counted on it as a deterrent force. This fear of the atom bomb was reduced but not eliminated by America's acceptance of a peacetime military alliance with Europe.

It was more than a year and a half after the signature of the North Atlantic Treaty before America agreed to increase its armed forces on the Continent and send General Eisenhower back to Europe to create a NATO command. During that period of a power vacuum in Europe there were a series of indiscreet and exaggerated speeches by a few bomb-brandishing American military men and politicians that gave Europe the jitters. Stalin made his own contribution to Europe's panic by erecting the Berlin blockade and concentrating troops on the borders of Yugoslavia.

There was a story making its way around the bars and cafés of Paris during this period that accurately describes the frame of mind of the French and of other Europeans. It was a story of three soldiers who had died in battle and had come to seek entry into Paradise. St. Peter asked each soldier in turn to describe the circumstances that had brought him to the Gates of Heaven.

The first soldier was a Russian, and, when St. Peter beckoned to him, the young Soviet soldier stepped forward, raised a clenched fist and shouted: "I died fighting for the brotherhood of men, for the liberation of the prisoners of starvation." The next soldier, an American, stepped forward, saluted smartly and said: "Sir, I died fighting for the dignity of man and for the liberation of all the oppressed."

The third soldier, a Frenchman, remained in the shadows, watching, listening, saying nothing. St. Peter motioned to him to step forward, and, when the Frenchman still hesitated, he said: "Come now, young man, don't be frightened. Step right up and tell me: what brought you to the Gates of Heaven?"

The Frenchman shrugged, pointed his finger and said: "They did."

Stories of this kind led many foreign observers to report that France was "anti-American" and "neutralist." There was considerable criticism of the United States in the French press and Parliament and a very vocal neutralist group active in politics. However, what really counts in foreign affairs are deeds, not words, and despite its verbal neutralism France in action was pro-American and deeply committed to the Western Alliance.

ᏔᏏᎣ

France's greatest concern was not about the Russians or the Americans. She was most worried about the Germans. Few Frenchmen were ready to believe that Russia was France's enemy number one, even though Stalin was poised for attack and Germany was still occupied and disarmed in 1949. One of the first and most hotly debated questions put to Foreign Minister Robert Schuman when he asked the Assembly to ratify the North Atlantic Treaty was: will Germany eventually become a part of NATO? The deputies demanded that Schuman give them a guarantee against German rearmament.

Schuman insisted that "there was no plan to rearm Germany," and technically speaking he was correct, for there was no specific plan at that time. However, it was obvious to anyone familiar with world affairs that NATO military commanders would begin to yearn for the reservoir of manpower in Germany.

The German question was not a new one by any means. In the aftermath of the First World War the French had proposed several solutions to the problem of an aggressive Germany. The League of Nations was a global framework to provide collective security against aggression. The Briand proposals for a United States of Europe, the Locarno Pact, the French attempt to persuade Britain to join a peacetime European Army on the Continent, the occupation of the Rhineland, were all different aspects of the same problem: how to contain Germany.

After the Second World War the United Nations was a revival of the League, the Morgenthau Plan was another form of the post-

Versailles occupation of the Ruhr and the stripping of German plants. The Marshall Plan, in a much more constructive and farsighted manner, repeated the earlier reversal of policies in Germany, substituting the carrot of economic aid for the big stick of occupation forces, as a means of inducing Germany to become a peaceful member of the Western family of nations.

The most important revival of old policies, which evoked the most enthusiastic response, was the revival of Briand's proposal to the League in 1929, that a European union be formed and recognized as a regional group, with common interests and aims.

Briand's ideas had been inspired by the crusade of a Danish nobleman and visionary, Count Richard Coudenhove-Kalergi, founder of the Pan-European Union movement. Some of Europe's greatest statesmen had joined the movement in the interwar years: Briand in Paris, Madariaga in Madrid, Beneš in Prague. In Berlin an obscure, young German lawyer, Konrad Adenauer, had become an enthusiast for the union of Europe.

Men had dreamed of *Europa* ever since Julius Caesar had created the first European union. From Charlemagne through Napoleon and Hitler, from Philip the Fair to Dante, Mazzini, Nietzsche and Hugo, soldiers, dictators, kings and poets had tried to fashion Europe. Some had briefly succeeded in uniting Europe by force of arms, but until the mid-twentieth century no man had ever succeeded in uniting the rival nation-states of Europe voluntarily in times of peace.

ᖆᚬ

Winston Churchill was the first great man of Europe to speak of European union after the Second World War, in fact during it. In 1943 Coudenhove-Kalergi induced Churchill to deliver a world-wide radio address, calling for the creation of a Council of Europe after the final victory over the Nazis. Churchill had remembered his promise after the war in his Zurich speech of September, 1946, in which he appealed for a United States of Europe.

A year and a half later, in May, 1948, Churchill convoked a Congress of Europe at The Hague. In July, French Foreign Minister Bidault proposed to his partners in the Western European military union that a Parliament of Europe be created. The next month a group of prominent Europeans, led by Churchill's son-in-law, Duncan

Sandys, created the European Movement, with its headquarters in Brussels. The idea of Europe spread through the Continent as rapidly as in its brightest moments of the idealistic twenties, when men were going to banish war and make the world safe for democracy.

Yet the same opposition to European union that had begun in the nationalistic thirties was forming its ranks for a counterattack. The first opposition came from the British, and from Churchill himself. This was not a paradox and Churchill had not changed his ideas. What had happened was what always happens when a vision is translated into a plan for action. Everybody agreed that there ought to be, had to be, a Europe, but each sought to create Europe in his own image, and to fit his own interests.

For Churchill, Europe was a civilization and a culture and a common cause. It was not a common institution, a single, integrated nation, one and indivisible. In any case, the British, with their Commonwealth commitments, could not become a European state.

For Georges Bidault and Robert Schuman, leaders of the French Catholic party, Europe was a group of nations united by Christianity as well as by a common cause. Adenauer in Germany and de Gasperi in Italy were leaders of Christian-Democratic parties with similar outlooks to Bidault's MRP in France. For French Socialists, however, this smacked of a revival of the Holy Roman Empire. For them Europe was an economic and social collectivity, a common market to provide jobs and prosperity for Europe's masses.

For the European Communists, however, Europe was a masquerade for American economic hegemony of the Continent and a means of recruiting European mercenaries for the American crusade against Russia.

The European Movement, thanks to Churchill's sponsorship, was the first to see its program translated into reality, when the "Council of Europe" came into being on August 8, 1949, in Strasbourg. However, the Council was then, and remained thereafter, nothing more than a debating society, without any power and with little prestige of its own. Many dedicated Europeans said the Council was nothing but a British Punch and Judy show, to distract Europeans from the real issue, which was the creation of a European community in acts and authority as well as in speeches.

The issue of European union reached a climax in the spring of 1950, when French Foreign Minister Robert Schuman won immortality for his name by proposing the "Schuman Plan" for a Coal and Steel Community, in which the member nations would not only put their power resources in a common pool but sacrifice a measure of national sovereignty to a supranational High Authority of the Community.

I was only one of a hundred reporters who heard Schuman make his historic declaration of May 9, 1950 in the famous Salon de l'Horloge at the Ministry of Foreign Affairs. Personally, I shall never forget what happened when Schuman finished speaking and I had begun to read through my notes.

An usher came over and told me that I was urgently wanted in the Foreign Minister's office. I looked up with surprise to see the Minister still standing at the end of the room, but the messenger insisted that I follow him at once to the Minister's private office.

I arose, made my way through the gilt-and-satin reception halls of the Quai d'Orsay to Schuman's office, only two rooms away from the Salon de l'Horloge. The usher opened the door and I walked in, to see three familiar faces smiling up at me, from the deep, red-silk armchairs of the Minister's baroque bureau: the thin, foxlike face of Pierre Uri, one of France's most brilliant political scientists and economists; the square, freckled, confidence-inspiring face of Etienne Hirsch, once a chemical engineer but now the top brain-truster of "the Plan," France's re-equipment and modernization Ministry; and, between the two, the shrewd, mandarin-like countenance of the High Priest of the Plan, Commissioner General Jean Monnet.

Jean Monnet, the *Eminence Grise* of the Fourth Republic, technician extraordinary, was almost unknown to the public outside France, and only a shadowy mystery man to the French themselves, yet no man in the twentieth century had ever influenced so many governments in Europe, America and Asia.

As I looked at him, sitting in Schuman's office, some of the great events and great ideas of the past began to flash through my memory: Churchill's dramatic offer of British citizenship to the French on the eve of the fall of France; Roosevelt's famous directive to American industry to "produce one hundred thousand planes"; Chiang Kai-shek's railway-organization plan that gave China modern communications. Behind them all was the brain, the vision of one man, Jean

Monnet, world broker of ideas, a poet who composes his odes in blueprints and columns of figures.

As I looked at Monnet sitting in Schuman's office, I realized that the project for a Coal and Steel Community was another one of his brain children. He had been watching me closely as I had entered and had waited for me to recover from my surprise. "Well," he said, "what do you think of it?"

I smiled in reply: "Congratulations on your new brain child."

Monnet frowned, waved away my remark, and in his curt, concise manner, said: "Don't joke, this is serious. It is vitally important that you reporters understand exactly what is at stake and what this can mean for the peace of the world. If you have a moment later this afternoon, please come to my office. I would like to talk to you about Europe."

Within the hour I was on my way over to his austere office on the Rue Martignac, in the cloistered quiet of the Commissariat du Plan, to hear about the Schuman Plan from its author, Jean Monnet. Monnet, himself, refused to discuss the question of authorship. He never sought public recognition. I found out later, however, that he had originally submitted the plan to Premier Georges Bidault, who had not found time to study it, and had then brought it in person to Foreign Minister Schuman. Schuman needed no persuasion. The plan corresponded exactly to his own concept of French foreign policy, particularly the need for a Franco-German reconciliation.

It was one of the strange accidents of history that Schuman and Adenauer should have been Foreign Ministers of France and Germany at that moment. Schuman had been born and raised in Lorraine, prior to the First World War, when that territory was German. He had only become a French citizen after the Versailles Treaty restored Alsace and Lorraine to France. Twenty-eight years later this German-born and German-educated lawyer was Prime Minister of France, and, in a succeeding cabinet, Foreign Minister.

His German counterpart, Chancellor Konrad Adenauer, was a Rhinelander, brought up on the right bank of the River Rhine, opposite the birthplace of Schuman. The Rhineland had always been the most French-influenced of the German states. In his youth Adenauer was an advocate of French-German union and an admirer of French culture. For Adenauer the Rhine had always been a natural link between, rather than a frontier dividing, France and Germany.

Jean Monnet, therefore, was not an originator of the idea of a French-German union, but rather its architect. Monnet was not an innovator nor an intellectual creator. He was a clever idea-engineer, with a perfect sense of timing. The spring of 1950 was the right time, with the right men in the right places, to make the dream of Europe come true.

"What is Europe?" Monnet asked, rhetorically, when I arrived at his office. "It is the peninsula of Asia, inhabited by some two hundred and fifty million peoples. This peninsula is favored by a temperate climate, fertile fields and natural communications without geographic barriers. All the barriers among the nations of Europe are man-made.

"Nature was bountiful and wise in its gifts to Europe and above all to France and Germany. The River Rhine is a natural reservoir of energy and a channel of trade. On the right bank are rich deposits of hard coal and on the left bank rich deposits of iron ore. Energy plus coke plus iron ore equals steel. You could not ask for a better, more convenient industrial complex than the Ruhr and Lorraine.

"Yet what has happened? The Germans have hoarded their coke, the French their iron ore, and each has erected trade barriers and fortresses on either side of the River Rhine. Instead of carrying barges loaded down with steel, the Rhine has run red with the bloated bodies of Frenchmen and Germans. This is not only criminal, it is mad. The time has come to end forever the wars between the Germans and the French.

"There is only one way to end wars between nations: that is to merge them into one."

Monnet waited for me to complete my notes and then continued:

"This Community of Coal and Steel that we have proposed is only the beginning. It must and will be extended to other areas of public affairs until some day a United States of Europe will emerge. That is why I see this Community as much more than an industrial pool. There would be nothing very new in that. International cartels and trusts have for years developed such mergers. This is not what we are seeking, in fact it is the very opposite.

"We want to break the power of those cartels and pool the natural resources of our countries in the interests of all the peoples of the

European Community. It is therefore necessary to give the Community governmental powers of its own, powers that transcend the national authority. This is the heart of the matter. Watch this development closely, for in the months and years ahead this embyro of Europe will either grow or die depending on this one essential element: integration—a union as complete as that of the federal structure of America—or extinction. As Clement Attlee, the British Premier, put it, Europe must 'federate or perish.' "

ᴄᴡᴐ

The Schuman Plan was well received in the French and European press, and above all in America, where it was regarded as the final success of the Marshall Plan goal of European self-help through economic union.

European steel producers were at first hesitant about the plan, particularly the Germans, for in the past they had profited by the cartel system. Monnet, however, won them all over. He persuaded the French steel men that they had everything to gain by achieving access on equal terms to German coke. Then he won over German producers by pointing out that the Community would bring about an end to wartime restrictions on German industry, and prepare Germany's entry into the Western Alliance. Adenauer needed no persuasion himself, and he had a majority in the Bundestag for political endorsement of the plan.

Within a year Monnet had achieved his goals. On March 20, 1951, the delegates of six nations—France, Germany, Italy and the three Benelux countries—met at the Quai d'Orsay to initial a Treaty Instituting a Coal and Steel Community of Europe. The treaty, a twenty-thousand-word document, provided for a fifty-year merger of the coal and steel industries of the member nations, under a High Authority, which would have supranational powers to regulate the industries, over and above the individual laws of the member nations. It included a clause which left the door open for any European nation to join the six charter members or be associated with the Community.

This clause was aimed primarily at the British, who had refused all of Monnet's many pleas for their adherence to the treaty. Only a few days before the final conference among the drafting powers, Monnet had held a private meeting with British representatives at his house outside Paris. The British had once again explained the impossibility of their joining any supranational organization that would put a strain on their Commonwealth ties and interfere with the sterling-zone preferential trade system.

Opponents of European union, particularly among the French Socialists and the Mendès-France supporters, were to use this British refusal as a pretext for attacking the Community, calling it derisively "*la petite Europe*." Without Britain and the Scandinavian countries, they argued, the Community had no right to call itself "European." Many a Frenchman also sincerely feared any community in which France would find herself face to face with a powerful Germany, without any counterbalance. Britain was regarded as an indispensable check on Germany.

Monnet agreed that Britain ought to be a member of the Community but he refused to delay the signing of the treaty until the happy but unpredictable day of British approval.

Monnet fought on against all opposition and on February 10, 1953, only two years after the initialing of the treaty, the common market came into effect. Jean Monnet, unanimously elected Chairman of the High Authority, announced the opening of the common market in coal and steel in an address from the studios of Radio Luxembourg, where the Community had set up its headquarters.

The first President of Europe told his fellow Community members: "From this morning on we have all become Europeans, all of us, Germans, Belgians, Frenchmen, Dutchmen, Italians and Luxembourgers. There is no more German coal, no more French steel, but only European coal and steel circulating freely among our countries, as though it were one country of one hundred fifty-five million consumers, as many as the United States or the Soviet Union."

Later that day, at a dinner for the international reporters, Monnet declared: "This new Community is a revolution in Europe, perhaps the greatest Europe has known. We are embarked upon a liberation of Europe from its past."

A few months later, the *Observer* of London paid tribute to Monnet's vision and energy and said: "A United Western Europe is, partly at least, a reality, no longer a dream. It is a wonderful achievement." The *Observer* went on, however, to express the doubts that many Europeans, particularly the British, still had about Monnet's dream: "And yet, a nagging feeling remains that this is all too much one man's glorious sleight-of-hand; that revolutions do not happen this way and that it may still all come undone. . . . It is still impossible to say whether this tale of a dashing and intrepid pioneer, now at its dramatic climax, is one of triumph or of tragedy."[3]

The *Observer's* comment was apt, for the Community had hovered between triumph and tragedy ever since its birth. The tragedy had its origins in an event that occurred far from Europe's shores and almost destroyed the entire world. It happened on the morning of June 25, 1950, when the North Koreans invaded South Korea. Only a few men in Europe knew what or where North Korea was but the Korean War changed the directions of Western policy.

The Coal and Steel Community managed to survive but the shock effects of the Korean War and the new policies it engendered stunted the Community's growth. It has done well within its own narrow field of operations but it did not evolve from the coal fields and steel mills to become a full economic and political community. The United States of Europe, of which Monnet dreamed in 1950, was still a dream as the world entered the second decade of its postwar history.

❦

The Korean War changed both the direction and the pace of world affairs. From economic recovery, slow-moving at best, the emphasis shifted to rapid rearmament. The Atlantic Community of guns and men became more urgent than the European Community of coal and steel.

Western Europe faced a serious shortage of military manpower at the outbreak of war in Korea. With America concentrating on Korea and France bogged down in Indochina, armed forces available for Western Europe were inadequate to provide a NATO cover against a Russian attack. There was, however, one still-untapped reservoir: Germany. Congressional leaders in Washington began to put pressure on Truman and Acheson to insist upon the rearmament of Germany, no matter how reluctant the French might be.

Acheson finally yielded to Congressional pressures, and raised the issue with the British and French at a conference in the Hotel Waldorf-Astoria, in New York, in September, 1950. I was present at that

[3] The *Observer*, London, April 10, 1953.

conference, which marked the turning point of postwar European affairs, and recall the observation of a pessimistic French official who said: "This is the end of the postwar period and the beginning of a new prewar period of European history."

I saw both Schuman and French Ambassador to Germany, André François-Poncet, at that conference and they made no effort to disguise their own pessimism about the crisis ahead in France, when the government informed Parliament of the decision to rearm Germany. "I do not know whether European union can survive this," Schuman confessed in a talk we had the day the conference ended.

Acheson and President Truman both understood and sympathized with French fears about German rearmament. The German Army had always been a threat not only to the French but to German democracy too and, in 1950, German democracy was still too fragile to be sure it could control a new Wehrmacht. German ambitions to unify the country and recapture the lost territories ceded to Poland would certainly become dangerous when they had an army that could be used to gain their goals.

American Congressional leaders, attempting to allay French and British fears of German rearmament, agreed to send an additional four American divisions to Europe. This also answered another major argument of our allies: that the two world wars might never have started had the United States been a member of a collective security organization, with American troops stationed on the Continent and committed to fight an aggressor. Acheson therefore told Schuman that Congress had a right to demand German troops, as a counterpart to America's concession to French and British demands.

Both the American and French theses were logical and sound, although mutually contradictory. German troops were obviously needed, but German troops were also a menace to the security of Western Europe and to the health of German's postwar democracy. Some synthesis had to be found to bring into harmony these two conflicting views.

French Premier René Pleven, whose problem it was to solve this dilemma, was a businessman from Brittany, leader of the small center party, the UDSR. Pleven, before the war, had worked for some time under the direction of Jean Monnet, in one of Monnet's many international banking projects. He was devoted to Monnet, and considered him to be one of the greatest men of our times. It was natural, there-fore, that Pleven should turn to the master planner of France, and ask him to devise a scheme for German rearmament, with safeguards against German militarism.

As in the case of economic union, Monnet was not called upon to originate a concept but rather to blueprint a practical realization. It was just the kind of operation at which he excelled. Monnet went to work immediately with his top brain-trusters, to sort out all the elements of the problem and to see how they could be reassembled neatly into one, smooth-fitting whole.

In six short weeks they came up with the answer. It was an inspired and inspiring solution, one of the most brilliant of French paradoxes: Germany must be rearmed but there must not be any German troops. Or, as one Paris wit put it: Germany must be given an army smaller than the French but bigger than the Russian.

The key to the riddle was an integrated European Army. Just as Monnet once said that there was no more German coal or French iron ore but only European steel, so could he claim that there would be no more German or French soldiers if they were merged in an inte-grated European Army.

The European Army, as he saw it, would be a complete merger of the armed forces of all the member nations, "on the lowest possible unit level." A European division would be composed of German, French and Italian regiments under a Belgian general, or any other formula that would so fuse the men, the weapons and the services of supply that no one nation would be able to call upon an army of its own to carry out its own national purposes. In brief: Germans would be rearmed but Germany would not be.

And so the "Pleven Plan" was born.

On October 24, 1950, René Pleven walked to the speaker's platform in the National Assembly to propose, for the first time in history, a French military alliance with Germany. The European Army, he said, would be the military counterpart of the Coal and Steel Com-munity. It would defend Europe "as far to the east as possible," in other words deep inside Germany, a concept designed to give comfort to the French, on whose soil the previous world wars had been fought.

The public in France was almost evenly divided between hope that this might end forever German invasions of France and fear that it might end forever the independent French Republic. Public opinion polls were run by French papers, and, depending on how the questions were framed, showed majorities both for and against the European Army scheme. One paper, *Paris-Presse,* asked its readers whether they would prefer a European Army in which German boys would hold the line against the Russians, instead of sending French boys to the Elbe. Some seven out of ten replied they would. However, the paper *Aurore* put the question this way: "Are you in favor of rearming the Germans, who have invaded France three times?" Obviously the *Aurore* poll showed a majority against the European Army.

The same basic conflicts of interests and ideals divided the military men and statesmen of the Western world. In Paris General Eisenhower at first called the scheme "a military monstrosity." French generals opposed it vehemently, charging that Pleven was destroying the French Army rather than creating a European one.

Jean Monnet, however, made a deep impression on Eisenhower, who admired the clarity of his mind and the sincerity of his aims. The Supreme Commander was also greatly influenced by the American Ambassador to France, David K. E. Bruce, one of the most able and respected representatives our country has ever sent abroad.

Under the guidance of Bruce and Monnet, Eisenhower became an ardent "European." In a conversation I had with the General at his SHAPE headquarters in the summer of 1951, he described his "conversion" to the European Army plan this way: "It is true that I was skeptical at first. It will not be easy, militarily, to make it an efficient, fast-moving army. But it can be done. The question is a simple one, really: do we want to end once and for all the French-German conflicts, and, do we want and need German armed forces in NATO? The answer is yes, and the only way we can achieve all of these aims is in the European Army. So, I'm for it."

Eisenhower was not only for the European Army; he was also against the reconstitution of the German Wehrmacht, which he considered was as great a danger to Europe as the Red Army. One of the most dedicated democrats ever to wear a uniform, Eisenhower was devoted to the principle of civilian control of a nation's armed forces. This was one of the best features of the European Army in his view, because it would put German forces under a Parliament of Europe, which could protect the young German Government from the influence of the industrial and military clique that had brought Hitler to power.

When I interviewed Eisenhower in that summer of 1951 he had just had a sharp exchange with Acheson on that very issue of control over a German Army. French delays in implementing Pleven's proposal of October, 1950 had so irritated Washington that Dean Acheson had cabled Eisenhower instructions to proceed with recruiting Germans immediately, while continuing the negotiations with the French.

Eisenhower promptly cabled back that this would be a disaster. It would mean that the Wehrmacht would be recreated, a step that he refused to take. Or, even more likely, he thought, the French would simply walk out of NATO. It is absurd, said Eisenhower, to put Germans into the front lines of NATO, if the French, who geographically occupy the center and rear areas, refuse to co-operate. Eisenhower sympathized with Washington's impatience; he himself was impatient, he said, but the only solution was to continue to persuade our allies to do what we think right, and not try to impose our will by force.

Eisenhower's prestige and patience prevailed over the impatience of Congressmen and the administration. However, despite all of his talent for conciliation, he could not finally bring the French around to the point of making a final decision on their own proposal. Weeks, months and years went by in negotiations on the EDC draft treaty.

The treaty was written and revised a dozen times before it was finally completed and signed by the member governments. However, by the summer of 1954, almost four full years after the Pleven proposal, and two years after Eisenhower had left SHAPE for the White House, no French Government had yet dared submit the treaty for a ratification debate in Parliament.

By then the world had changed radically. Churchill, who had called on Britain to lead in the creation of a European Army, in August, 1950, when he was the leader of the Opposition in Commons, had been re-elected Prime Minister and had changed his policy with his role. As the King's First Minister, Winston Churchill refused to merge His Majesty's forces in a Continental Army. Stalin had died

in March, 1953, and the new rulers of the Kremlin had changed the
Moscow scowls of war into beguiling smiles of peace. The Korean
War, which had precipitated the issue of German rearmament, had
ended. So had the war in Indochina.

The man who had ended the Indochinese War decided that the
time had come to end the dispute over the European Army.

Pierre Mendès-France announced that his government would submit the EDC Treaty to the National Assembly by August. Mendès,
who had built his political program on the thesis, "To govern is to
choose," meant to force his countrymen to make their choice on the
German question.

ᔕᓬ

Inside France the battle of EDC set Frenchmen against Frenchmen and split every political party into dissident factions. In one
public debate I heard General Jacques Chaban-Delmas, mayor of
Bordeaux and a prominent Gaullist deputy, tell his followers: "I am
appalled at what the EDC is doing to our country. The Communists
call government ministers American recruiting sergeants. The Catholics and liberals jeer back at them, calling the Communists Russian
spies. Patriots, I appeal to you, are there no more Frenchmen left in
France?"

Mendès-France, too, was appalled by the fact that France was being
torn apart by the EDC dispute. He had told his fellow deputies in
Parliament, in his investiture speech of June 18, 1954, that he refused
to believe it impossible to reconcile Frenchmen to the question of
German policy. This was the first real indication that Mendès-France
had given of his own position on EDC. It meant that he had not committed himself to the treaty, that he was ready to revise it, in the
course of finding a compromise that would reconcile divided France.

Allied statesmen were immediately suspicious of Mendès. Their
suspicions turned into open distrust when Mendès sent a memorandum to London and Washington, informing them that he planned to
call for a conference with the Russians between the ratification of
EDC in the Assembly and its final endorsement in the Senate. He
seemed to them to look on the EDC Treaty as a commodity of diplomatic trade with Russia.

Anglo-American diplomats in Paris, who deliberately "leaked" this memorandum to reporters, told us that Sir Winston Churchill and John Foster Dulles had sent scathing replies back to Mendès. Churchill, we were told, threatened to disavow him publicly if he dared call a meeting with Russia before ratification of EDC. Dulles was said to have sent the most violent message to an ally in the history of American diplomacy, virtually threatening to break relations with France. The leading exponents of the EDC Treaty began to attack Mendès in the press, notably Catholic Robert Schuman, the "Father of Europe," and Socialist André Philip, both of whom denounced Mendès on the day he flew to Brussels for a six-power conference of the Coal and Steel Community ministers, for a final attempt to reach an understanding before the EDC debate.

Mendès found himself virtually alone representing France at the conference table. The other Foreign Ministers, strengthened by the divisions of France, stiffened their resolve to reject any amendments to the treaty. They heard Mendès out, as he presented a new "protocol" to the treaty, and then one by one tore into his protocols and ripped them to pieces. There was a sharp clash between Mendès and Spaak and Mendès and Adenauer. Mendès walked out of Brussels, pale, tight-lipped and defeated but, as always, firmly convinced that he was right and everybody else was wrong.

Mendès then flew to London to see Churchill and Eden. But he found no sympathy in London. Churchill told him that he would not intervene on his behalf. Churchill said that Britain expected the French Government to honor its country's signature on a treaty negotiated in good faith.

Mendès flew back to Paris shaken, for the first time, by the failure of his international talks. He did not have a friend left among the political leaders of Western Europe and very few inside his own country. By the time the debate ended and EDC died, Mendès-France had become public enemy number one in the eyes of the Western allies.

૭∿૭

The rejection of EDC was inevitably interpreted throughout the world as a victory for the Soviet Union and a defeat for the United States. It precipitated the gravest crisis of the Atlantic Alliance since its birth five years before. Although the treaty had died on a procedural technicality, without being submitted to a substantive vote, everyone understood that France had rejected the idea of European Union and had decided to pursue an independent, nationalistic foreign policy.[4]

In Germany something very close to panic seized the democratic leaders of the Federal Republic. Adenauer had staked his future and the future of a democratic Germany on a reconciliation with France and on the prevention of any rebirth of an uncontrolled German militarism. With the rejection of EDC by the French Parliament, which then went blithely off on vacation, Germany was left in a vacuum of confusion.

In Washington the President and Congressional leaders surveyed the wreckage of American policy in Europe with gloom and then with anger. Mr. Dulles, who had publicly warned the French a dozen times that "there is no alternative to EDC," began to prepare his agonizing reappraisal of American foreign policy. He flew to London and Bonn, deliberately by-passing Paris to demonstrate the fact that France was now the pariah of the Alliance and that Germany would be rearmed anyway, without France's consent.

British Foreign Secretary Anthony Eden also went on a flying tour to Europe to see what could be saved. In Paris he told Mendès that Britain would participate in a Western European Union if a new treaty could be quickly drafted, but without the supranational features of EDC. He suggested a conference be convened rapidly to end the crisis of the Atlantic Alliance. Mendès, by then genuinely alarmed at France's isolation, agreed to co-operate fully with Eden.

At the end of September, Mendès went to London for a nine-power conference (the six European nations of the Coal and Steel Community plus Britain, America and Canada) to construct a new policy for European unity. Out of that conference came a decision to revive the old Brussels Treaty of 1948, which had been the forerunner of the Atlantic Pact, and to extend its membership to include Germany and Italy in a "new" Western European Union. Mendès signed the London accords on October 3, and four days later went before the Assembly in Paris. He won a vote of confidence authorizing him to proceed with the drafting of a treaty.

A week later, on October 19, Mendès met the German Chancellor at La Celle–Saint Cloud, near Paris, to work out the terms of an

[4] See pages 125-26 for description of the EDC debate.

accord to "Europeanize" the Saar, the last major obstacle on the road to reconciliation of France and Germany.

When Mendès agreed to hold a referendum to allow the Saarlanders to decide whether they wished to be an autonomous territory in the Western European Union, it was the beginning of the end of French control over the Saar. Strong and prosperous Germany was a greater magnet than weak, depressed France, above all to the Germanic peoples of the Saar. Had France ratified EDC and formed an integrated European Community with Germany, then the Saar too would have been part of a common pool. By rejecting EDC and accepting a so-called Western European Union, which was no more than a loose coalition of national states, France gave the Saar back to Germany.

The referendum later bore out advance predictions when the Saar majority rejected a European status and the pro-German parties defeated the European parties. The Saar question was finally settled once and for all in June, 1956, when France and Germany signed an agreement providing for the transfer of the Saar back to German sovereignty by January 1, 1957.

ᘒ

The final step to be taken after the Saar agreement between Mendès and Adenauer was the drafting of the Treaty of Western European Union and its submission to the French Assembly for ratification. Mendès had promised Eden that there would be no more delays by France. He had only one more mission to accomplish before liquidating the German question: a visit to America to heal the wounds that had been opened by the defeat of EDC.

Mendès flew to Washington in November and in a few days' time the force of his personality had captured the American people. From a villain, who had destroyed Europe and almost wrecked the Atlantic Alliance, Mendès became a hero who had saved the free world. Mr. Dulles, ecstatic at the last-minute rescue from his agonizing reappraisal, called Mendès a "superman."

Mendès flew back to Paris from his triumphant tour to discover that he still had a tough fight ahead, for, in his absence, the opposition to any rearmament of Germany had organized for the final test of strength in the scheduled year-end ratification debate.

Christmas week was a nightmare for Mendès-France and caused

new jitters in London and Washington. On the day before Christmas, the National Assembly rejected the first paragraph of the Ratification Bill, authorizing the creation of a German Army. Mendès jumped up immediately, demanded a second reading of the bill on a confidence motion. He won his point and the bill passed by the meager margin of 287 to 260, a plurality, but twenty-seven votes less than a majority of the legislature.

The epitaph to Western European Union was pronounced by Conservative deputy Pierre André, who commented: "Not brilliant, eh?"

∾

Brilliant or not, the crisis was over.

In London, Churchill expressed his "satisfaction at this happy result." In Washington President Eisenhower said that "this was most satisfactory news for the whole free world."

In Paris, Mendès-France, exhausted and depressed, sat down to write a letter to Churchill, to warn him that the French acceptance of a German armed participation in NATO was not the end of the problems of the Alliance but the beginning of a new and more difficult problem: the search for peace. The Soviet reaction to German rearmament would undoubtedly be sharp. It was necessary, Mendès felt, to take immediate steps to reassure the Russians that the West had no aggressive plans. Mendès suggested in his letter that there be a joint, Western invitation to the Soviet Government for a Big Four Conference.

Churchill read the letter with disbelief and dismay. Mendès had not said a word about completing the ratification process by submitting the treaty to the French Senate. Once again, as in his summer memorandum on a meeting with the Russians, Mendès seemed to be ready to use European Union as a diplomatic trading-instrument to bribe the Soviets into peace.

The British Prime Minister sent back a reply on January 12 that made Mendès wince. Rarely has there been such an exchange between two closely allied chiefs of government. Churchill wrote: "Although we have every sympathy with you in your difficulties and admiration for your exertions, the fact should be accepted that I and my colleagues are wholeheartedly resolved that there shall be no meeting or invitation in any circumstances . . . until the London-Paris agreements have been ratified by all the signatories." Churchill then warned Mendès that Britain and the United States were prepared to proceed without France: "Indeed, I fear that an indefinite process of delay may well lead to the adoption of other solutions, which are certainly being studied on both sides of the Atlantic."

To leave no doubt what he meant by "other solutions," Churchill went on to make an open threat: "I myself am very much opposed to the withdrawal of all American and British troops from the Continent. You may count on me to oppose, to the best of my ability, the strategic concept known as 'peripheral.' *On the other hand, I should feel bound, whether as Prime Minister, or as a private member, to support the policy known as the 'empty chair,' although this would involve large changes in the infra-structure of NATO, both military and political.*"

Churchill could not have been more brutally frank: if France did not ratify the rearmament of Germany, Britain and America would cancel their commitments to defend France and would write France out of the Atlantic military alliance.

This letter was not made public until March, 1955, a month after Mendès had been overthrown by the Assembly. It was not, however, addressed to him alone, but to all France, and Mendès' successor, Edgar Faure, understood this. One of the first things Faure did when elected was to assure the British and American Ambassadors that his government's first priority was ratification of Western European Union in the Senate.

Faure carried out his promise. At dawn on March 27, 1955, after an all-night debate, France completed the ratification of Western European Union. Immediately after the Senate vote Premier Faure made this statement to me in a television interview: "This is one of the most important decisions in French history. It guarantees the preservation and strengthening of the Atlantic Alliance, with the addition of German armed might."

Faure then announced that this "was not the end of the road but rather the beginning of a new search, for the only true security of mankind, the search for peace." He said: "France, like your own country, the United States, desires sincere talks with the Russians. A recent declaration of President Eisenhower shows that you

Americans, like the French and the British, believe that the time has come to seek *rapprochement* with the East. My government asks, with insistence, that every effort be made, in the shortest delay, to bring about East-West talks, for security and for peace."

༄

Faure's demand for peace talks with the Russians was well timed. It was not, however, the beginning of the search for peace, nor had France been the first to call for East-West talks. A year before, in July, 1954, Winston Churchill had flown to Washington to discuss with President Eisenhower the urgent need to explore the chances of peaceful coexistence with the Russians.

Churchill, in a July 13 report to Commons on his mission to Washington, revealed that it had been prompted by "the stupefying revelations" of America's atomic experiments at Eniwetok. The power of the H-bomb, possessed by both America and Russia, terrified all the smaller nations, even a nation like Britain which did have atomic bombs of its own.

President Eisenhower, a month later, tried to reassure America's allies by stating emphatically that America rejected the idea of preventive war against Russia. At a news conference in Washington on August 11 the President said that preventive war was completely unthinkable in this age of atomic and hydrogen weapons. He said there is no such thing as "preventive" war. There is only war or peace, said Eisenhower, and the United States was dedicated to the search for peace.

A year later President Eisenhower flew to Geneva for the first "Peace Conference" of the cold war. The Geneva Conference came only three months after France's ratification of German rearmament and was hailed in France as an answer to Faure's appeal for an immediate attempt to seek an East-West *rapprochement*.

The French, however, played almost no role at that conference, nor at the two succeeding Conferences of Geneva in the turning-point year of 1955. The rejection of EDC had cost France her chance to achieve not only leadership in Europe but to regain a major voice in world affairs. As the spokesman for a united Europe, as big as America or Russia, France would have commanded attention and respect at any conference table. As the spokesman for a small nation, weakened by internal divisions and colonial wars, France was lost and alone in the strange, new world of 1955, as she had been back in 1945.

Only ten years had gone by, from the unconditional surrender of the Nazis to the unconditional acceptance of Germany as a free and equal partner in the Atlantic Alliance. Stalin and Roosevelt had died but the new leaders of Russia and America had no greater regard for the French, as a world power, than the wartime leaders had. General de Gaulle was engrossed in his history of the liberation and Mendès-France was again isolated politically in his old role of Cassandra. There was no outstanding French statesman to recapture prestige for France.

There was, however, one man left, who had never lost hope, who had never stopped dreaming. He was no statesman, no politician, but no Frenchman had ever won such world-wide acclaim as he had. Jean Monnet, Mr. Europe, came home, for one more attempt to make his dream come true and to open the eyes of his countrymen to the realities of a changed world.

Monnet resigned as President of the Coal and Steel Authority after the ratification of Western European Union, which he regarded as the very opposite of a European Community. He resigned his post but did not quit his mission in life, the creation of Europe, for he had another idea, another one of his fabulous plans. This one had a catchy name: Euratom.

Again, the idea of an atomic pool was not an innovation of Monnet's. It had been discussed for years by the Organization for European Economic Co-operation. In December, 1953, the OEEC instructed a French technician, Louis Armand, research and planning director of the National Railways, to report on means to reduce the cost and increase the availability of power for European industries by development of atomic energy. After months of intensive study Armand had sent in a report recommending the creation of a common organization to develop industrial use of the atom. This was the germ of the Euratom idea.

It was as natural and logical as the merger of German coal and French iron ore, for each of the European countries had something to contribute to an Atomic Community. France and Germany had some of the world's leading atomic scientists, as well as highly developed chemical industries. Belgium, of course, owned one of the world's richest supplies of uranium in the Congo. Norway was the home of heavy water, Holland and Switzerland of precision instruments. Great Britain was one of the three major atomic powers of the world. Euratom could easily rival America or Russia in a few years' time, if the countries of Europe would agree to pool their skills and resources.

Once again, as in the case of the Coal-Steel and European Defense communities, Great Britain refused to join a European organization that would interfere with its other interests, particularly its close atomic partnership with the United States. Once again Jean Monnet insisted that Euratom would be a failure if it were not an integrated, supranational community.

This time a huge majority of Frenchmen agreed with Monnet. Perhaps it was a belated realization of what they had lost in EDC; perhaps it was the fear of the destructive power of the atom, and the conviction that it could only be contained by taking it out of the hands of a small group. Whatever the reason, Euratom captured the imagination of the French and the five other members of the Coal and Steel Community, who had already learned to work together successfully, in their limited field.

Monnet worked through an "Action Committee for a United States of Europe," which, by January, 1956, had won the adherence of parliamentary group leaders in each of the six countries. On July 11, 1956, the French Assembly authorized the Mollet Government to negotiate a supranational Atomic Community, to be known as Euratom. The vote was 342 to 183.

Only a week later, on July 18, the Organization for European Economic Co-operation moved to compete with Euratom, with a plan of its own, a limited project for a seventeen-nation Nuclear Energy Committee. OEEC members felt it was more likely that Britain would co-operate with the Continental nations in a non-supranational organization.

Monnet, undaunted, pushed ahead with his own plan, more convinced than ever that there was nothing to gain and everything to lose by waiting for the British.

At the time of this writing both projects are still in the early stages of discussion. There is, however, no longer any doubt that some kind of a Continental atomic-energy pool will emerge, if only some common pilot plants for the separation of uranium isotopes or the chemical treatment of irradiated fuels. Whether or not Monnet's dream of Europe is any closer to realization is a matter for pure speculation.

World affairs do not proceed in an unbroken line; they move in zigs and zags, impossible to predict on a day-to-day or month-to-month basis. However, even the zigs and zags, while shifting from side to side, can also move forward or backward. It is my conviction that Europe is moving toward unity, in the Monnet sense of the concept, despite the shifts of French policy.

I believe that Frenchmen are slowly realizing that France has no future as a small nation-state. France cannot retire from the world, cannot become a larger Switzerland, living in a prosperous, prophylactic Paradise, inside a protective mountain fortress. France is an integral part of Europe and cannot escape its destiny.

Once France could deny its European origins by dreaming of Empire and then of a great Union of Overseas France. That dream is only the dimmest memory as the Fourth Republic enters its second decade of life. The French have not yet admitted the end of their long period of eminence as an imperial power, but most Frenchmen know in their hearts that they have come to the end of the road. It is always difficult for any generation to admit it can no longer protect the heritage and traditions of the past. Thus the French continue to live by yesterday's standards while searching for their place in the world of tomorrow.

France's search for a better tomorrow is symbolic of every man's search for peace and progress. The entire world is groping blindly and fearfully through the terrifying dusts of the atomic era, in a search for peace, freedom and dignity that transcends national interests. It is a search for the survival of mankind.

CONCLUSION

18 A Change of Life

for France

France may be lonely and lost in the strange, new world of the mid-century but France is not alone among the great powers to suffer confusion and humiliation in a world of violent change.

The Soviet Empire began to disintegrate in the year 1956. The Poles loosened their chains, drove Soviet Marshal Rokossovsky from their government and then publicly defied Khrushchev when he flew to Warsaw to stop the Titoist rebellion. The Hungarians attacked Soviet tanks with their bare hands, singing the Marseillaise as they waved the flag of revolution—the old, tricolor banner of Hungary with the red star ripped out of it.

Western rejoicing at this long hoped-for challenge to Soviet imperialism was mitigated by signs of simultaneous disintegration of the Atlantic Alliance. The Germans, in defiance of strong American recommendations, tore up their commitment to raise an army of 500,000 men for NATO. Tiny Iceland ordered mighty America to withdraw from NATO air bases there. American leadership of the West had never been more seriously challenged in the postwar decade.

It thus became evident in the year 1956 that the postwar period of world history had reached a turning point. The era dominated by the rivalry of East and West, with two powerful, hostile camps, led by Russia and America, was on its way out. Anglo-French influence in Arabia, Africa and Asia was waning rapidly. North Africans and South Africans, Egyptians, Israeli, Vietnamese and Sudanese all turned on their mentors or tormentors. The star of nationalism was on the rise, from Port Said to Warsaw, from Rabat to Reykjavik. This has been the year of the little man, the year of the turning of the worm.

The chain reactions of revolt did not mean the final triumph of

321

good over evil, of liberty over slavery. The Russians counterattacked, brutally crushing the Hungarian rebels. Nor were all the rebels freedom-loving democrats. In some cases, the rebellions marked a return to anachronistic chauvinism and retrograde feudalism. Nasser was not an Arab George Washington. Gomulka is no Thomas Jefferson, and Strijdom, to say the least, is not an Abraham Lincoln. All of the revolutions, however, did share one common characteristic: the small nations, for better or for worse, will no longer be bribed or bullied into carrying out the policies of the big nations.

The Russians could not frighten the Hungarians into submission. They had to use force, had to destroy the myth of a Communist "People's Democracy." The British and French, too, had to use force against Nasser. None of the great powers could impose its will by threats alone, as once they could. One of the most extraordinary results of this change was the Canadian plan for a United Nations police force, composed of troops from the small nations alone, excluding the great powers. This was a complete about-face from the original concept of the UN Charter, which was based upon the principle that world peace could only be preserved by the Big Five. The peace of the world still depends upon the atomic powers but they have lost their *exclusive* initiative to direct the course of world affairs. The small nations no longer cower helplessly in the shadow of the atom bomb. It is the great powers who have become fearful of the adventures into which they are being plunged by the rebellious little peoples. The basic premises of international life have been radically altered and some new power equation must be devised.

It is in France, more than in any other country, that this startling reversal of roles can be most clearly discerned and sharply felt. France is a microcosm, a political, social and diplomatic laboratory, in which all the passions that move men everywhere can be seen and studied in almost pure form. France is both a big power and a small nation and can thus appreciate the emotions of each. France is the only small nation that is a member of the Big Four and has veto power in the United Nations. Yet France is the only member of the Big Four that does not have a stock of atomic bombs to give validity to its membership and power to its veto. France, therefore, has a schizophrenic reaction to almost every international crisis: a small nation's resentment of big-power domination and a big-power determination to impose its will and direct the course of events. For the past decade France has been unable to decide whether she was the biggest of the small nations or the smallest of the big powers. The French have consequently been unable to construct a consistent foreign policy or to adjust to the shifts of world affairs.

France is the last of the colonial powers to cling desperately to her imperial domains. Britain could grant freedom to India and still remain influential in world councils, for Britain had the Commonwealth behind her. Holland could lose Indonesia without suffering a psychological shock or a feeling of humiliation, for Holland is beyond question a small country and could not be expected to hold a big empire in revolt. The French, unlike the British and the Dutch, had neither a commonwealth to turn to nor the excuse of being too small to act as an imperial power. The French were trying to build a commonwealth and thus felt they had to hold on to Indochina. When the French Army was defeated at Dien Bien Phu it was a national humiliation for the once powerful French. They could not, like the Dutch, resign themselves to defeat, could not accept a reduction to the status of a small European nation. So they fought back in North Africa and then reached a peak of do-or-die bravado in the decision to invade Egypt, risking a general war, the destruction of the Atlantic Alliance and of the United Nations in one of the most daring gambles of French history.

Neither big enough to hold on nor small enough to give up, the French have condemned themselves to such acts of desperation in lieu of a reappraisal of their true role in the world. For the past decade France has been staggering around in the world arena like a punch-drunk fighter, whose vision is clouded, whose body is bruised and bleeding but who will not quit, because a once-great champion must go down fighting. If the French could rid themselves of this romantic delusion they could live a long and prosperous life. If not, then France may come to a tragic end, broken in body and spirit.

∽

A contemporary evaluation of any society is generally risky and unreliable, particularly in so volatile a country as France. Every time

I speculate upon the future of France there comes to my mind the image of a foreign correspondent in the year 1871, trying to forecast the future of a France that lay prostrate under the Prussian boot. Would he, I keep wondering, have foreseen the renaissance of France in a few years' time, the conquest of the world's second largest empire, the rise of a mighty army that assumed the leadership of the democratic world and beat back the superior forces of the Kaiser's bravest soldiers at Verdun?

I have spent many days at the Bibliothèque Nationale in Paris reading through the papers and histories of that period, searching for evidence of any contemporary forecast of the late nineteenth-century renaissance of French power. Among the generally gloomy commentators of the day there were two who refused to lose faith: Georges Clemenceau in France and Walt Whitman in America. Clemenceau never accepted the defeat as final and always believed in the eventual liberation of Alsace and Lorraine. Walt Whitman chose the moment of defeat to write one of the most stirring tributes to the glory and grandeur of France.

With a poet's blind faith Walt Whitman rejected the "facts" of history and saw France, purged by defeat, rising stronger than ever:

O star of France . . .
Dim, smitten star,
Orb not of France alone, pale symbol of my soul, its dearest hopes,
The struggle and the daring, rage divine for liberty,
Of aspirations toward the far ideal, enthusiast's dreams of brotherhood . . .

Again thy star, O France, fair, lustrous star,
In heavenly peace, clearer, more bright than ever,
Shall beam immortal.

The poet's faith was swiftly vindicated. Within a decade the star of France had risen brightly in the heavens. Clemenceau, too, was vindicated. He had voted against the peace treaty cession of Alsace and Lorraine to Germany, and had lived to march back and raise the tricolor again over the lost provinces. The miracle of French recovery, so many times in history, should give pause to any contemporary commentator of French affairs. Whether one has faith in France or not, none can deny the rage for liberty and life of the historically indomitable French.

Yet, despite this record of resiliency, only a poet can truly believe in the immortality of France. France's recoveries have been miraculous but no nation has a guaranteed immortality. History abounds in evidence to disprove Walt Whitman's faith in an eternal star. Where is the glory that was Greece, the power that was Rome? From Angkor to Crete, from Baalbek to Carthage the land is studded with the ruins of once dazzling cultures and mighty empires. South of the Pyrenees the empty, rock-strewn plateau of Spain is a close and fresh warning to the French of the decline and fall of a proud people. France may not be dying, as the pessimists claim, but France can die despite the faith of the poets.

の

The present is one of those critical moments of history when either the pessimist or the poet may be right. Our diagnosis of the Fourth Republic's state of health has revealed evidence that might substantiate either one of two conflicting theories: that France is dying; that France is rising "clearer, more bright than ever."

The rebellion in Algeria, swiftly following upon the war in Indochina, is surely the last death agony of the French Empire. The graph of industrial production is just as surely evidence of a strong pulse beat, indicating a healthy body fighting off the fever. The rising birth rate is another sign of regenerative powers. For the first time in modern history France's birth rate has passed that of Italy, Germany and Great Britain. By 1980 France will have one of the largest active populations in Western Europe.

The pessimist tends to give weight to the symptoms of decline, while the poet looks only at the rising curve of progress; thus both arrive at mutually exclusive conclusions from the same set of findings. This is not surprising since the best economic diagnosticians of Europe have been unable to decide whether the future will find France suffering from depression or enjoying rapid recovery. France, the sick man of Europe, is obviously tossing through the phase of disease that doctors fear most: the high fever that signals the final crisis; when the fever breaks the patient will either be cured or dead.

It is in that sense that the agonies of the French Empire are not necessarily the death agonies of France herself. France may emerge from the colonial struggles healthier than ever because the abscess has been lanced. The loss of the Empire may be the best thing that ever happened to France. With the dead weight of empire off her shoulders, freed of world responsibilities beyond her power to bear, France may, for the first time in centuries, realize to the full her potential for expansion within her own frontiers.

This does not mean that France can ever again attain her former status as the richest, strongest nation in the world. It does mean, however, that France has an opportunity to provide her people with the richest, fullest life they have ever enjoyed. The natural resources of France and individual skills of the French have never been fully realized. If ever they were efficiently organized and used for the betterment of the people, instead of for the illusory grandeur of the nation, the French would achieve a material well-being as great as the cultural heritage and spiritual freedom that have always been their most precious possessions.

No one can say with any certainty that the French will, or will not, some day achieve this fullest expression of their capacity and genius. It would be a higly hypothetical prediction even if the French held the power of decision in their hands alone. The French can do much to influence their own destiny but their fate is not independent of the destiny of other peoples. France is no Switzerland living in splendid isolation behind an Alpine wall. France lives on the crossroads of the world and cannot retire from it. France is no tiny Holland or Belgium either. The French are committed to playing an influential role in European and in world affairs, even though they can no longer play the dominant role. The historian who would predict the future course of French affairs must be prepared to predict the future of Britain, Germany, Russia and America. If it is true that the hopes and plans of many nations depend on the rise or fall of France, then the reverse is equally true.

This observer will not attempt anything so rash and fundamentally valueless as to play the prophet. It has been difficult enough to explore the present and try to chart the course of French affairs, without attempting to predict a future that only time can verify. Our children and our children's children will know, in due course, how France and Western civilization have fared. Perhaps some day my great-grandson will write about the history of the Tenth Republic or, perhaps, the one-hundredth anniversary of this Fourth Republic. If mankind itself is to survive I would guess that future historians will be recording the birth of the First Republic of the World. I would guess, too, that if that happy millennium is ever reached it will have been a Frenchman who first proposed or drafted the World Constitution. There will probably be another Frenchman who will deliver the most brilliant analysis of its errors and vote against it. And somewhere in the stratosphere, carrying delegates to the first meeting of the World Government, there will be a rocket plane from Paris flying through an infrared stopbeam because its pilot is a man and not a machine.

index